ROYAL HISTORICAL SOCIETY

STUDIES IN HISTORY

New Series

LAND AND NATION IN ENGLAND

PATRIOTISM, NATIONAL IDENTITY,
AND THE POLITICS OF LAND, 1880–1914

LAND AND NATION IN ENGLAND

PATRIOTISM, NATIONAL IDENTITY, AND THE POLITICS OF LAND, 1880–1914

Paul Readman

THE ROYAL HISTORICAL SOCIETY
THE BOYDELL PRESS

First published 2008

A Royal Historical Society publication
Published by The Boydell Press
an imprint of Boydell & Brewer Ltd
PO Box 9, Woodbridge, Suffolk IP12 3DF, UK
and of Boydell & Brewer Inc.
668 Mt Hope Avenue, Rochester, NY 14620, USA
website: www.boydellandbrewer.com

ISBN 978-0-86193-297-9

ISSN 0269-2244

A CIP catalogue record for this book is available
from the British Library

This publication is printed on acid-free paper

Printed in Great Britain by
CPI Antony Rowe, Chippenham, Wiltshire

FOR KRISTINA

Contents

Acknowledgements

I was inspired to pursue the academic study of history by James Ryan, one of my teachers at Newpark Comprehensive School in Dublin, and to him I owe my first and perhaps greatest debt. He once told me that I would write a lot of books. Given the time it has taken me to write my first one, I am not sure that he was correct, and in the course of writing it I have relied on a great many people and institutions for help of various kinds. I must acknowledge the financial assistance of the British Academy, the Cambridge European Trust and Christ's College, Cambridge. The Governing Body of Christ's also elected me into a Junior Research Fellowship, which I held for three very happy years and for which I am enormously grateful. At Christ's I was brought into contact with Susan Bayly, Sir John Plumb, David Reynolds and Miles Taylor, who in rather different but not altogether incompatible ways had a great influence on my development as an historian. I was fortunate to have Jon Parry as my PhD supervisor. Jon was and remains an unfailingly reliable source of ideas, wise counsel and moral support, even if in the past I did not always listen to him as attentively as I now know I should have done. I hope that this book serves as some recompense for the kindness he has shown me over the years. That this is not the book of a doctoral thesis has much to do with David Cannadine and Peter Mandler, who examined my PhD. Peter's usefully bracing criticism was particularly important and I am deeply grateful to him for it.

The writing of the book was carried out after I had arrived at the History Department of King's College London, where since September 2002 I have benefited from the intellectual stimulation of the best set of colleagues for which one could wish. I would particularly like to thank Arthur Burns, who as Head of Department provided much needed help and encouragement at crucial times. Arthur arranged a term's research leave for me in 2005–6, which together with matching Arts and Humanities Council-funded leave gave me the time to complete the first full draft of the manuscript. I am very grateful to King's and the AHRC for their assistance in this regard. At King's, Jim Bjork, Laura Clayton, Serena Ferente, Anne Goldgar, Ian McBride, Richard Vinen and Jon Wilson provided support, advice and therapeutic diversions of different kinds. Activities such as highly competitive bouts of table football proved vitally important in the academic year 2006–7, a very busy and demanding one for me. Outside of King's, other friends and colleagues also rendered valuable assistance. They know who they are, but I especially want to thank Matthew Cragoe and Kathryn Rix, fellow historians of modern Britain and providers of endless ideas, references and conversations over many years. More recently, Jon Lawrence has done much, as my academic editor, to sharpen and improve the arguments put forward in this book, and I am immensely thankful to him for the time and effort he has put into reading various drafts. I would also like to thank Christine Linehan for her expert copy editorial help during the final stages of completing the manuscript.

A great deal of the research for this book was carried out in the Cambridge University Library. Wonderfully conducive to study and serendipity, and a source of reliably excellent cheese scones, it is one of my favourite places in the world. I owe a considerable debt of gratitude to its staff. I would also like to thank the staff of the British Library, particularly those of the Newspaper Library at Colindale, where I have spent many months-worth of research over the last few years. Thanks are also due to the librarians and archivists of Christ's College, Cambridge; the Bodleian, Oxford; the libraries of Birmingham, London and Reading Universities; Trinity College Dublin; the House of Lords Record Office; Cumbria Record Office and the Surrey History Centre.

I am grateful to Oxford University Press and Cambridge University Press for permission to reproduce some passages from articles of mine published in *Twentieth Century British History* (OUP), the *English Historical Review* (OUP) and *Rural History* (CUP). In addition, I must also thank the Institute of Historical Research and Blackwell Publishing for permission to reproduce material from an article of mine published in *Historical Research*.

The remaining debts I need to acknowledge are to my family. My parents have always encouraged my study of the past (those Ladybird history books have a lot to answer for) and have been a constant source of unconditional support over the years. I have no words, really, to express my gratitude. I would also like to thank Ben and Dan for putting up with a perhaps sometimes irritatingly academic sibling, while simultaneously showing a convivial brotherly interest in what I do and allowing me to tell them about it. Finally, my wife Kristina deserves special thanks for her love and encouragement throughout the vicissitudinous course of completing this project. She attended to my worries, helped me work out difficult points, read and re-read various sections, and kept my spirits up. This book is for her.

Paul Readman,
Cambridge and London,
January 2008

This book is produced with the assistance of a grant
from Isobel Thornley's Bequest to the University of London

Abbreviations

ALU	Agricultural Labourers' Union
AOS	Agricultural Organisation Society
ASHA	Allotments and Small Holdings Association
BL	British Library
CLA	Central Land Association
CLHC	Central Land and Housing Council
CPS	Commons Preservation Society
ELRL	English Land Restoration League
ELTV	English League for the Taxation of Land Values
FLL	Free Land League
HLRO	House of Lords Records Office
ILP	Independent Labour Party
JJ Coll.	John Johnson Collection, Bodleian Library, Oxford
JP	Justice of the Peace
LLRA	Land Law Reform Association
LNS	Land Nationalisation Society
LYL	League of Young Liberals
MP	Member of Parliament
NAU	National Agricultural Union
NLF	National Liberal Federation
NLHL	National Land and Home League
NUCCA	National Union of Conservative and Constitutional Associations
RLL	Rural Labourers' League
SDF	Social Democratic Federation
SDP	Social Democratic Party
USRC	Unionist Social Reform Committee
AgHR	*Agricultural History Review*
CIP	*Cambridge Independent Press*
CR	*Contemporary Review*
DE	*Daily Express*
DN	*Daily News*
EcHR	*Economic History Review*
EDP	*Eastern Daily Press*
EHR	*English Historical Review*
ELC	*English Labourers' Chronicle*
FR	*Fortnightly Review*
HJ	*Historical Journal*

HR	Historical Research
IR	Independent Review
JBS	Journal of British Studies
JICH	Journal of Imperial and Commonwealth History
LaL	Labour Leader
LL	Land and Labour
LM	Liberal Monthly
LP	Land and People
LV	Land Values
MG	Manchester Guardian
NC	Nineteenth Century
NR	National Review
ODNB	Oxford dictionary of national biography
P&P	Past and Present
PLG	Primrose League Gazette
QR	Quarterly Review
RW	Rural World
TCBH	Twentieth Century British History
TE	Taunton Echo
TRHS	Transactions of the Royal Historical Society

Introduction

In late Victorian and Edwardian England, the politics of land loomed large. Prompted by fears about the faltering rural economy and the effects of large-scale migration from the countryside to the towns, as well as the demands of pressure groups and newly enfranchised agricultural labourers, politicians paid increased attention to agrarian matters. As never before, issues relating to the land were raised in parliament, with the marquess of Salisbury's Conservative government finding it necessary to create a Board of Agriculture in 1889 – a department the head of which, Arthur Balfour, observed six years later, 'more questions are asked ... than of any other except the Irish Secretary'.[1] And if the English land question played a prominent part inside parliament, it had still greater extra-parliamentary prominence. Agrarian issues were of considerable importance in constituency politics, featuring strongly in the appeals of candidates for urban as well as rural areas at all general elections between 1880 and the First World War, with the exception of 1886.

The English land question has attracted some attention from historians, although not as much as its Irish, Scottish and Welsh equivalents. It has received treatment in a number of chronological surveys, which have provided narrative accounts of the party political side of the subject. Recently, more detailed studies dealing with specific debates, personalities and legislation have added to this overview literature. Ian Packer's *Lloyd George, Liberalism and the land*, which focuses on the Liberal 'Land Campaign' of 1913–14, is one important example here.[2] As a consequence of this work, historical understanding of the parliamentary land question has been much augmented: there is no longer any pressing need for detailed accounts of proposed and enacted legislation, or the behind-the-scenes wrangling that led to its formulation. But there is a pressing need for further examination of the ideological content of debates on the land question, without which any understanding as to why they were of such contemporary political significance will remain incomplete.

This book provides a thematic treatment of the political debates on the English land question in the thirty-five years before the First World War. It examines what was at issue in these debates, paying particular attention to their ideological content. The principal focus is the relationship between political engagement with land issues and patriotic and nationalistic ideas.

1   Cited in E. H. H. Green, *The crisis of Conservatism: the politics, economics and ideology of the British Conservative party, 1880–1914*, London 1995, 99.
2   I. Packer, *Lloyd George, Liberalism and the land: the land issue and party politics in England, 1906–1914*, Woodbridge 2001.

This focus is novel. As yet, historians have paid scant attention to the inter-action between the politics of land and the politics of Englishness. Indeed, no book-length study exists on the subject. On the face of it, this scholarly neglect is astonishing. After all, scholarly interest in patriotism and national identity remains extraordinarily high, as made evident by the rapidly-growing quantity of general and theoretical literature on the subject. Furthermore, in the field of British history, elucidations of the connections between land and nation in the Irish, Scottish and Welsh contexts are not hard to come by.[3] It is also true that in the English context there is a strong a priori case for regarding ideas about patriotism and national identity as bound up with land, landscape and the rural: 'England is the country, and the country is England', as Stanley Baldwin famously remarked.[4] The publication of Martin Wiener's English culture and the decline of the industrial spirit (Cambridge 1981) spawned a voluminous literature on the relationship between land and nation in the cultural sphere. Representations of rural and usually reactionary forms of Englishness are now routine subjects of study for cultural historians and historical geographers, being identified in painting, photography, architec-ture, music, literature and the 'heritage' dispensation, among other contexts. In a recent historical survey of the development of English national identity, Krishan Kumar has claimed that by the late nineteenth century, 'the essen-tial England was rural', a judgement with which most scholars working on the subject would concur.[5] Yet, despite all this work, which has done much to establish the historical connections between Englishness, patriotism and the rural, political historians have been reluctant to consider its implica-tions for their own field of study. Accounts of the politics of land have been oddly silent on the question of national identity. Some of the reasons for this silence are suggested in the next chapter, but for the moment it is sufficient to observe that if cultural ideas of land and nation were closely intertwined, then it appears highly likely that political ideas were as well.

All this is not to say, however, that this book sets out to support the view of Englishness presented in the cultural literature. As I have argued else-where, there is no doubt that patriotic concern for land and landscape played an important part in late nineteenth- and early twentieth-century English culture. However, this concern (as expressed though the preservationist movement, for example) was not suffused with antipathy for modernity, as Wiener and those influenced by him have suggested; rather it represented a desire to come to terms with the rapid pace of social and economic change

---

[3] P. Bew, Land and the national question in Ireland, 1858–82, Dublin 1978; P. Bull, Land, politics and nationalism, Dublin 1996; D. Howell, Land and people in nineteenth-century Wales, London 1978; M. Cragoe, Culture, politics, and national identity in Wales, 1832–1886, Oxford 2004; E. A. Cameron, Land for the people? The British people and the Scottish Highlands, c. 1880–1925, East Linton 1996.
[4] S. Baldwin, On England, London 1926, 5–6.
[5] K. Kumar, The making of English national identity, Cambridge 2003, 211.

by maintaining a sense of continuity with the English past, so preserving a durable sense of national belonging.[6] And if this was the case, it has implica-tions for the political study of land and nation. If cultural Englishness was not necessarily as conservative as has been claimed, then it would seem likely that a similar ideological heterogeneity is to be found in the political discourse. The following chapters confirm this supposition. It is true that reactionary languages of land and nation existed in the political sphere, as they did in the cultural, finding expression in backbench Tory veneration of a *quondam* 'Merrie England' of large-scale arable farming, class harmony and landlord paternalism, where everyone knew his place and was content with his station in life. But in the context of the progressive democratisation of the political nation, other languages existed too, even within political Conservatism, and much of the time they exerted greater influence. One such, for example, was a democratic vision that upheld the self-sufficient smallholder, free from the control of the squire, as the ideal Englishman and the embodiment of national virtue.

This perspective stands in contrast to Hugh Cunningham's argument that by the late nineteenth century, the 'language of patriotism' had fallen under the control of the Conservative party, largely thanks to the nationalist and imperialist rhetoric employed by Disraeli in the 1870s. 'In the age of imperialism', Cunningham claimed, 'the patriot was above class, loyal to the institutions of the country, and resolute in defence of its honour and inter-ests. Liberals, radicals and socialists who protested their own patriotism were singularly unsuccessful in wresting the initiative from the right. Patriotism was firmly identified with Conservatism, militarism, royalism and racialism.'[7] Cunningham's view has been hugely influential, regularly being cited in support of claims that the Tories had an undisputed monopoly on political discourses of patriotism in the three or four decades before the First World War.[8] Yet, it is becoming increasingly apparent that there are problems with this interpretation. Since the publication of Raphael Samuel's *Patriotism* (1989), a wonderfully eclectic collection of essays on subjects ranging from the image of Britannia to the nationalist dimension of history teaching in schools, it has been clear that the vocabularies of patriotism current in the

---

[6] P. Readman, 'Landscape preservation, "advertising disfigurement", and English national identity, c. 1090–1914', *Rural History* xii (2001), 61–83, and 'The place of the past in English culture, c. 1890–1914', *P&P* clxxxvi (2005), 147–99; cf. P. Mandler, 'Against "Englishness": English culture and the limits to rural nostalgia', *TRHS* 6th ser. vii (1997), 155–75.

[7] H. Cunningham, 'The language of patriotism, 1750–1914', *History Workshop Journal* xii (1981), 24.

[8] Even scholars working in fields quite outside modern British history have called on Cunningham in support of their generalisations. See, for example, M. Viroli, *For love of country: an essay on patriotism and nationalism*, Oxford 1995, 156–7.

wider culture assumed a variety of different forms.[9] And while it has taken some time for historians of British politics to grasp the implications of this for their own research, scholars are now beginning to recognise the diverse character of political patriotisms. Paul Ward's work on late nineteenth- and early twentieth-century socialist engagement with patriotic ideas, for example, would seem to invalidate Cunningham's contention that it was at this time 'impossible to demarcate a patriotism of the left'.[10]

By emphasising the ideological heterogeneity of patriotic debate, what follows builds on this recent trend in the historiography, while also extending its approach into new areas. The focus on the relationship between land and nation is novel, but so too, more generally, is the focus on party politics. Although patriotism is attracting more attention from scholars, the role that it played in debates within and between the political parties in the late Victorian and Edwardian periods remains remarkably under-explored.[11] Ward's research has done something to remedy this with regard to the left (although he has surprisingly little to say about Labour and socialist rural policies), but the patriotic dimension to Liberal and Conservative party politics has not got much beyond the occasional scholarly article on particular topics, or general treatment in textbook surveys.[12] The present study aims to do something towards addressing this deficiency: parliamentary and extra-parliamentary political debate on the English land question was an important vehicle for the contestation of the language of patriotism on a variety of levels. Inspired by competing visions of ruralised Englishness, Liberals, Conservatives and socialists presented their land policies as addressing issues of patriotic concern, many of which were connected to the late nineteenth-century phenomenon of rural depopulation. These issues included the contagion of social disunity and class conflict, the decay of national character and racial fitness, the salvation of the 'national industry' of agriculture, and the squalor and alienation of urban-industrial capitalism.

First and foremost, then, this book focuses on the ideological significance of patriotic debates on the land question. However, in examining the char-

---

[9] R. Samuel (ed.), *Patriotism*, London 1989. Published around the same time as Samuel's three volumes, J. H. Grainger's neglected *Patriotisms*, London 1986, also took a pluralist approach.

[10] P. Ward, *Red flag and Union Jack: Englishness, patriotism and the British left, 1881–1924*, London 1998; cf. Cunningham, 'Language of patriotism', 27.

[11] The mid-Victorian period is better served: M. Taylor, *The decline of British radicalism, 1847–1860*, Oxford 1995; M. Finn, *After Chartism: class and nation in English radical politics, 1848–1874*, Cambridge 1993; J. Parry, *The politics of patriotism: English Liberalism, national identity and Europe, 1830–1886*, Cambridge 2006.

[12] H. Cunningham, 'The Conservative party and patriotism', in R. Colls and P. Dodd (eds), *Englishness*, London 1986, 283–307; P. Readman, 'The Liberal party and patriotism in early twentieth century Britain', *TCBH* xii (2001), 269–302, and 'The Conservative party, patriotism, and British politics: the case of the general election of 1900', *JBS* xl (2001), 107–45; P. Ward, *Britishness since 1870*, London 2004, 93–112.

acter of these debates, it also seeks to shed light on the relationship between languages of land and nation, on the one hand, and patterns of political change and party allegiance, particularly in the English countryside, on the other. Much scholarly work has of course been done on electoral and popular politics, both in urban and rural areas – and the flood of publications shows no sign of abating. Yet this research has often shied away from close examination of the connections between political language and electoral behaviour. There are good reasons for this. After all, even when a particular ideological vocabulary can be identified with precision, assessment of the extent of its impact on voter choice and political change is fraught with difficulties, given all the other factors at play. There exists no easy way of separating out the political effect of one issue, policy or ideology from that of another, or indeed of evaluating the relative importance of platform appeals and party organisation. In all likelihood these methodological problems have contributed to historians' reluctance to consider the impact of political language on party politics. But there is a further reason for this reluctance. At least until quite recently, scholars took the view that the party allegiances and political identities of nineteenth- and twentieth-century Britons were not much influenced by ideology, or what politicians said at election time. Rather, they were held to be determined by social relations and structures. These included the deference communities that supposedly prevailed in early to mid-Victorian England, which formed the basis of the political power of traditional elites, and the rise of urban working-class consciousness from the late nineteenth century onwards, which spawned the Labour movement while also prompting the Edwardian radicalisation of Liberalism.[13]

As borne out by the work of Jon Lawrence, Miles Taylor and others, a revisionist critique of this sociologically determinist scholarship is now well underway.[14] Research on electoral politics now pays far more attention to issues and ideology than it did previously. This is as true for work focusing on rural as on urban England. D. C. Moore's claim that rural social relations sustained a 'politics of deference' after 1832 has been the subject of especially devastating criticism. The work of R. W. Davies, Edwin Jaggard and others has established beyond doubt that early and mid nineteenth-century rural politics had more to do with issues and principles – and were more sharply divided on partisan lines – than the older scholarship had supposed.[15]

---

[13] Key works include H. J. Hanham, *Elections and party management: politics in the time of Disraeli and Gladstone*, London 1959; H. Pelling, *Social geography of British elections, 1885–1910*, London 1967; P. F. Clarke, *Lancashire and the new Liberalism*, Cambridge 1971; and D. C. Moore, *The politics of deference: a study of the mid-nineteenth century English political system*, Hassocks 1976.

[14] J. Lawrence and M. Taylor (eds), *Party, state and society: electoral behaviour in Britain since 1820*, Aldershot 1997.

[15] Moore, *Politics of deference*. Cf., for example, R. W. Davies, *Political change and continuity, 1760–1885: a Buckinghamshire study*, London 1972, and 'The mid-nineteenth-century electoral structure', *Albion* viii (1976), 142–53; E. Jaggard, *Cornwall politics in*

And while the politics of the late Victorian and Edwardian countryside have received comparatively less attention, recent research on this topic has also emphasised the importance of issues, language and ideology to political change. According to an important recent study by Patricia Lynch, there were two main reasons for Conservative dominance in English rural constituencies in the twenty years after 1886. One was the Liberal party's 'abandonment ... of the language of rural reform' that had swept them to victory at the polls in 1885. The other was a tension between Liberal political culture and the rural 'culture of community' prevalent in the English shires. With its emphasis on vigorous partisanship and debate, popular Liberalism was seen as divisive in many villages; hence it often failed to put down strong roots. Popular Conservatism, by contrast, proved far more successful, as its inclusive yet hierarchical values conformed to the rural community ideal. It was only in 1906, Lynch argues, that the Liberals rediscovered the language of rural radicalism, which propelled them back to a position of strength in English county seats.[16]

This book offers a different perspective on the determinants of political change in rural England at this time. It suggests that Lynch exaggerates the Liberals' downplaying of their agrarian radicalism after 1886, and also the purchase of a socially conservative village community ideal. Throughout the late nineteenth and early twentieth centuries, the discourse of land politics was hotly contested by both parties at national and constituency level. These debates were hotly contested because they involved patriotic issues and values, and their outcome had a tangible impact on the ebb and flow of party politics in the countryside. At first, in the aftermath of the Liberal split over Irish home rule, traditionalist Conservative discourses of land and nation held sway. Over time, however, popular languages of Liberal agrarian patriotism, combined with the democratisation of political culture, forced Tories to adapt their appeal, which they did in dramatic fashion following their landslide defeat at the general election of 1906. By the outbreak of the First World War, both main parties were vying for the votes of the rural electorate using language premised on democratic conceptions of nationhood, and on democratic visions of rural Englishness.

Given the focus on language, it should come as no surprise that this book deals with what individuals said and published: their speeches, lectures and addresses; what they wrote in books, journals and newspapers. It deals, there-

the age of reform, 1790–1885, Woodbridge 1999; and J. R. Fisher, 'The limits of deference: agricultural communities in a mid-nineteenth century election campaign', JBS xxi (1981), 90–105. For a useful overview of the debate see D. Eastwood, 'Contesting the politics of deference: the rural electorate, 1820–60', in Lawrence and Taylor, Party, state and society, 27–49.

[16] P. Lynch, The Liberal party in rural England, 1885–1910, Oxford 2003, quotation at p. 118.

fore, with coherent patterns of thought, language and rhetoric, or 'discourses'.[17]
In recent years, interest in the recovery and analysis of discourse has grown
rapidly. On the whole, it is a trend to be welcomed. The new 'linguistic'
emphasis of modern scholarship has added much to our understanding of the
past. But it has also presented problems. Influenced by postmodernist theory,
some historians now assert that discourse constitutes all of historical 'reality':
in the field of modern British history Patrick Joyce has argued this most
trenchantly.[18] Although it is still the case that few would go as far as Joyce,
there is now a tendency towards the view that the retrieval of discourse
is the core element of the historian's craft. As Adrian Jones has recently
noted, 'History as a form of rhetoric is ascendant nowadays ... Discourses
and tropes, dramas and "thick" descriptions are all the rage ... Some claim
that history itself and history's subjects are only ever discourses; "there is
nothing beneath the text".'[19] Literal interpretation of Michel Foucault's 'Il
n'y pas de hors-texte' can lead to what Jones has called 'hollow words-only
history'. This sort of history presents us with a profusion of discourses, but
its relativising epistemology inhibits proper evaluation of these discourses'
significance. Scholars are now increasingly unwilling to probe beneath their
sources, to situate them in historical context. Although understandably keen
to assert the importance of their research, many historians are reluctant to
make any real attempt at assessing the contemporary importance of their
subject matter – the extent to which it 'counted' to people at the time.
Too often, what Peter Mandler has aptly called the 'throw' of the discourses
recovered by modern scholarship is presumed rather than proved.[20] This
book makes no such presumption. Throughout, 'language' is not recovered
divorced from its historical context, but linked to the individuals who used
it, and to their (and others') actions and activities. Moreover, the first of its
eight chapters is explicitly devoted to assessing the contemporary currency
of political ideas about the English land question. Judgement, explanation,
generalisation, even quantitative methods have not been abandoned for
the merely rhetorical recapturing of late nineteenth- and early twentieth-
century discursive forms.

It follows from this that the approach to the sources used in this book has
an empirical base. This is not to say that discursive notions of 'the actual'
have been rejected. Myths, images and other forms of representation preva-

---

[17] 'Discourse' is now a notoriously problematic term for historians to use. In this book,
'discourse' should be taken to mean a pattern of 'language' practice. It is not meant in
the Foucauldian sense of a form of 'power/knowledge'.
[18] See his *Democratic subjects*, Cambridge 1994, and 'History and post-modernism I', *P&P*
cxxxiii (1991), 204–9.
[19] A. Jones, 'Word *and* deed: why a *post*-poststructuralist history is needed, and how it
might look', *HJ* xliii (2000), 534.
[20] As Mandler has shown, this problem is perhaps especially prevalent in the field of
cultural history: 'The problem with cultural history', *Cultural and Social History* i (2004),
94–117.

lent in the past cannot be dismissed as 'unreal' and therefore unworthy of the attention of serious historians, just because they might have conflicted with contemporaries' day-to-day experiences. Nor is it to say that the classical positivist view has been adopted: that sources 'speak' directly and historians can be entirely 'objective' in their interpretation of them. Sources do not speak for themselves, graciously yielding up facts to the patient researcher, who approaches the evidence with his or her mind a *tabula rasa* cleared of personal views and preferences. Historians select material from archives and libraries with their minds freighted with preconceptions of various kinds, including hypotheses they wish to test, questions they want to answer, ideas about topics and issues they want to explore or understand.

The hypotheses, questions and ideas I had formulated when I approached the sources used for this book were to a certain extent informed by dissatisfaction with the ways other scholars had understood public debate on late nineteenth- and early twentieth-century land politics. To my mind there seemed a strong *prima facie* case for land, landscape and the rural being importantly connected to ideas about patriotism and national identity. Yet, despite demonstrating this connection in the Irish and Scottish contexts, political historians had failed to consider whether or not patriotic ideas played any part in the English 'land question', and this oversight seemed all the more extraordinary in the light of the very ruralised interpretation of English identity that had been developed by cultural historians. Spanning more than three decades of history, the research for this inquiry involved the selection of material from numerous primary sources, many of which have not received the scholarly attention they deserve. Given the focus on political ideas and debate, published primary sources are used extensively, particularly pamphlet collections (such as those preserved in the John Johnson Collection at the Bodleian Library), the still under-exploited *Hansard*, local and national newspapers, and specialist periodicals. Publications associated with various political organisations and pressure groups figure prominently; little used by scholars, they offer striking illustrations of different ideological perspectives and positions (examples include the National Agricultural Union's *Cable*, the Rural Labourers' League's *Rural World*, the Allotments and Small Holdings Association's *Land and People*, and the Land Nationalisation Society's *Land and Labour*). Periodicals such as the *National Review*, the *Nineteenth Century* and the *Fortnightly Review*, to which politicians and other opinion-formers regularly contributed, yield much information about Liberal and Conservative thinking on agrarian issues. In addition, the National Liberal Club's collection of election addresses, which are conveniently available on microfilm, is a crucial tool for examining the electoral appeal of politicians involved in debates on land reform.

This book is divided into eight chapters. Chapter 1 provides a chronological narrative of the politics of the English land question in the period under study, as well as some further historiographical commentary. This chapter is designed to serve as the basic point of reference for factual information on the politics of land, and should be particularly useful for those readers lacking detailed knowledge of the subject. Its purpose is to set out the main political events and legislative landmarks, so removing the need for repetition later. The remaining seven chapters constitute essays on various themes. These chapters are grouped into two parts: the first deals with 'Land Politics and National Issues', the second with 'Land Politics and Visions of England'. In part I, the various national and patriotic issues central to the politics of land are discussed. Chapter 2 is concerned with the relationship between the land system and the social and constitutional stability of the nation. In the context of the democratisation of the political nation wrought by the Second and Third Reform Acts, which gave the vote to many men who owned no land, politicians presented legislation for the creation of a numerous class of small occupying owners as a patriotic imperative. Peasant proprietorship was upheld as a means of forestalling class conflict, national disunity and the undermining of the constitution by revolutionary agitation. Liberals were susceptible to this line of thinking in the early part of the period; later on, it became an approach most closely associated with the Conservative party.

Land politics were also closely associated with concerns about the English national character, and this inter-relationship is explored in Chapter 3. In the analysis of Liberal reformers, the monopolistic land system was inimical to that spirit of independence which 'freeborn Englishmen' so prized: unable to gain access to an allotment or a smallholding, forced to work for meagre wages as a farm labourer, denied decent accommodation and hence a proper home, deprived of any sort of control over the affairs of his parish, the countryman was being driven from the land. As a consequence, it was claimed, the English race was deteriorating. In the cities, overcrowded and unsanitary conditions were rife, with speculative urban landlords often withholding vacant land that might be used for building purposes, so forcing prices up at the cost of the nation's health and strength. Numerous reforms were advocated to remedy this situation. In the 1880s and 1890s Liberals pushed for rural local government reform as a means of striking at the 'tyranny' of the squire, so loosening the bonds of 'serfdom' that so degraded the character of Hodge and stimulated his migration to the town. Coupled to this, they advocated legislation to create allotments and smallholdings, which were regarded as being conducive to individual self-sufficiency and moral virtue, as well as acting as disincentives to rural-urban migration. Later on, land value taxation gained in popularity, particularly as a means of combating the urban 'land monopoly' and its destructive effects on health and character. As for the Conservatives, while they were initially sceptical about the need for reform, their attitude changed over time, as concerns mounted about 'racial' degeneration and the magnitude of rural depopulation. By the 1900s the idea that peasant proprietors could function both as bulwarks against social upheaval and as guarantors of racial health was a commonplace in Conservative discourse.

Debate about land politics encompassed debate about agriculture. Chapter 4 discusses the political response to the late nineteenth-century agricultural depression, which saw a catastrophic fall in prices and a widespread shift from arable farming to pasturage. This response was bound up with patriotic concern. Many agrarian Tories regarded agriculture as the 'national industry'; unlike other industries, it provided the foundation for England's existence as a nation. This argument could take a number of forms, often being related to the question of food supply: Britain's dependence on imported produce fuelled fears that the nation could face starvation in wartime. From here it was a short step to nationalistic advocacy of domestic production, tariff reform and autarky, which Tories – as well as some Liberal Unionists like Jesse Collings – presented as a patriotic alternative to the free trade commercialism associated with political Liberalism. Yet, as this chapter shows, Liberals also advanced economic arguments in support of their land reformist schemes, particularly towards the end of the period, when Lloyd George's demand that land be put on a 'business footing' assumed some prominence in the political language of the 'People's Budget' and Land Campaign.

In the 1900s many of Lloyd George's Conservative critics alleged that his party had embraced a novel and dangerous collectivist (or even socialist) doctrine, one based on the 'confiscation' of private property; and in their eyes the radical land measures proposed by the Liberals seemed powerful evidence of this. However, as chapter 5 demonstrates, examination of reformers' positions on property rights does not lend much weight to the view that Liberals had adopted socialist or quasi-socialist ideology – indeed it even calls into question the influence of collectivist 'new Liberal' thinking on agrarian issues. It is true that Liberals sought to impose limits on the rights of property in land, not least by introducing compulsory purchase legislation, but this aim drew upon and developed already-existing traditions of Liberal-radical thought. The idea, for example, that private land use was limited by considerations of public interest had a long pedigree in Liberal political discourse, and indeed was supported by jurisprudential precepts, which laid down that in the final analysis all land in England belonged to the state; and it was the state's job to ensure that it was used in the best interests of the nation as a whole. This perspective exerted a powerful influence on Liberal demands that interference in the current system of landholding was justified on the grounds that it did not conduce to the welfare of an increasingly democratic political nation. Popular patriotism, not confiscatory collectivism, informed that conviction of radical Liberal land reformers that an Englishman did not in fact have 'the right to do as he liked with his own'.

Political engagement with the land question was informed by various visions of ruralised Englishness. These visions are the concern of part II of the book. In most cases, they derived from differing conceptions of the national past. As shown in chapter 6, Liberals drew on two patriotic visions in particular; one centred on the self-governing village communities of pre-

Conquest England, with their folk moots and communal system of land-holding; the other on rural England before the enclosure movement of the late eighteenth and early nineteenth centuries. Both were upheld as offering inspiration for land reform. However, evocations of the Anglo-Saxon past diminished in importance in Liberal land reform discourse as time wore on, with Liberal reformers placing increased emphasis on the pre-enclosure past, extolling the virtues of a prosperous and peopled countryside, where even the humble enjoyed access to the soil and hence to a self-sufficient livelihood. Common land played a crucial part here. It was the commons that provided ordinary Englishmen with an independent way of life, free from the drudgery of wage-slavery and landlord tyranny. But with enclosure, Liberals contended, this way of life had been brutally extinguished. Hence, land reform was presented as a means of making amends for the past crime of enclosure, not least by repairing the breach it had made in the continuity of the English national *telos*. This project of restoring the English people's 'birthright' in the English soil reached its apotheosis in the Edwardian period, with the Liberal government's smallholdings and land tenure legislation and, most tellingly, the Land Campaign of 1913–14. Yet, despite their clear orientation towards the past, Liberal visions of rural renewal did not reflect an anti-modern, retrogressive mindset.

By contrast, the Conservative visions of the rural nation discussed in chapter 7 had a more reactionary bent. Like their Liberal counterparts, they too drew heavily on the past. Moreover, they also took two main forms. That which was longest established venerated a rural England of large-scale arable farming, class harmony and landlord paternalism. Still in the ascendancy in the early 1880s, this 'pure squire Conservatism' was informed by a Tory version of a *quondam* 'Merrie England', where good-natured fellow feeling coexisted with a hierarchical social structure moderated by top-down benevolence, which ensured that everyone knew his place and was content with his station in life. Such Tory ruralism had many exponents within the ranks of the party, forming the basis of an attitude of hostility towards many proposals for reform – particularly those concerning land tenure and small-holders, which were damned as economically mischievous and destructive of good social relations. Despite its persistence throughout the period, however, the significance of the national vision embodied in pure squire Conservatism fell away over time. Political democratisation, agricultural depression and the rising tide of radicalism led Conservatives and Liberal Unionists to an alternative vision of rural England, one centred on the peasant or 'yeoman' proprietor who had in times past formed the mainstay of the land system and (so it was said) the nation's strength and stability.

Chapter 8 considers Labour and socialist responses to the land question. Often neglected by historians, left-wing land politics formed an integral part of a wider crusade against capitalism – a crusade that was animated by a spirit of 'welfare patriotism'. But socialist land reformism was also animated by distinctive patriotic visions of its own. Here, too, history loomed large.

For many on the left, the English past provided inspiration for a vision of national life which stood in sharp contrast to contemporary reality. The late medieval period was singled out for special attention, being presented as a 'Golden Age' of popular freedom and prosperity which had sustained a race of masterless men, largely thanks to a land system that conferred free access to the soil by means of commons and the charity of the pre-Reformation Church. In its (relatively) collectivist social organisation, it also served as evidence that the roots of English socialism lay deep in English history, thereby giving substance to the claim that socialism was no 'alien' import inconsistent with national traditions. The corollary to this vision of a felicitous Golden Age, which might serve as inspiration for future progress in a socialist direction, was the idea that it had been brought to an end by the emergence of modern capitalism, which had robbed the people of their commons, driven them from the countryside and transformed them into a wage-receiving proletariat, condemned to a degraded life of alienation and squalor in urban slums. Land nationalisation was advocated as a means of restoring the people to their inheritance in the soil, and by so doing effecting national renewal by stimulating the decentralisation of population and industry. This project of national renewal was bound up with concern for the health and character of the 'race', as it was for Liberals and Conservatives. It was also connected to a distinctively socialist emphasis on production rather than trade or finance, based on the ideological conviction that labour applied to land was the source of all real wealth. For many on the left, this position shaded into autarkic economic nationalism and hostility to the free trade 'Manchester School' dispensation, a tendency of thought that throws doubt on the interpretations of those scholars who have argued for the near-identity of Liberal and Labour approaches to the land question in the Edwardian period.

1

The English Land Question, 1880–1914

'This question of the land has been talked and written about *ad nauseum*':
H. Brockhouse, *The curse of the country*, London 1909, 1.

Contemporary debate on land reform and 'the land question' generally was
varied, multifaceted and conducted across a wide spectrum of opinion both
in and out of parliament. This chapter has two main aims. First, to provide
an outline summary of the principal debates and legislation to which reference will later be made; second, to demonstrate the importance of the
land question in late-Victorian and Edwardian politics. This second aim is
important, as political languages of land and nation only tell us anything
meaningful about conceptions of Englishness if the patriotic concerns they
expressed had real contemporary resonance. Before making any claims about
the significance of the discourse of land politics, it is first necessary to show
that these politics were themselves of significance, that they were not just
the concern of an unrepresentative minority. The chapter ends with a short
inquiry into the treatment of the land question by historians. It is suggested
here that there is a need for a shift in focus away from the details and effects
of legislation and the machinations of parliamentary politics, and towards
the languages that influenced and found expression in the views of interested
politicians. In general, scholarly treatment of the land question has tended
to neglect these languages, particularly those that spoke to conceptions of
patriotism and national identity. Proper recognition of their political importance is now overdue.

Land politics: an overview

Land politics before 1880

Land had long played a part in English politics. Between the 1830s and the
1850s there was considerable debate over the question of supplying agricultural labourers with allotment gardens.[1] These years also witnessed the
emergence of schemes of land reform centred on 'home colonisation', an
idea which originated with the Chartists and was carried on by a number
of radical politicians throughout the 1850s and 1860s. For many of these
reformers, the establishment of a sober, honest, hardworking and self-

---

[1] J. Burchardt, *The allotment movement in England, 1793–1873*, Woodbridge 2002.

sufficient class of small proprietors exerted considerable appeal. Its attraction increased markedly after the publication, in 1848, of W. T. Thornton's *Plea for peasant proprietors* and – in the same year – of John Stuart Mill's *Principles of political economy* (four chapters of which were devoted to peasant proprietorship and *petite culture*).[2]

The writings of Mill and Thornton were hugely influential and fed into the developing campaign for 'Free Trade in Land'. This centred on a conviction that primogeniture, strict settlement and the costly and cumbersome system of land transfer were evils that urgently required redressing. Such arrangements were thought to foster under-cultivation of the soil, the argument being that tenants-for-life of overburdened estates, denied the financial relief that sale of land (impossible due to the terms of settlement) would have afforded them, lacked the capital to invest in productivity-enhancing improvements. Furthermore, they were also believed to concentrate land in large estates, and therefore to militate powerfully against the emergence of the class of small landowners whose supposed merits had been set out by Mill and Thornton. By removing these 'artificial' restrictions on the buying, selling and inheritance of land, the market would be allowed to operate 'naturally'. This, so it was hoped, would lead to a wider distribution of property in land and the development of a numerous peasant proprietary.

In retrospect, Free Trade in Land was certainly misguided in some of its assumptions, but this was not apparent to many reformers at the time, and it became increasingly important in Liberal and radical discourse on the land question as the century progressed. Following a hiatus in the 1850s, the issue gathered momentum in the middle of the following decade. At Rochdale in November 1864, in the last of his great public speeches, Richard Cobden advocated the establishment of a league for Free Trade in Land.[3] Responding to the call of the veteran radical, Mill, Sir Charles Dilke, Henry Fawcett and others established the Land Tenure Reform Association (LTRA) in 1869. However, in addition to advocating the abolition of primogeniture and strict settlement, and reform of the land transfer system, the association also proposed more radical measures. These included state purchase of land for the direct provision of smallholdings, legislative action for the preservation of commons, and taxation of the 'unearned increment'.[4] In fact, the League's programme was considerably more advanced than mainstream Liberal or radical opinion would tolerate, and it disappeared soon after Mill's death in 1873. Yet while the 1870s saw the demise of the LTRA, the more moderate agenda of Free Trade in Land increased in strength. Published in 1876, Lord Derby's *Return of the owners of land* revealed that over one-quarter of the

---

2   W. T. Thornton, *A plea for peasant proprietors*, London 1848; J. S. Mill, *Principles of political economy*, London 1848.

3   J. Morley, *The life of Richard Cobden*, London 1881, ii. 456.

4   D. Martin, 'Land reform', in P. Hollis (ed.), *Pressure from without in early Victorian England*, London 1973, 154–5.

land area of England and Wales was owned by 710 people.[5] Presented in accessible book form by John Bateman, the statistics generated by the *Return* added weight to the argument of reformers that restrictions on the inheritance and transfer of land concentrated property in the hands of a few.

Many of those involved in the movement for Free Trade in Land also supported land tenure reform, the Liberal MP G. J. Shaw Lefevre being one prominent example.[6] For such individuals, the stringent conditions of tenure that landlords imposed on farmers were not only restrictive of personal liberty, but also inimical to agricultural efficiency and progress. Particular causes of complaint were the insecurity of the farmer's tenure and the lack of compensation available to him for any improvements he might have made to the land he had cultivated. So too, notoriously, were the game laws, which denied tenants the right to kill game on the land they farmed. Mounting pressure for reform led to legislative action. In 1875 a bill was passed providing tenants with compensation for improvements. But because it was possible for landlords to contract out of its provisions, the act was virtually a dead letter and its ineffectiveness provoked demands for more radical measures, particularly from practising agriculturalists. In 1879, with farmer discontent exacerbated by the onset of depression, an extra-parliamentary organisation for land tenure reform came into being and this 'Farmers' Alliance' soon became a political force that was taken seriously by both parties.[7]

Not only had the 1870s seen the emergence of an organised farmers' lobby, however. In this decade, agricultural labourers and their interests came to play a far greater part in politics. Joseph Arch founded the Agricultural Labourers' Union (ALU) in 1872 to campaign for better wages and working conditions for farmworkers. In its early years, these aims remained the union's primary objectives. In addition, however, the ALU emphasised the labourer's need for a 'stake in the soil'. As a means by which this stake could be established, it advocated the extensive provision of allotments and smallholdings at decent rents and increased security of tenure.[8]

Land politics, 1880–1914

The demand that 'land ... be as free as commerce'[9] resulted in the passage of the Settled Lands Act of 1882. This allowed the tenant-for-life of an entailed estate to sell land subject to the entail on condition that the proceeds were held in trust for the heir. However, because park and mansion were

[5] J. Bateman, *The great landowners of Great Britain and Ireland* (London 1883), London 1971.
[6] See G. J. Shaw Lefevre, Lord Eversley, *Agrarian tenures*, London 1893.
[7] J. R. Fisher, 'The Farmers' Alliance: an agricultural protest movement of the 1880s', *AgHR* xxvi (1978), 15–25.
[8] N. Scotland, 'The National Agricultural Labourers' Union and the demand for a stake in the soil, 1872–1896', in E. F. Biagini (ed.), *Citizenship and community: Liberals, radicals and collective identities in the British Isles, 1865–1931*, Cambridge 1996, 152–4.
[9] H. Fisher, *The English land question*, London 1883, 6.

exempted from its provisions, and as strict settlement and primogeniture were left unabolished, the measure did not end demands for reform. Arthur Arnold's establishment of the Free Land League (FLL) in 1885 testified to the continued importance of Free Trade in Land as a political issue for Liberals.[10] Yet, despite the foundation of the FLL, Free Trade in Land was on the wane as an issue from the mid-1880s on. Land transfer was no longer so serious a bone of party contention, with the later 1880s and early 1890s witnessing a number of attempts by members of both parties to get reforms onto the statute book. As for the abolition of strict settlement and primogeniture, although still strongly urged by some moderate Liberals as late as the mid-1890s, many party members thought that they did not go far enough. Along with the institution of land title registration, they were increasingly regarded as insufficiently radical shibboleths of an out-of-date Liberalism. In an 'Eighty' Club speech of May 1891, Richard Haldane asked his audience, 'Who hears a word in the constituencies now about the abolition of settlements and entail or the cheapening of the transfer of land, or any other of those fine things that used to occur in the programme of the Free Land League? Sometimes an old-fashioned politician echoes them.'[11] Haldane's remarks reflected the development of widespread (and well-founded) scepticism as to whether Free Trade in Land would really do anything tangible to encourage the diffusion of landed property; increasingly, a more extensive range of agrarian legislation was deemed necessary.

Among this legislation was land tenure reform, the need for which many Liberals persistently affirmed in the 1880s, 1890s and into the 1900s. Spurred on by extra-parliamentary pressure, Gladstone's second government passed a Ground Game Act in 1880. This granted tenants the right to kill hares and rabbits on their farms and, as Roland Quinault has observed, it effectively 'put an end to the game question as a major political issue'.[12] Three years later a more wide-ranging Agricultural Holdings Bill provided tenants with increased rights to compensation for improvements. In the 1890s reforming Liberals led by George Lambert, MP for the Devonshire division of South Molton, kept up the pressure for further legislation. After an ineffective Conservative measure in 1900, substantial reform finally came with the Agricultural Holdings Act of 1906. Among other benefits, this measure enhanced the level of compensation available in return for improvements, granted the tenant freedom of cropping and provided compensation for disturbance in cases where the landlord evicted 'for reasons inconsistent with good estate management'.

Land tenure reform, of course, had been central to the programme of

[10] Arnold was among the more important advocates of Free Trade in Land and author of *Free land*, London 1880, perhaps the most influential publication on the subject.
[11] Eighty Club, *Social problems*, London 1891, 14.
[12] R. Quinault, 'Warwickshire landowners and parliamentary politics, c. 1841–1923', unpubl. DPhil. diss. Oxford 1975, 172.

the Farmers' Alliance, whose influence peaked in the run-up to the 1883 act. After this time, the Alliance's importance declined and it eventually folded in 1888. Its disappearance did not mark the demise of the 'farmers' interest', however. As the agricultural depression deepened, more farmers felt the reform of land tenure to be insufficient as a remedy for their woes and many landlords, hit by falling rent receipts, added their voices to the clamour for action. Direct intervention in the workings of the agrarian economy was demanded of government and many looked to the Conservatives rather than the Liberals as the party to provide it. A start was made in 1889 when in response, in part, to the lobbying of the Central Chamber of Agriculture and its allies, Salisbury's administration created the Board of Agriculture and installed Henry Chaplin as its first president. But this was widely regarded as insufficient on its own. Indeed, ever more vociferous calls for drastic action were heard from farmers and landlords, with the reduction of railway rates, the relief of local taxation and the imposition of duties on certain sorts of imported produce being the expedients many had in mind. This agrarian discontent prompted the establishment of an extra-parliamentary movement – the earl of Winchilsea's National Agricultural Union (NAU) – to press for a more substantial political response. Although the NAU only survived until 1901, it did achieve some success in heightening political awareness of farmer and landlord grievances – and, in the event, parliament did take some action. In 1896 the Unionists passed the Agricultural Lands Rating Act, which reduced by one-half the rates paid on agricultural land.

However, while farmers and landlords welcomed rate relief, it did not put an end to their grievances. Indeed, despite the Rating Act, they and their spokesmen considered the turn-of-the-century Houses of Parliament to have perpetuated their long-running neglect of agriculture. The two Royal Commissions established in 1879 and 1894 did not result in much legislative activity. And although the tariff reform campaign Joseph Chamberlain launched in May 1903 received some agrarian support, this was always muted. Few Tory farmers trusted 'Brummagem Joe' or took to the imperialist rationale behind his proposals, which in any case were primarily addressed to urban and industrial audiences – 'made on behalf of the towns', as H. Rider Haggard caustically put it.[13] Up to a point, the belief of farmers and landlords that politicians had neglected their welfare was a function of the increased importance of the agricultural labourer in political life. The Third Reform Act of 1884 had given the vote to large numbers of rural labourers, and this alone forced both Liberals and Conservatives to pay greater attention to their demands. For many Liberals in the mid-1880s the legislative provision of allotments provided a key means by which these demands could be met. Reformist agitation had led to the passage of the Allotments Extension Act of 1882, which directed the trustees of charity lands to provide allotments to

---

[13] R. H. Rider Haggard, *Rural England*, 2nd edn, London 1906, i, p. xv.

'cottagers and labourers'. However, the very limited impact of this measure stimulated radicals to press for further reform. Chamberlain's Birmingham ally Jesse Collings was a key player here. In 1883, Collings set up the Allotments Extension Association (later the Allotments and Small Holdings Association). An influential body very well connected to the Liberal party, it boasted Sir Charles Dilke, Henry Broadhurst, J. T. Brunner, J. E. Ellis and Lord Carrington among its vice-presidents, organised regular conferences and other meetings, and published its own newspaper (*Land and People*). The agitation generated by Collings and his association culminated in Chamberlain's 'unauthorised programme', set out in the run-up to the 1885 general election. Though Chamberlain's proposals were not exclusively concerned with rural matters, the most prominent of them was that which would have compelled landlords to make available to agricultural labourers plots of land for rent as allotments.[14] Somewhat misleadingly dubbed 'three acres and a cow', the idea had an enormous impact, especially in rural areas.

Radical reformers were not the only ones to advocate allotments. As was the case earlier in the century, allotments also appealed to a number of landlords, among them Tory peers such as the earl of Onslow, the duke of Bedford and the Lords Wantage and Tollemache. Actuated by a desire to demonstrate the redundancy of compulsory legislation, maintain social peace in the aftermath of the Third Reform Act and display paternal solicitude for the well-being of the agricultural labourer, such individuals urged and practised the voluntary provision of allotments. In 1886 Onslow established the Land and Glebe Owners' Association for the Voluntary Extension of the Allotments System, an organisation that aimed to publicise the benefits of independent action on the part of landlords. However, mounting demands for reform, not least from those Liberal Unionists who had parted company with Gladstone over home rule, left Salisbury's government with little choice but to legislate. In 1887 an act gave local authorities the power to buy or rent land, even compulsorily, for letting in allotment plots of one acre. Although some authorities were reluctant to take action, the measure made a significant impact. After the first steps had been taken by local authorities to obtain allotments, it frequently happened that landlords proved willing to supply them 'voluntarily'. A Parliamentary Return of 1890 showed that allotment numbers had risen to 453,000, an increase of 96,000 over the 1886 figure.[15] Allotment provision was further improved by an amending act of 1890 and, later on, by the Local Government Act of Gladstone's fourth administration.[16]

[14] A. Simon, 'Joseph Chamberlain and the unauthorized programme', unpubl. DPhil. diss. Oxford 1970, 222–66.

[15] Shaw Lefevre, *Agrarian tenures*, 74–5.

[16] The 1890 act gave allotment-providing powers to county councils; the 1894 Local Government Act extended those powers to the newly-created parish and district councils.

Closely associated with the issue of allotments was that of smallholdings, which also gained prominence in the mid-1880s. Like allotments, small-holdings were seen as a means of combating rural depopulation, promoting virtues such as thrift, hard work and self-reliance, and fostering social cohesion. However, they were also seen as a means of fundamentally altering the existing land system by promoting the development of a class of small farmers, akin to the much-vaunted 'yeomen' of old. As confidence in the capacity of Free Trade in Land to stimulate the growth of such a class of persons diminished, the belief strengthened that there was a need for direct legislative action by the state. For reformers like Collings, this was the only effective way of establishing a numerous peasant proprietary. In the 1880s Liberal Bills for the creation of peasant owners were introduced into parliament, as well as being strongly urged outside it by the press and bodies such as the Allotments and Small Holdings Association (ASHA). Following the defection of Collings and other agrarian radicals from the Liberal party after 1886, however, reform schemes were also pressed upon (and heard from) the Conservative side of the House, and in 1888 Salisbury's government established a select committee on the subject.

Unsurprisingly, many Tory landed grandees were in private rather luke-warm about smallholdings, but others in the party were far more positively disposed, seeing them as a means of encouraging property ownership. In 1892 the broadly favourable attitude of such individuals and the similarly favourable *Report* of the select committee combined with Liberal Unionist pressure and electoral calculations to produce a reform proposal from the party's normatively cautious leadership. This measure, which became law as the Small Holdings Act in the same year, gave county councils the ability to purchase or lease plots of land each of up to fifty acres in extent for sale to individuals as smallholdings.[17] Though it was considered by members of both political parties to be a groundbreaking piece of legislation, the act had a limited effect owing to the absence of compulsory clauses.[18]

Partly for this reason, calls for the further promotion of peasant proprietorship were still heard from Unionist politicians after 1892. Particularly voluble was the indefatigable Collings and the Rural Labourers' League (RLL), which he had set up in 1888 following his departure from the Gladstonian ASHA. Yet, while somewhat isolated in the 1890s, Collings and his radical associates were never completely without supporters within the Unionist alliance and, as time passed, increasing numbers rallied to their cause. Indeed, in the Edwardian period many Unionists rediscovered the peasant proprietor, among them Austen Chamberlain, Lord Milner and even

---

[17] Each purchaser was to find one-fifth of the cost of their holding, the remainder to be paid back in instalments over a period of fifty years.
[18] According to one estimate, only 881 acres were supplied by the act before 1908: N. R. Smith, *Land for the small man: English and Welsh experience with publicly-supplied small holdings, 1860–1937*, New York 1946, 59.

Lord Lansdowne, Unionist leader in the Upper House. In a 1909 speech Balfour committed his party to the legislative creation of smallholdings.[19] At the general election of January 1910, four-fifths of Unionist candidates for English county constituencies mentioned what many termed 'the land policy of Mr Balfour' in their election addresses.[20] A few years later, some MPs connected with the Unionist Social Reform Committee (USRC) went so far as to advocate responding to Lloyd George's Land Campaign with an alternative scheme for an agricultural minimum wage. But if this was too extreme a step for many, the democratisation of rural property owner-ship proved more congenial to a broad spectrum of party opinion, especially insofar as it was regarded as a much-needed bulwark against social upheaval. Milner's 1912–14 committee on land policy concluded that more peasant proprietors were required 'if the present social order is to endure'.[21]

If after 1886 Unionists moved towards the institution of peasant propri-etorship, their Liberal opponents moved away, preferring to advocate small-holding tenancy rather than ownership. Along with land tenure reform and parish councils, smallholdings were at the heart of the party's plan for rural regeneration in these years. Throughout the 1880s and 1890s, ASHA kept up pressure on the Liberal parliamentary party, as did the Land Law Reform Association (LLRA), the more radical successor to the FLL established in 1896. With the election of a Liberal government in 1906, reform came in the shape of an act enabling local authorities and centrally appointed commissioners to compulsorily acquire land for letting as small farms. This measure (the Small Holdings and Allotments Act) was combined with existing smallholding legislation in a consolidating act of 1908 and by 1914 over 205,000 acres of land had been provided under its provisions.[22]

Though the effect of the 1907–8 legislation was far from insignificant, it did not achieve the transformation of the English land system for which many had hoped. Yet there were those who had never entertained such hopes, people who believed that only very radical reform could deliver real change. For these individuals, the solution to many of the contemporary problems of town and country was land nationalisation. As is sometimes overlooked by historians, this was a major item on the political agenda of the early socialist movement. From its foundation in 1881, H. M. Hyndman's Social Democratic Federation (SDF) placed considerable emphasis on land reforms aiming towards nationalisation, as did Robert Blatchford's *Clarion* movement and also the Fabian Society. So too did Labour MPs, particularly

19 *The Times*, 23 Sept. 1909, 7.
20 Calculated from 234 addresses in *British political party general election addresses*, Brighton 1984–5, 28 microfilm reels, pt 1, 1892–1922, reel 5 (1910).
21 I. Packer, 'The Conservatives and the ideology of landownership, 1910–1914', in M. Francis and I. Zweiniger-Bargielowska (eds), *The Conservatives and British society, 1880–1990*, Cardiff 1996, 47.
22 C. S. Orwin and W. F. Darke, *Back to the land*, London 1935, 22–3, 28.

those associated with the Independent Labour Party (ILP), Philip Snowden and James Ramsay Macdonald being prominent examples. It is true that in 1913–14 the parliamentary Labour party leadership rejected left-wing calls for the adoption of immediate land nationalisation as official party policy.[23] However, as the party's own Land Enquiry report of January 1914 made plain, nationalisation – by means of the progressive increase of publicly-owned land – remained the ultimate objective.[24] In any case, nationalisation of the land (along with railways and canals) frequently featured in the electoral appeals of Labour and socialist politicians: at the general election of 1900 it was the third most commonly mentioned issue in candidates' addresses.[25]

But land nationalisation was by no means confined to the leftist fringes of politics. Having exerted considerable influence over radical elements of the Liberal party from the early 1880s on, this influence grew more widespread as time passed. The genealogy of Liberal support for land nationalisation can be traced back to the American social thinker Henry George and the famous British naturalist Alfred Russel Wallace. Their books on the subject, Wallace's *Land nationalisation* (1882) and particularly George's *Progress and poverty* (1880) had an enormous impact on progressive opinion.[26] The ideas advanced in these writings found expression in two organisations, the Land Nationalisation Society (LNS) and the English Land Restoration League (ELRL). Founded in 1881, the LNS followed Wallace in advocating the state-financed purchase of all real property. It also stressed the need for small-holdings, being more concerned with specifically rural affairs than the ELRL. Established in 1883 as a breakaway group of the LNS, the Georgeite ELRL favoured land nationalisation through the taxing rather than the buying out of property owners. Proposing the taxation of land values as 'the first step along the road which leads to Land Restoration', its concern was largely with towns and cities.[27] The land value of a plot of land was its base value aside from that accruing from improvements made to it by its user and, according to the ELRL, land values rightfully belonged to the entire community. The League hoped that ultimately, 'the whole annual value' of land would be taken 'for the public benefit', which would enable 'the English people themselves' to become 'the landlords of England', as there would no longer be any reason to own land except for personal use.[28]

---

[23] M. Tichelar, 'Socialists, Labour and the land: the response of the Labour party to the Land Campaign of Lloyd George before the First World War', *TCBH* viii (1997), 127–44.

[24] Labour party, *The Labour party and the agricultural problem*, London 1914.

[25] P. A. Readman, 'Patriotism and the general election of 1900 in Britain', unpubl. MPhil. diss. Cambridge 1998, 56.

[26] A. R. Wallace, *Land nationalisation* (1882), London 1892; H. George, *Progress and poverty* (1880), New York 1987.

[27] F. Verinder, *The land question*, Manchester 1901, 18.

[28] ELRL manifesto, JJ Coll., 'Land and the people', box 1; H. LeR. Malchow, *Agitators and promoters in the age of Gladstone and Disraeli*, New York 1983, p. xvi.

Although many moderate Liberals could not countenance land nationalisation, either now or in the future, the taxation of land values emerged as an important element of the party's appeal in the 1890s. It found a place in the Newcastle Programme of 1891 and became a staple element of the lists of reforms outlined in many candidates' platform appeals. At the 1895 general election, 25 per cent of Liberals standing for English seats mentioned land taxes in their addresses; by the time of the 1900 election, the figure had risen to 48 per cent and by 1906 it was 52 per cent.[29] In the Edwardian period, land value taxation proved especially popular as a proposal for tackling the problem of urban overcrowding and was the subject of many parliamentary debates, as well as important speeches and publications by prominent Liberals.[30] In 1902 added impetus was given to the movement by the reconstitution of the ELRL as the English League for the Taxation of Land Values (ELTV), an organisation to which numerous Liberal politicians belonged. (At the 1906 general election, forty-five members of the ELTV were returned to the Commons as Liberal MPs.)[31]

The land tax fed into Lloyd George's 'People's Budget' of 1909 and his Land Campaign of 1913–14. Lloyd George had been sympathetic to land value taxation for some time, and the notorious Land Clauses of the Budget were intended to lay the foundations for its eventual introduction. Under their provisions, the capital value of undeveloped land was to be subjected to a tax of half a penny in the pound (the Undeveloped Land Duty). In addition, the unearned increment of land values was to be taxed at 20 per cent, and lessors were to be liable to a 10 per cent reversion duty payable in cases when a lease terminated to their advantage. But the details of these measures were in a sense unimportant; the amount of money they were designed to raise was extremely small, amounting to under 5 per cent of the total increase in taxation proposed under the Budget.[32] What was significant was that these taxes required the comprehensive valuation of all land in the country, an undertaking which would allow the imposition of heavier land value taxation in later years. Thus to their Conservative critics, and also some of their more radical supporters, the Budget Land Taxes provided an apparatus for the institution of land nationalisation some time in the future. Soon after the People's Budget and before the controversy it had generated had abated, came the culmination of pre-war Liberal agrarian policy. In the

[29] Figures for 1895 and 1900 calculated from 600 addresses (321 for 1895, 279 for 1900) in *Election addresses*; figure for 1906 taken from A. K. Russell, *Liberal landslide: the general election of 1906*, Newton Abbot 1973, 65.

[30] For example *Hansard*, 4th ser., 1902, ciii. 475–544; 1904, cxxxi. 857–912; LV, Feb., Apr. 1903; C. Trevelyan, 'Land taxation and the use of land', in W. T. Stead (ed.), *Coming men on coming questions*, London 1905, 338–72; and A. J. A. Morris, *C. P. Trevelyan, 1870–1958*, London 1977, 55–6.

[31] *LV*, Feb. 1906, 176.

[32] R. Douglas, *Land, people and politics: a history of the land question in the United Kingdom, 1878–1952*, London 1976, 144.

summer of 1912, Lloyd George established committees of enquiry into the land question in town and country. The committees' reports were published in 1913 and 1914, providing the evidential basis for a great Liberal crusade against 'landlordism'. This was the famous Land Campaign, which Lloyd George launched in a speech at Bedford in October 1913. Here, and in subsequent speeches, Lloyd George and other prominent Liberals proposed a wide range of reforms. These included an agricultural minimum wage, further land tenure reform, increased provision for the compulsory purchase of land for public purposes, leasehold enfranchisement, and the institution of land value taxation as the basis of local rating. The leadership's oratorical efforts were followed up with an enormous propaganda campaign by the Liberal party organisation. A new body (the Central Land and Housing Council) was set up to co-ordinate activities, which soon reached a high pitch of intensity. By May 1914 between 90 and 120 meetings were taking place every day, and nearly three million booklets and leaflets had been distributed before the outbreak of war in August that year brought the Land Campaign to an abrupt end.[33]

The place of the land question in English politics, 1880–1914

Having delineated the principal features of the late Victorian and Edwardian 'land question', it is now necessary to establish the place it occupied in the politics of these years. How important were the debates just described? Did agrarian issues typically lie at the centre of the appeals mounted by Liberal and Conservative politicians? Or were they only of real significance at isolated points in time, or in particular places? In short, did land politics really matter? Generally speaking, the answer is that they did. Though land had always played some part in English politics, the early 1880s saw it rise to an unprecedented level of prominence. There were a number of reasons for this. There was a mounting perception of severe agricultural depression, this being associated with a conviction that 'something' ought to be done to assist what many still termed 'our greatest national industry'. In addition, there was more general anxiety about the depopulation of the countryside. Although rates of rural-urban migration had been steadily increasing since the 1850s, it was not until the 1880s that the scale of the demographic trend to the towns was properly appreciated. This was in large part due to the findings of the 1881 census and the 1879–82 Royal Commission on Agricultural Depression. Among other disquieting statistics, the census showed a 10 per cent decline in the number of tenant farmers since 1871, while the Royal Commission revealed that 700,000 people from the families of

---

[33] Packer, *Lloyd George, Liberalism and the land*, 125.

farm labourers had emigrated over the previous nine years. [34] In this context, books and articles warning of the grave dangers of allowing the 'rural exodus' to continue became commonplace. (Not least among the perceived dangers of rural depopulation was the effect it was held to have on urban life. High rates of migration led, so it was thought, to overcrowded slum conditions in towns and cities, the unwholesome character of which were graphically described in Andrew Mearns's *Bitter cry of outcast London*, and in other similarly alarmist publications of the time.)

Certain political developments also helped to propel the land question to the fore. Since the 1874 general election, which saw something of a Liberal collapse in rural constituencies, members of that party had grown infuriated by what they regarded as the entrenched Toryism and underdeveloped political culture of the English countryside. At and after the election of 1880, Whigs as well as radicals advocated county government reform to break the power of unelected JPs, Free Trade in Land to give the agricultural labourer liberating access to the soil, and further franchise reform to give him the vote.[35] The agitation of the Farmers' Alliance also served to push land up the political agenda in the 1880s, as did growing concern about the radical agrarianism of George, Wallace and others.

The early 1880s thus marked something of a watershed in land politics. At this time the land question drew an unprecedented level of public attention from Liberals in particular. While Whigs were sympathetic to moderate measures like the simplification of land transfer, Gladstonians and radicals emphasised land tenure reform and allotments. The enfranchisement of agricultural labourers and Chamberlain's 'unauthorised programme' ensured the prominence of land at the 1885 general election, especially in rural areas – where 'three acres and a cow' was almost the sole issue. With good reason did G. J. Goschen declare in one of his campaign speeches that 'the question of the land' was the 'subject … which is foremost, perhaps, in the minds of most men on both sides at this present moment'.[36] Soon after Goschen made these remarks, Gladstone announced his conversion to home rule for Ireland. Historians have seen the crisis this provoked as causing a serious and long-term decline in the importance of the politics of land. The Liberal split over Ireland deprived the party of several of its most important land reformers, including both Chamberlain and Collings, who left to help form the Liberal Unionists. Insulated from the potentially radicalising influence of such individuals, so it is argued, the 'leadership turned away from the subject of rural reform' and increasingly towards that of home rule. As Patricia Lynch has recently claimed, the result was that 'with one brief exception – the Local

---

34 Douglas, *Land*, 41.
35 J. Parry, *The rise and fall of Liberal government in Victorian Britain*, New Haven 1993, 241–3, 281–2.
36 G. J. Goschen, *Political speeches*, Edinburgh 1886, 7.

Government Act of 1894 – the party on a national level ignored the land question for most of the next twenty years'.[37]

There is some truth in this assessment. That home rule was the single most important issue in English politics in the ten or so years after 1885 is undeniable. Even at the general election of 1895, after the retirement of Gladstone, it figured more prominently than any other question in the political appeals of both parties' candidates.[38] Moreover, land was not a subject that provoked anything like unalloyed excitement from those at the apex of the Conservative or Liberal party hierarchies. Even before the decisive reorientation of his politics towards the lodestar of Irish self-government, Gladstone was not especially enthusiastic. Although amenable to certain moderate reforms and personally interested in *petite culture*, he was reluctant to countenance compulsory legislation for the creation of allotments or smallholdings. The public indifference and private distaste that Chamberlain's 'unauthorised programme' elicited from Gladstone dismayed the radical section of his party.[39]

Yet, while home rule might have moved into the forefront of late-Victorian politics in 1885–6, the continuing importance of the English land question cannot be denied. Leading politicians on both sides of the Commons urged the need for agrarian legislation and however reluctant Gladstone and Salisbury might have been, their calls did not go unheeded. A case in point is the Conservative administration of 1886–92. Under pressure from the Liberal Unionists, not least Collings and Chamberlain, it enacted measures for allotments and smallholdings and reformed the system of local government in the counties, in addition to establishing a Board of Agriculture.

The parliamentary prominence of agrarian issues bore testimony to their relevance to a broad spectrum of opinion. Newspapers and periodicals persistently advocated land reform, and there is substantial evidence to suggest that this advocacy reflected not just the views of the elite, but of the English people more generally. In many rural areas, demand for increased access to the land was considerable. In her *Lark Rise to Candleford*, Flora Thompson highlighted the appeal allotment cultivation had for the labouring population of Juniper Hill, the Oxfordshire village where she spent her youth in the 1880s and 1890s.[40] Its appeal evidently extended to other places too, as

---

[37] Lynch, *Liberal party*, 118–20; H. Newby, *Country life: a social history of rural England*, London 1987, 149–50.

[38] P. A. Readman, 'The 1895 general election and political change in late Victorian Britain', *HJ* xlii (1999), 469–71, 474–5, 492–3.

[39] Chamberlain regarded Gladstone's 1885 election address (which did not mention compulsory land purchase) as 'a slap in the face to us'. In a letter to Granville, Gladstone described the radical proposals for land reform as amounting to 'compulsory expropriation': C. H. D. Howard, 'Joseph Chamberlain and the "unauthorised programme"', *EHR* lxv (1950), 486. For Gladstone's espousal of the merits of *petite culture* see F. W. Hirst, *Gladstone as financier and economist*, London 1931, 257–61.

[40] F. Thompson, *Lark Rise to Candleford* (1945), London 1973, 62–4.

illustrated by the fact that immediately following the passage of the 1887 bill, 1,600 men in the Spalding division of Lincolnshire petitioned three Boards of Guardians for provision of allotments under the measure.[41] In 1891 the author of the Daily News's influential series of reports on rural England, entitled Life in our villages, found that allotments were readily taken up even when offered on quite unreasonable terms. None of the many allotment grounds he visited on his tour around England were unable to find tenants.[42] A comparable level of demand existed for smallholdings. Within four months of the legislation of 1907 coming into force, the government had received applications for land totalling 210,000 acres.[43] Rural local government reform also seems to have been welcomed by the inhabitants of the countryside,[44] and it is surely significant that allotments and smallholdings figured largely in the politics of county, parish and district council elections. According to one contemporary commentator, at the first set of county council contests in January 1889, 'allotments were made the test question, and upon "allotments" or "no allotments" every constituency was fought'.[45]

The popularity of land reform was not lost on politicians, many of whom were sensitive to the electoral benefits of its promotion. The Conservative government's legislation of 1887 and 1892 was drafted with half an eye on garnering votes in rural areas,[46] as indeed were the agrarian proposals of Campbell-Bannerman's and Asquith's Liberal administrations. In March 1907 a deputation of MPs told their Chief Whip that they were 'quite convinced … if we have nothing in the matter of Small Holdings and Rural Housing … the Liberal county members will be overwhelmed at the next general election'; the smallholdings bill passed the same year did something to assuage such concerns.[47] Similarly, the Land Campaign of 1913–14 was also influenced by partisan considerations. The success of radical land-taxer candidates at by-elections in North West Norfolk, Holmfirth and Hanley in the summer of 1912 did not go unnoticed – either by Lloyd George or the Liberal leadership generally.[48]

Thus it should be unsurprising that home rule notwithstanding, the land question retained a good deal of its importance in the electoral appeal of the two main parties after 1885. This was particularly true for the Liberals. While

41 R. Winfrey, Great men and others I have met, Kettering 1943, 41.
42 [G. F. Millin], Life in our villages, 3rd edn, London 1891, 63–4.
43 A. Adonis, 'Aristocracy, agriculture and Liberalism: the politics, finances and estates of the third Lord Carrington', HJ xxxi (1985), 893.
44 M. K. Ashby, Joseph Ashby of Tysoe, 1859–1919, Cambridge 1961, 183, 186–7.
45 J. F. Wilkinson (1894), cited in Smith, Land for the small man, 54.
46 J. R. Fisher, 'Public opinion and agriculture, 1875–1900', unpubl. PhD diss. Hull 1972, 780–1.
47 C. B. Harmsworth to G. Whiteley, 5 Mar. 1907, cited in J. Brown, 'Ideas concerning social policy and their influence on legislation in Britain, 1902–11', unpubl. PhD diss. London 1964, 265.
48 Douglas, Land, 156–8.

Ireland predominated in their candidates' campaigns at the election of 1886, land returned to play a far greater part in that of 1892. The early 1890s had seen a sharp increase in Liberal interest in the land, to which the proceedings of NLF conferences, the speeches of politicians and the *Daily News*'s *Life in our villages* bore compelling testimony.[49] This interest was reflected in party propaganda. By 1892 land reform had become almost as popular as home rule as subject matter for Liberal pamphlets. It was certainly much more popular than other items on the party's programme: disestablishment, education, temperance, social reforms and free trade all featured far less prominently in political literature.[50] During the election campaign, Liberal candidates put considerable emphasis on the land question, with parish and district councils being presented as potent engines of rural reform and renewal. Under Liberal proposals they would be given wide-ranging powers to acquire land for small-holdings and allotments. Some candidates gave agrarian matters top billing: for Hugh Luttrell in Tavistock there was 'no more important question than that of the treatment of our land'; for Frederick Cheetham in the High Peak division of Derbyshire the expeditious introduction of land reform was 'of vast consequence to the nation'.[51] Outside rural constituencies, land reform also featured in Liberals' appeals, where increasing the agricultural labourer's access to the soil (and thereby decreasing his propensity to migrate to the town) was – along with land value taxation – presented as a means of easing overcrowding and wage competition in urban areas.[52]

Emphasis on the urban relevance of the land question was still more pronounced at subsequent general elections. In 1895 and 1900 land value taxation and/or other land reforms appeared in 44 per cent (1895) and 64 per cent (1900) of the addresses of candidates standing for English boroughs.[53] In respect of county constituencies, the equivalent figures were 65 per cent

[49] Millin, *Life in our villages*; NLF, *Annual reports and council proceedings, 1877–1936*, Hassocks 1975 (microfiche), cards 9–12 (1891–2); Liberal Publication Department, *The condition of the rural population*, London 1891.

[50] In 1892 the National Liberal Club published a list of pamphlets on 'the chief points of the Liberal and Radical Programme'. The pamphlets were listed in subsections of varying size, each pertaining to a particular political issue. After 'Home Rule for Ireland', which filled 4½ pages, easily the largest subsection was 'the land question', which took up 3 pages (nearly 3½ if 'parish councils' are counted). This compared to 'disestablishment' (1 page), 'the labour question' (¾ page), 'education' (½ page), 'local option' (< ½ page), 'House of Lords' (¼ page): *List prepared under the direction of the Political Committee of the National Liberal Club of pamphlets, &c. on the chief points of the Liberal and radical programme*, London 1892, JJ Coll., 'Creeds, parties, policies', box 18.

[51] *Election addresses*, reel 1 (1892), 11, 9.

[52] For example, E. H. Bayley (North Camberwell) and C. Norton (West Newington): ibid. 15–16, 31–2.

[53] Figures calculated from 174 addresses ibid. (1895) and 144 addresses in reel 2 (1900).

and 57 per cent.[54] Indeed, it is telling that even in the contest of 1900, which was dominated by the South African War, land reform stood out as one of the more important domestic concerns of Liberal politicians. It was certainly of greater prominence than home rule, which was mentioned in just 20 per cent of addresses.[55] The importance of land reform had increased still further by the time of the 1906 general election, when many Liberals in both town and country insisted that a radical solution to the land question was, as one candidate put it, 'perhaps the chief social necessity of our time'.[56] According to Arnold Herbert, who successfully contested the normally Tory seat of Wycombe, 'no subject was listened to with more rapt attention, nothing aroused greater interest than the exposition of a scheme of land reform which would open a career to the villagers in the country they knew so well'.[57] In all, over two-thirds of candidates for English seats made reference to land reform in their election addresses.[58] 'Above all', one scholar has written, 'land reform ran through Liberal election addresses throughout Great Britain, ranging from advocacy of tenant right and the importance of small-holdings – so that sometimes the party appears as a small-holders, peasant party – to land nationalisation'.[59] The general elections of 1910 added to this impression; in the first of these, 67 per cent of candidates for English county constituencies mentioned land policies in their election addresses.[60]

So much for the Liberals: land was relatively less prominent in the electoral appeals of Conservatives and Liberal Unionists. However, it did occupy a significant presence. This was true even for the single-issue elections of 1886 and 1900, where in the English counties it remained one of the more important domestic items of politicians' appeals.[61] In 1892 and 1895 Unionists pushed land forcefully before the electorate. In 1892 the Allotments and Smallholdings Acts took pride of place on the list of government legislation retailed by candidates for county constituencies in their election addresses.[62] And, like their Liberal opponents, urban Tories such as Claude Hay and

---

[54] Figures calculated from 148 addresses ibid. reel 1 (1895) and 138 addresses in reel 2 (1900).
[55] Figure calculated from 279 addresses ibid. reel 2 (1900).
[56] W. B. Luke (Devon, Honiton); D. Williamson (Camberwell, Dulwich), W. Claridge (West Bradford), E. H. Lamb (Rochester): ibid. reel 3 (1906).
[57] A. Herbert, 'The three planks of progress', in C. F. G. Masterman and others, *To colonise England*, London 1907, 13.
[58] Russell, *Landslide*, 65.
[59] R. E. Ellins, 'Aspects of the New Liberalism, 1895–1914', unpubl. PhD diss. Sheffield 1980, 268.
[60] Figure calculated from 221 addresses in *Election addresses*, reels 4, 5 (1910).
[61] In the 1900 election agriculture and agrarian issues were mentioned in 20% of Unionist candidates' addresses. By contrast, the figures for disestablishment, workers' compensation, education, housing and temperance were 12%, 6%, 15%, 12% and 13% respectively: figures calculated from 209 addresses ibid. reel 2 (1900).
[62] Ibid. reel 1 (1892).

Walter Goldsworthy promoted land reform as a means of improving the job opportunities and overcrowded living conditions of working-class city-dwellers.[63] In 1895, however, the focus was overwhelmingly rural. Following the lead of the 'manifesto' delivered by Salisbury in a House of Lords speech given just before the dissolution of parliament, Unionists stressed their conviction that the crisis-hit agricultural industry 'must receive special and immediate attention'.[64] Though some were rather vague as to what form this attention should take, the relief of local taxation, the remission of railway rates and the enactment of moderate land reform were evidently the expedients most had in mind.[65] Throughout England as a whole, agrarian issues were mentioned in 45 per cent of Unionist addresses: in counties, the figure was 67 per cent (rising to 72 per cent in those counties that experienced a contest).[66] After 1895 there followed something of a hiatus in the electoral presence of land politics on Unionist platforms. In 1900 the Boer War squeezed domestic issues to the sidelines, while in 1906 land policy was subsumed within the overriding debate about fiscal reform, having little presence outside of this.[67] The elections of 1910, however, were a rather different matter. Drawing on Balfour's public commitment to the legislative encouragement of peasant proprietorship, Conservative and Liberal Unionist candidates gave great prominence to the land question in their appeals. Of those Unionists standing for English county seats in January 1910, 82 per cent dealt with land policy in their addresses.[68]

The sustained prominence of the language of land politics in the political appeals of Liberals and Unionists after 1885 was reflected by its electoral significance. Political commitment to various land policies sprang largely from conviction (Collings provides the classic example), but considerations of electoral benefit also played a part in explaining politicians' motivations. As they were well aware, the Third Reform Act had democratised rural political culture, giving the vote to about 75 per cent of agricultural labourers.[69] In this context, languages of land politics that were both popular and patriotic were increasingly seen as a key means of winning votes in many county constituencies. As we have seen, there is little doubt that such considerations had an influence on many of the land reforms promulgated in

---

[63] C. G. Hay (Shoreditch, Hoxton) and W. T. Goldsworthy (Hammersmith): ibid.

[64] H. V. Duncombe (Cumberland, Egremont): ibid. reel 1 (1895).

[65] Only 1% of candidates standing for English constituencies advocated protective tariffs: figure calculated from 417 addresses ibid.

[66] Figures calculated from 221 addresses for county and 196 addresses for borough constituencies in England, ibid.

[67] Russell, *Landslide*, 83.

[68] Figures calculated from 234 addresses in *Election addresses*, reel 5 (1910).

[69] P. F. Clarke and K. Langford, 'Hodge's politics: the agricultural labourer and the Third Reform Act in Suffolk', in N. Harte and R. Quinault (eds), *Land and society in Britain, 1700–1914*, Manchester 1996, 125–6.

this period, from the Conservative government's allotments and smallholdings legislation of 1887 and 1892 to Lloyd George's Land Campaign.

Furthermore, there is also little doubt that politicians were right to assume
that attractive land policies could confer considerable benefits at the polls.
In 1885 the Liberals made massive gains in country seats, hitherto dominated by the Conservatives. Of the ninety-eight seats defined as 'rural' by
Neal Blewett, the Liberals won fifty-two.[70] While there is evidence to suggest
that Liberal responsibility for passing the Third Reform Act drew the support
of many rural voters, the vigorous championing of land reform by Liberals of
all political shades made the decisive impact.[71] Indeed, the extent to which
Liberal success in rural seats rested on land policy was revealed the following
year, at the election of 1886. The catastrophic reduction of Liberal representation in rural seats to just fourteen MPs was largely a consequence of many
voters in these seats regarding the policy of home rule as having derailed, or
even betrayed, the cause of land reform – not least by precipitating the exit
of prominent radicals like Collings and Chamberlain from the party.[72]

In a recent book, Patricia Lynch has offered an important interpretation
of Conservative electoral dominance in rural England after 1886. In her
analysis, the Tories exploited Liberal abandonment of land reform for the
cause of home rule by extolling the values of a harmonious, hierarchical
and politically quiescent 'rural culture of community'. Such conservative
communitarianism loomed large in the party's political discourse, not least in
the language of the Primrose League, which was especially strong in English
county constituencies.[73] According to Lynch, this agrarian Tory rhetoric
correlated with the inclusive, communitarian values of rural inhabitants
who disdained the confrontational, divisive politics of Liberal radicalism and
thereby played a key part in the party's electoral success in country areas
between the mid-1880s and the 1900s.

That Lynch has exaggerated the extent to which Liberal commitment
to land reform declined in the years after 1885 has already been noted (the
1886 election was something of an exception), but there is a further problem
with her argument – this being that she has misunderstood the nature of
rural politics more generally. Her view that a socially conservative village
community ethos prevailed in rural England bears some similarities to the
earlier work of D. C. Moore and Howard Newby, both of whom argued for
the persistence of 'deferential' social relations into the Victorian period.[74]

---

[70] For N. Blewett's classification of seats as 'rural' see *The peers, the parties and the people:
the general elections of 1910*, London 1972, 488–94.
[71] Clarke and Langford, 'Hodge's politics', 130–1; Howard, 'Joseph Chamberlain', 477–
91; Simon, 'Joseph Chamberlain', 247–8, 265–6, 430–1.
[72] For J. Collings's view of home rule as 'betrayal' of labourers' interests see *Land reform*,
new edn, London 1908, 182–3.
[73] Lynch, *Liberal party*, esp. pp. 84–5.
[74] H. Newby, *The deferential worker: a study of farm workers in East Anglia*, London 1977,
esp. pp. 47–55; Moore, *Politics of deference*.

Table 1
Election results in rural seats, 1885–1910

Election	No. of rural seats/98 won by Unionists	Unionist % of poll in rural seats	Unionist % of poll in England as a whole
1885	46	49.0	48.7
1886	84	57.4	54.5
1892	64	53.5	52.0
1895	81	56.6	55.6
1900	78	55.9	56.1
1906	32	47.6	44.5
1910 (Jan.)	70	53.6	49.4
1910 (Dec.)	69	53.3	50.0

Source: Blewett, *Peers*, 495–6.

Table 2
Swing to Unionists at general elections, 1886–1910

Election	Swing in rural seats	Swing in England as a whole
1886	8.4	5.8
1892	−3.9	−2.5
1895	3.1	3.6
1900	−0.7	0.5
1906	−8.3	−11.6
1910 (Jan.)	6.0	4.9
1910 (Dec.)	−0.3	0.6

Source: Blewett, *Peers*, 495–6.

But just as Moore and Newby misread the early and mid nineteenth-century political culture of rural England, so has Lynch misread its late nineteenth- and early twentieth-century equivalent. It is simply not true to say that Tory politics in the English countryside – as exemplified by the Primrose League – tended strongly towards communitarian inclusivity and away from partisan divisiveness. Despite its genteel tea-parties and fetes, the Primrose League was aggressively partisan: the inculcation of 'sound political principles' by means of policy-specific propaganda remained central to its agenda throughout.[75]

[75] As one prospective Conservative MP put it in a letter to the *Primrose League Gazette*, 'The Primrose League is essentially a political and educational organisation for carrying out certain principles': *PLG*, 1 Apr. 1897, 5. This was borne out by the League's propaganda activities, which included the establishment of circulating libraries (stocked with political tracts as well as novels) and the issuing of political leaflets – two million of which were distributed in 1891 alone. (For a list of League leaflets see *PLG*, 1 Oct. 1894, 17.) 'Social and entertaining meetings' were important, but principally insofar as they provided a congenial context for the partisan indoctrination of voters and their families. Even the most apparently apolitical of Primrose League activities were laden

But it was prepared to use more directly confrontational tactics too, which were quite at odds with the pieties of any socially harmonious village 'culture of community'. In 1889 the Liberal Lord Spencer reported that members of the League in Northamptonshire had taken to engaging in 'exclusive dealing and social isolation of individuals against political opponents'.[76] Three years later he attributed the reduction of his half-brother's majority in mid Northants to 'constant Primrose Leaguing for 5 years ... They had "habitations" in villages altogether belonging to me, and of course I could say nothing to tenants who took this line'.[77]

That the Primrose League was not above subverting ties between landlord and tenant for Conservative political gain is just one indication of the importantly partisan character of rural politics at this time. Writing of his efforts to promote NAU activity in Norfolk, A. H. H. Matthews averred that

> No one has any idea of the care necessary in starting a work like this in a strange village ... To have seen the clergyman of a parish first, is enough to prevent every nonconformist from attending your meeting. If a Conservative takes any active part the Radicals avoid it like poison, and *vice-versa* ... It would be laughable were it not so detrimental to the progress and to the dignity of a village, which from its size cannot afford to be divided, but regardless of consequences it must needs split itself up into such cliques and parties, both in religion and politics, that anything like 'Union' was out of the question.[78]

Although Matthews suggested that this 'strained feeling' was not apparent everywhere, his observation shows how after the enfranchisement of agricultural labourers in 1884, village politics were increasingly confrontational, divisive and partisan. The socially conservative 'culture of community' described by Lynch did not dominate rural political culture and neither – as the Primrose League demonstrates *a fortiori* – was it a leitmotif of the Conservatives' appeal to country voters.

From the late 1880s, Conservative opposition to land reform based on a traditionalist defence of the agrarian *status quo* lost ground to the idea of

with partisan import. As the *Illustrated London News* reported in 1887, the concerts, 'community singing' and dancing held in rural schoolrooms under the aegis of labourers' social superiors might have marked 'a return to Merry England's traditions for the village folks', but nevertheless these activities were 'politics all the same. Every woman, as well as every man there, will feel a degraded and contemptible traitor if, when the election comes, they fail to work for "the Primrose Cause"': *Illustrated London News*, 19 Nov. 1887, repr. *PLG*, 26 Nov. 1887, 3.

[76] Speech of John Spencer, 5th Earl Spencer at Reading, 6 Feb. 1889, cited in *The red earl: the papers of the fifth Earl Spencer, 1835–1910*, ed. P. Gordon, Northampton 1981–6, ii. 210 n. 3.

[77] Spencer to Sir William Harcourt, 15 July 1892, ibid. ii. 210.

[78] *Cable*, supplement, 5 June 1897, 3.

peasant or 'yeoman' proprietorship. In the context of growing labour unrest and increasingly violent attacks on landed property by the Land Nationalisation Society and others, many Conservatives had come to present the traditional objections to small ownership as vitiated by pressing national needs, not least that of 'anchor[ing] the institutions of the state' in response to the rising tide of extremist ideas.[79] By the end of the Edwardian period, small-holdings had become a major item on the Unionists' rural agenda. Some party members – Liberal Unionists especially – claimed that the legislative encouragement of a numerous class of small owners (not local authority tenants, as in Liberal plans) was an effective way of preserving the character and health of Englishmen. Others continued to emphasise its utility as a bulwark against serious social upheaval. In an increasingly democratic political culture, the expansion of property-ownership rather than the maintenance of paternalism was offered as the means through which social peace and harmony in the countryside would be preserved.

The reconceptualisation of Unionist land policy along more democratic lines paid electoral dividends. Balfour's 1909 declaration in support of a purchase policy was a not insignificant factor behind Unionist success in English rural constituencies at the general election of January 1910.[80] In 1906 the Conservatives and Liberal Unionists had won just thirty-two out of ninety-eight such constituencies; in January 1910, by contrast, they won sixty-nine. The average swing to the Unionists in these rural seats (6.0) was also significantly higher than that across England as a whole (4.9).[81] This being the case, was the democratisation of Unionist rhetoric on the land question anything more than a vote-winning ploy? Some historians think not, taking a sceptical view of the party's profession of commitment to land reform. For Matthew Fforde, it amounted to little more than an opportunistic policy, one consistent with Conservative traditions and formulated as a defensive response to Liberal radicalism. In his interpretation, Tories' support for occupying ownership did not indicate conversion to a radical vision of a regenerated and socially transformed countryside; they merely hoped that a smallholdings policy would do something to bolster the position of landlords (by giving them property-owning allies), while also furnishing their party with an attractive electoral appeal with which to combat the collectivist new Liberalism of their opponents.[82] In his high political study of the

[79] Lord Salisbury, speech at Conservative Party conference, Nottingham, The Times, 27 Nov. 1889, 6.

[80] J. Collings to A. Balfour, 29 Jan 1910, Austen Chamberlain papers, Birmingham University Library, AC8/5/2.

[81] Analysis based on the figures given in Blewett, Peers, 495–6.

[82] 'A handful of Conservatives looked to the creation of yeoman and peasant proprietors as a method of repopulating the countryside. But all the signs suggest that the adoption of land purchase by the Conservative party after 1906 was animated by a bulwarkian and opportunist aspiration, rather than by Collings's dream of a more intensely inhabited rural sector': M. Fforde, 'The Conservative party and real property in England, 1900–1914',

Unionist party in opposition after 1905, David Dutton has taken a similarly sceptical view, arguing that there was little real enthusiasm for constructive land reform within the party leadership, whose position basically remained one of negative hostility to change.[83]

There are grounds for taking this view of Unionist policy. That party members increasingly saw land reform as an effective means of winning votes in rural areas cannot be doubted, and the hope that an increase in the numbers of land owners could strengthen the traditional social order of the countryside probably did play a part in the thinking of some Tory grandees. But considerations of electoral benefit were not incompatible with the arguments of more radical Unionists like Collings, who was never backward in urging the adoption of his proposals for these reasons anyway. As Collings wrote to A. D. Steel-Maitland in the aftermath of the crisis over the Parliament Act,

> The rural voters care little or nothing about what is termed the constitutional question, nor are they interested in high politics. What they do care about are matters connected with the land. They will always listen to the programme of the Rural League, which is understood and popular everywhere. Their interest is constant and abiding in the policy of creating ownerships of land by means of State aid.[84]

Yet while Unionist land reformers saw the policy of small-ownership as a means of bolstering the institution of private property, they did not see it as a means of bolstering the institution of landlordism; the aim was the transformation of rural England to conform with new social and political realities, not the preservation of the old order. And despite the claims of Fforde and Dutton, mainstream Conservatives and Liberal Unionists developed genuine sympathy for this position, as will be shown in later chapters.

Real ideological change thus combined with a felt need for an electorally-effective appeal to meet the challenge posed by a rejuvenated rural Liberalism; the two processes were not incompatible, but went hand in hand. As for the nature of this challenge, it is clear that the rural radicalism of Campbell-Bannerman and Asquith's Liberal party had strong echoes of 1885. For Lynch, the Edwardian revival of radical agrarianism was combined with a new emphasis on community: a vigorous anti-aristocratic agenda fused with a defence of the national community against the sectional aims of Unionists

unpubl. DPhil diss. Oxford 1985, 200–1. See also his *Conservatism and collectivism, 1886–1914*, Edinburgh 1990, 117–19, 136–9, 152–3.

[83] D. Dutton, '*His Majesty's loyal opposition': the Unionist party in opposition, 1905–1915*, Liverpool 1992, 274–6.

[84] Collings to A. D. Steel-Maitland, 18 Sept. 1911, Joseph Chamberlain papers, Birmingham University Library, JC22/53. See also Collings to J. Chamberlain, 17 Oct. 1890, JC5/16/25; Collings to J. Chamberlain, 22 Nov. 1908, JC22/45; Collings to M. Chamberlain, 20 Mar. 1910, JC22/48; and T. A. Jenkins, 'Hartington, Chamberlain and the Unionist alliance, 1886–1895', *Parliamentary History* xi (1992), 134 n. 131.

(especially tariff reformers). This, Lynch says, was a winning combination at the polls and formed the basis of Liberal strength in rural areas before 1914.[85] Liberal land policies in the 1900s were compatible with the party's patriotic defence of the nation's welfare against the selfish claims of business, clerical and landlord interests, as I have argued elsewhere.[86] But the national community to which Edwardian Liberals appealed with such success had little in common with the 'resolutely apolitical ideal of the harmonious village community' cited by Lynch as one of the key obstacles to the advance of rural Liberalism in the twenty years after 1886.[87] The Liberals had neither stolen the clothes of their Tory opponents, nor had they suddenly stumbled on a new and potent rhetoric for the winning of votes. The language of land reformism articulated by Liberals in 1906 was suffused with a democratic vision of a village community of self-sufficient, independent cultivators. This vision, which drew upon English history, inspired policies aimed at addressing pressing national issues (such as race deterioration), and had done so since the early 1880s – if not earlier. The Liberal recovery in the English counties in 1906 was achieved by means of an appeal that had in essence been before the electorate for some time. That it had not met with any great success for much of the twenty years after 1886 – with the exception of the victory in 1892, for which it took some of the credit – was largely due to extraneous factors. In 1886 and 1900 it was eclipsed by home rule and the Boer War respectively, as was everything else; in 1895 its impact was vitiated by the fissiparousness and disorganisation of the Liberal party.[88] By the 1900s, Unionist divisions over tariff reform combined with a new sense of party purpose and cohesion among Liberals to help ensure the success of their languages of land and nation.

Historians and the language of land politics

The politics of land have not always attracted a level of scholarly interest commensurate with their contemporary significance. In the 1960s and 1970s those historians working on the subject could lament that theirs was a neglected field. Speaking to the Royal Historical Society in 1965, F. M. L. Thompson suggested that a primary reason for this state of affairs (at least with regard to the nineteenth century) was that 'alone among the great Victorian movements the land reform agitation possesses no great monuments recording its later successes'.[89] He had a point. The legislative action

[85] Lynch, Liberal party.
[86] Readman, 'Liberal party', 269–302.
[87] Lynch, Liberal party, quotation at p. 220.
[88] D. C. Savage, 'The general election of 1886 in Great Britain and Ireland', unpubl. PhD diss. London 1958; Readman, '1895', and 'Conservative party', 107–45.
[89] F. M. L. Thompson, 'Land and politics in the nineteenth century', TRHS 5th ser. xv

and political debate outlined in this chapter had relatively little effect on English society. Despite the intentions of reformers, demographic trends and the pattern of landownership remained largely unchanged: rural depopulation continued, and neither peasant proprietorship nor small tenancy came to replace the existing system. Nor were the land laws fundamentally altered: primogeniture, strict settlement and the cumbersome method of land transfer survived into the twentieth century. More tangible, perhaps, was the direct impact on the welfare of the rural population. Farmers benefited from land tenure and game law reforms, and the distress caused them by agricultural depression was mitigated by rate relief (a measure which also eased the pressure on landlords). In the shape of more extensive provision of allotments and smallholdings, labourers enjoyed something of that increased access to the soil that they had long demanded. But these qualifications aside, the politics of land (even those of the period 1900–14) can hardly be said to have produced any revolutionary social or economic changes worthy of lapidary commemoration.

Although a lack of memorable socio-economic achievements might help explain the comparatively minor place assigned land politics in the historical record, it does not necessarily follow that this placing is justified. While the legislation enacted ultimately had a relatively small effect on society, contemporaries unaccustomed to governmental intervention in agrarian matters took it extremely seriously. In 1893 Shaw Lefevre felt confident that his book on land reform demonstrated 'how fully Parliament has recognised the defects of the present system of land tenure in England and Wales and of the distribution of land, and how manifold and varied have been the efforts to mitigate them'.[90] These efforts might ultimately have been ineffective, yet, as Thompson himself argued, the English land question was still 'central to an understanding of nineteenth-century political history'. For Thompson, this was because the debates it produced represented one aspect of a wider struggle for power between the historical incumbents of this power, the landed elite, and those Liberals and radicals who sought to wrest it from them.[91]

Whether or not Thompson's reading of the political significance of the land question was entirely correct is a moot point. What is beyond doubt, however, is that his paper helped prompt much research into the subject. There followed a large number of books, articles and doctoral dissertations on the politics of land in the late nineteenth and early twentieth centuries. Reliable overview treatments of the parliamentary land question have now been produced, as have numerous more detailed studies of specific debates, personalities and legislation.[92] In addition, a good deal of work on trade

---

(1965), 23.
[90] Lefevre, *Agrarian tenures*, 88.
[91] Thompson, 'Land and politics', 23–4.
[92] For example, Douglas, *Land*; J. R. Fisher, 'Agrarian politics', in E. J. T. Collins (ed.),

unionism and pressure group activity has appeared.[93] However, there still remains some truth in Matthew Fforde's claim, made in his *Conservatism and collectivism* of 1990, that 'a deafening silence surrounds the land question in many of the secondary works on these years'.[94] Textbooks and general surveys do still fail to pay sufficient regard to the politics of land, with Richard Shannon's *Age of Salisbury* being one fairly recent example.[95] Moreover, it remains the case that the English land question is accorded less attention than its Irish, Scottish and Welsh equivalents – though the work of Ian Packer has done something to remedy this deficiency for the Edwardian period.[96]

There is, however, a further and arguably more significant shortcoming in the extant literature. Despite Thompson's arguments, historians have found it difficult to deal with the limited socio-economic impact of the measures passed by parliament. The continuing ineluctability of this fact has inhibited scholars from formulating compelling conclusions assertive of the significance of land politics. So too has their view – for which there exists substantial evidence to the contrary – that many proposals for land reform had a very restricted appeal.[97] As a result, much of the historiography has a bathetic feel to it. The reader can wade through detailed descriptions of pressure group activities, or party political debates, or legislative activity, only to be told that it was all of little account, all heat and no light. Whatever the nature of their intentions, historians have done little to dispel the impression railed against by Thompson: that, ultimately, the politics of land were of relatively minor importance. One writer has claimed that because nothing concrete resulted from Liberal and radical schemes of land reform, the debate they generated constituted a mere 'pantomime of politics'.[98] And while few are as dismissive as this, even those scholars who take land politics with greater seriousness find it difficult to advance beyond similar conclusions. Historians of the land question have searched for what in another context Raphael Samuel once called 'the reality content', and found it somewhat lacking.[99] A good case in point is provided by their treatment of the measures passed by Lord Carrington, Liberal President of the Board of Agriculture between

The agrarian history of England and Wales, VII: *1850–1914*, Cambridge 2000, i. 321–57; Adonis, 'Aristocracy'; and Packer, *Lloyd George, Liberalism and the land*.

[93] For example, J. P. D. Dunbabin, *Rural discontent in nineteenth-century Britain*, London 1974; A. Howkins, *Poor labouring men: rural radicalism in Norfolk, 1872–1923*, London 1985; N. Scotland, *Agricultural trade unionism in Gloucestershire, 1972–1950*, Cheltenham 1991; Fisher, 'Farmers' Alliance', S. D. Ward, 'Land reform in England, 1880–1914', unpubl. PhD diss. Reading 1976; and Fisher, 'Public opinion'.

[94] Fforde, *Conservatism*, 19–20.

[95] R. Shannon, *The age of Salisbury, 1881–1902*, London 1996.

[96] Packer, *Lloyd George, Liberalism and the land*.

[97] See, for example, Douglas, *Land*, 106–7, 120.

[98] S. Hogg, 'Landed society and the Conservative party in the late nineteenth and early twentieth centuries', unpubl. DPhil diss. Oxford 1972, 126–7.

[99] Samuel, *Patriotism*, iii, p. xxvii.

1905 and 1911. In his study of Carrington's rural politics, Andrew Adonis remarks that the earl hoped that his smallholdings legislation of 1907 would 'cause a peaceful agricultural revolution' by 'restor[ing] to the agricultural labourer some of the conditions under which he lived in the earlier part of the [nineteenth] century'. However, stemming from an unrealistic 'nostalgic vision' of a lost rural England, Carrington's hopes were disappointed by the failure of his act to have more than a relatively inconsequential effect on the overall distribution of land; it was, Adonis concludes, little more than 'a romantic irrelevance'. In his analysis, paving the way for Lloyd George's Land Campaign seems to have been its primary significance.[100] Similarly, Packer's recent book on Edwardian land politics also downplays the importance of Carrington's rural reforms. In his interpretation, both the Agricultural Holdings Act of 1906 and the Smallholdings Act of 1907 were legislative 'failures', political initiatives of secondary historical significance.[101]

Yet what is clearly missing from the literature is a satisfactory explanation of the reasons why people at the time saw land politics, even supposedly 'failed' measures like those of 1906 and 1907, as important. And it is only by examining the language they used that such an explanation can be provided. Historians have so far paid limited attention to the language of the land question. Scholarly writing has too often confined itself to telling the parliamentary story of proposed and enacted agrarian legislation, and the institutional history of reformist movements and trade unions. As a consequence, it has had the effect of leaving some of the key ideas that informed the politics of land relatively unexplored. Many of these ideas were shot through with patriotic sentiment of various sorts, as subsequent chapters will discuss. This is not something that would surprise cultural historians, accustomed as they are to the view that the language of English patriotism was inflected by rural themes. Yet it has not drawn much in the way of acknowledgement from political historians. Some, indeed, have denied that patriotic or nationalistic ideas had much influence on English land politics. Packer, for example, has expressed scepticism as to their significance before 1914, as has Adonis, in his belittling of the 'nostalgic vision' of a lost rural nation entertained by Carrington in the 1900s.[102] Others have recognised the significance of such visions, but have proved reluctant to discuss them in any detail. In his contribution to volume vii of the *Cambridge agrarian history*, for example, J. R. Fisher suggests that 'the importance of the land question' in late nineteenth- and early twentieth-century politics 'was due at least in part to the almost mystical appeal it exerted among the politically conscious'.[103] Regrettably, however, Fisher does not elaborate upon this observation, and he is not alone in his reticence. Even those historians who

100   Adonis, 'Aristocracy', 894–5.
101   Packer, *Lloyd George, Liberalism and the land*, 41–8.
102   Ibid. 195–6; Adonis, 'Aristocracy', 894–5.
103   Fisher, 'Agrarian politics', 351.

have perceived a 'mystical' (or 'romantic', or 'nostalgic') dimension to the politics of land have shied away from discussing its meaning or purchase in any depth.

The lack of adequate attention paid to political language and rhetoric has had the effect of leaving unexamined many of the key arguments and ideas employed in the debates surrounding the late Victorian and Edwardian land question. These arguments and ideas cannot simply be described in vague catch-all terms such as 'mystical', 'romantic' or 'nostalgic'. Nor can they be written off as irrelevant to the substantive business of agrarian politics: they were central to the business of articulating popular electoral appeals. To be sure, many were mystical, romantic or nostalgic, and some combined all three. But these attributes did not constitute their defining quality. What defined these arguments and ideas was their intimate connection to and use of patriotic sentiment. In a real sense, debates about agrarian issues and reform were debates about the nation and the character of its people, about the very nature of Englishness. Perhaps more than anything else, it was this that explained their contemporary importance. Land politics might not have altered the fabric of English society, but they bore close relation to patterns of political change and party allegiance. That this was the case is one of the reasons why languages of land politics so excited the interest of contemporaries. The main reason, however, was the fact that they spoke to patriotic issues and visions closely connected to English national identity.

PART I

LAND POLITICS AND NATIONAL ISSUES

2

Land Reform and National Stability

'The peasant proprietor is the spoilt child of theorists; his artificial creation by the stroke of the pen is the favourite panacea of a large section of land reformers. Towards this end ... all theoretical reforms appear to tend': R. E. Prothero, *The pioneers and progress of British farming*, London 1888, 124.

A stern critic of agrarian radicalism, Rowland Prothero had good reason for making this remark. Since the lavish attentions bestowed upon him in the political economy of Mill and Thornton, the peasant proprietor had bulked large in debates on the land question. Emblematic of the 'sturdy yeoman' of popular myth, he exerted a considerable appeal over the minds of politicians. In part this appeal was based on his supposed physical attributes and character – his healthiness, industry, thrift, independence and so on – and these smallholder virtues will be discussed in the next chapter. But also important in explaining the attraction of the peasant proprietor was the conviction that he belonged to a class of men whose existence (in large enough numbers) was a powerful force for the social and constitutional stability of the nation. As a property-owner with a stake in the soil of his native country, he was considered unlikely to be led astray by extremist movements. Hence the advocacy of smallholdings legislation formed part of a patriotic defence of the constitution: at a time of advancing democracy, broadening the distribution of property in land was seen as a means of preventing social unrest and even revolution. Unsurprisingly, this point of view came to find favour with Conservative opinion, being compatible with their patriotic self-image as the 'constitutional' party. However, it also formed part of Liberal arguments for land reform, particularly in the earlier part of the period, and it is with the Liberals that this chapter begins.

Liberal reformers and social conservatism

It might seem surprising that it was Liberals and radicals rather than Conservatives who first promoted legislation for the encouragement of peasant proprietorship. Yet, as historians should perhaps remind themselves more often, fear of social unrest and a protective attitude to the constitution extended to members of both main parties in the Victorian and Edwardian periods. After all, as Jonathan Parry has emphasised, mid-Victorian Liberalism was animated by an agenda of class harmony, coupled with affectionate regard

43

for the constitution and its traditions.[1] And despite Gladstone's conversion to home rule, patriotic constitutionalism and desire for cross-class national unity persisted as elements of Liberal political discourse, exerting a significant influence on land policy. In the 1880s, with the growing influence of the land nationalisation and socialist movements generally, and Henry George's ideas in particular, a wide variety of Liberals began to perceive new revolutionary threats. Actuated by patriotic concern for the social and constitutional stability of the nation in the context of political democratisation, they responded by urging the expansion of small-scale landownership. As G. W. E. Russell, the radical parliamentary secretary to the Local Government Board, argued in a speech of June 1885, 'the more they increased the number of those having a direct and conscious interest in the soil of the country, the more they would add to the material well-being of the people, and the less likely they would be to listen to revolutionary and socialistic doctrines from the other side of the Atlantic'.[2]

Moderate supporters of Free Trade in Land were similarly inclined to this line of thinking. Reformers like the Cobdenite George Brodrick and Arthur Arnold, president of the FLL, set themselves against the rising tide of 'communistic' argument. A crucial aim of these campaigners was the inculcation of social stability, on which all national progress was held to depend. Drawing on the statistics generated by Lord Derby's 1876 *Return*, they claimed that the tendency of the land system was to concentrate property in progressively fewer hands. This might have been acceptable in the past, when parliament was controlled by an aristocratic elite which legislated in its own interest. But the danger was, as Arnold put it, that the Britain of the 1880s combined 'a medieval land system' with 'representative institutions of a practically democratic character'.[3] This was, he felt, an extremely dangerous disjuncture, antithetical to the historic constitutional relationship between property ownership and parliamentary representation. Violent unrest and the forcible plundering of the haves by the have-nots was a real possibility: 'when millions rule, the ownership of land may not safely be confined to a few thousands'.[4] Thus, far from providing a defence against 'communism' and revolution, these great landowners only served to undermine the security of property and with it the English constitution. Elevated to high position through unjust land laws (the 'class legislation' of their ancestors) and living rent-sustained lives of indolent luxury, monopo-

---

[1] Much Liberal hostility to Disraeli in the 1870s stemmed from fear that he was attempting to subvert these traditions by introducing an 'alien' style of government: J. P. Parry, 'The impact of Napoleon III on British politics, 1851–1880', *TRHS* 6th ser. xi (2001), 147–75.
[2] *The Times*, 1 July 1885, 10.
[3] Arnold, *Free land*, 40.
[4] Ibid.

listic landlords only provided justification for confiscatory and revolutionary doctrines.

For Arnold and his ilk, the solution lay in encouraging a wider distribution of property in land, so broadening the base of the 'social pyramid', creating 'a contented, prosperous, intelligent and conservative rural population', and averting 'the grave political danger' threatened by the present system. Legislation to 'make' peasant proprietors by force of law was ruled out.[5] In fact, any direct intervention by the state, from the drastic action contemplated by the LNS downwards, was condemned as contrary to the security of property upon which economic progress and social stability was founded. Schooled in a radical tradition of hostility to state action, supporters of Free Trade in Land saw legislation as the problem, not the solution. In their view, land needed to be exposed to the free play of 'economic law' in like manner as had been international trade, once hobbled by restrictive tariffs. In this interpretation, which followed Cobden's analysis of 1864, England's 'feudal' system of land tenure was an evil analogous to the Corn Law. Like the Corn Law, it interfered with the beneficent action of 'natural' market forces, to the detriment of the nation. Instituted to meet the dynastic needs of medieval society, primogeniture and strict settlement prevented the disposal of families' landed property. Their abolition, contended reformers, would release large amounts of land onto the market, not least because many indebted landlords would be only too willing to sell. The envisaged result of this was the inevitable multiplication of smallholders as large estates were broken up; and so the unfettered action of economic forces would provide England with a large class of peasant proprietors, men with a tangible stake in their country and unlikely to be led astray by revolutionary doctrines.[6]

Advocates of Free Trade in Land presented this wider distribution of real property as harmonising with 'the democratic tendency of the age' yet at the same time 'conservative in the best sense of the term'.[7] Brodrick looked forward to the day when 'a new order of county society will grow up in country districts, and a landed democracy will gradually establish itself side by side with the landed aristocracy'. In this way, the rigidly tripartite social structure of rural England – landlord, tenant farmer, labourer – would be replaced by one more complexly stratified, with many levels of gradation

---

[5] J. Kay, *Free trade in land*, 2nd edn, London 1879, 18–22; G. C. Brodrick, 'The law and custom of primogeniture', in J. W. Probyn (ed.), *Systems of land tenure in various countries*, new edn, London 1881, 146; Arnold, *Free land*, 287–8, 310–11.

[6] For example, Shaw Lefevre at Maidstone, *The Times*, 28 Sept, 1885, 12, and 'The question of the land', NC xviii (1885), 515–18; I. S. Leadam, *Agriculture and the land laws*, I: *Ownership*, London 1881, esp. pp. 28–9; S. Moss, *The English land laws*, London 1886, esp. pp. 61–3; and Arnold, *Free land*, 280ff.

[7] G. C. Brodrick, cited in P. C. Gould, *Early green politics: back to nature, back to the land, and socialism in Britain, 1880–1914*, Brighton 1988, 108; Shaw Lefevre, 'Question of the land', 522.

between squire and farmworker, rich and poor.[8] To the Tory objection that such a change ran counter to English traditions, reformers responded that the existing system was in fact no 'indigenous product of the soil'.[9] An 'artificial creation' which crushed out of existence the old English yeomen, it had destabilised society through the creation of a landless working class, vulnerable to the blandishments of socialistic demagogues. With property less the preserve of a remote elite, this damage would be undone and Englishmen would be united through their common possession of the nation's land. By offering an opportunity to acquire a tangible stake in the national domain, supporters of Free Trade in Land sought to supply a prophylaptic against social unrest and violent change of a decidedly un-English variety. As one Liberal told London artisans in a Sunday evening lecture in 1884, the abolition of primogeniture and entail was required to avoid 'convulsion' and the forcible seizure of the land by the people, as occurred in the 'great and awful French Revolution'.[10]

In the 1880s these arguments were quite prominent in Liberal political discourse. During the months before the 1885 general election, they featured strongly in the speeches of moderate and even Whiggish Liberals, including Cabinet-ranking politicians. Goschen and Shaw Lefevre were two notable examples, both being alarmed by the land nationalisation movement, whose 'crude panaceas' they feared could prove popular among the propertyless rural voters newly-enfranchised by the Third Reform Act. In addition, they were concerned to provide a reformist alternative to the interventionist agrarian policy trumpeted in Chamberlain's 'unauthorised programme', which they regarded as dangerously drastic both in terms of substance and rhetorical presentation. With these objects in mind, they presented Free Trade in Land as a means of shoring up the defences of the nation against social and political unrest.[11] Dismissing Chamberlain's calls for local authorities to be given compulsory powers to acquire land for small proprietors as 'utopian', Goschen urged that land be made 'as saleable as Consols'. This would effect a natural dispersal of landed property, so providing a 'great safeguard for the owners and for the general public'.[12]

Soon after he uttered these words, Goschen and a number of other moderate Liberal advocates of Free Trade in Land (among them Lord Hartington) left the party over Irish home rule. This dealt a blow to the cause, but it retained a significant presence in Liberal political argument until the end of the century – thanks in large part to the activity of Arnold's FLL. Founded in 1885, it had in its early years the support of several dozen MPs,

[8] G. C. Brodrick, *The reform of the English land system*, London 1883, 22, 27–8.
[9] Ibid. 5.
[10] E. White, *Land reform and emigration*, London 1884, 8.
[11] *The Times*, 2 Feb. 1885, 7 (Goschen); 2 Apr. 1885, 10, 26 Sept. 1885, 7 (Shaw Lefevre).
[12] *The Times*, 2 Feb. 1885, 7.

some of whom, like Shaw Lefevre, were prominent figures.[13] Speaking at the eighth annual meeting of the FLL in 1894, Shaw Lefevre pointed to the political unwisdom of the 'aggregation of land in a few hands' and re-iterated the argument of his *Agrarian tenures* (1893) that Free Trade in Land was far superior to newfangled plans for smallholdings legislation.[14] Doubtless this was music to the ears of his audience, but Shaw Lefevre was swimming against the general current of party opinion and had been doing so for some time.

In large part this was due to Chamberlain and Collings. Although they too were to leave the party over home rule, their 'three acres and a cow' campaign of 1883–5 decisively shifted the Liberal agenda towards compulsory legislation and a more aggressively anti-landlord stance. Chamberlain's oratorical assault on those 'who toil not, neither do they spin' doubtless played a part here; but neither it nor its contribution to the radicalisation of Liberal agrarian discourse should be allowed to obscure his socially conservative aims. In common with more moderate reformers in the 1880s, Chamberlain and Collings feared social unrest and revolution, and they too, as Collings told the Commons in July 1883, saw the encouragement of peasant proprietorship as a means of averting 'a war of classes', so ensuring 'the safety of the nation'.[15] Unlike more moderate reformers, however, they argued that Free Trade in Land would not be sufficient for these purposes: state intervention to break up the land monopoly and create small proprietors by force of law was urgently required.

The radicalism of this proposal should not be underestimated, and it certainly appeared alarmingly extreme to many: Whigs like Hartington were horrified by the large-scale compulsory purchase of land it appeared to involve, their private concerns freely spilling over into public statements and speeches.[16] From the perspective of Chamberlain and Collings, however, it was a necessary response to a grave national crisis. In their analysis, Britain – and England in particular – was menaced by rural decay and depopulation, and the landless urban proletariat that was a function of this imperilled the constitutional stability of the nation, especially when the doctrines of George and others were winning many working-class supporters. Collings set forth this argument repeatedly, insisting that the situation was a consequence of the land system, which denied labourers access to an independent living on the soil and forced them to migrate to the slums of the towns. 'Grave national dangers', he told readers of the *Times* in a November 1885 article, 'are likely to ensue' unless urgent action was taken. For,

---

13 Almost 70 MPs backed the FLL in Jan. 1886: *ELC*, 30 Jan. 1886, 3.
14 *DN*, 15 Mar. 1894, 3; cf. Shaw Lefevre, *Agrarian tenures*, 286–93.
15 *Hansard*, 3rd ser., 1883, ccxxxii. 101.
16 For example, *The Times*, 31 Aug. 1885, 8 (Hartington); 12 Oct. 1885, 10, and *Hansard*, 3rd ser., 1886, cccii. 492–504 (Goschen).

Side by side with widespread poverty and misery we see vast and increasing wealth possessed by a comparatively few persons. We have a proletariat in this country such as exists nowhere else in Europe; a peasantry, which it is the fashion to call the backbone of the country, rapidly disappearing; while in our towns we have overcrowding and other crying social evils, together with the keenest struggle by the masses of the people for a bare subsistence. At the same time education is spreading and making the feelings of the poor more poignant and their perceptions more keen. Privations which were formerly accepted as a matter of course will no longer be patiently endured.[17]

Chamberlain's message was similar. Like Collings, he was anxious about the social effects of rural depopulation, which he blamed on an iniquitous land system. Also like Collings, he was determined to offer a constructive response to the appeal of the land nationalisers, about which he was genuinely alarmed. Chamberlain's solution to these twin problems was 'peasant proprietorship ... on a large scale', which would break the land monopoly and act as 'the antidote to the doctrines of confiscation which are now making converts'.[18] Despite the famously controversial anti-landlord rhetoric in the two years before the 1885 election, Chamberlain aimed to bolster the security of private property. This was apparent even from his most inflammatory speeches, in which he asserted how, over centuries, landowners had robbed the poor of their stake in the land through enclosure.[19] Chamberlain told this story to expose what he saw as the moral illegitimacy of present arrangements, which by concentrating land in the hands of an aristocratic elite only served to undermine the security of property in an increasingly democratic political culture. By asking 'what ransom will property pay for the security which it enjoys', he was demanding reform to correct this historical injustice, which had seen 'the birthright of the English people... bartered away for a mess of pottage' – and legislation to create peasant proprietors was largely what he had in mind. This, Chamberlain hoped, would provide restitution for past wrongs and so put 'the rights of property on the only firm and defensible basis'.[20]

Chamberlainite radicals were clear that their proposals involved an element of sacrifice on the part of great landowners, who would be adversely affected by the compulsory nature of the reforms (restitution, after all, was necessary); but they were also clear that it was in the interests of landed property generally that such a sacrifice be made. A just land system, in which popular right of access to the soil was acknowledged and property more

[17] J. Collings, 'The land question from the labourers' point of view', The Times, 19 Nov. 1885, 4.
[18] Cited in Smith, Land for the small man, 48–9; Simon, 'Joseph Chamberlain', 225–7, 239; P. T. Marsh, Joseph Chamberlain, New Haven 1994, 163–4.
[19] See, for example, The Times, 10 Nov. 1885, 10; 17 Nov. 1885, 10.
[20] Speeches at Birmingham (5 Jan. 1885) and Ipswich (14 Jan. 1885), repr. in Mr Chamberlain's speeches, ed. C. W. Boyd, London 1914, i. 137, 142.

widely distributed, was one that could better resist the claims of nationalisers and socialists. Not the least reason for this was that it would create an
identity of interest between squire and peasant: both would have something
to lose from the triumph of 'communism'. As Collings and Henry Broadhurst
made clear in a parliamentary debate on peasant proprietorship in 1883,
were action not taken to create a large class of smallholders, there would
be too few landowners to resist the soon-to-be 'formidable power' of revolutionary agitation. If reforms were instituted, however, 'when the great storm
reached this country ... the upper classes would find themselves backed by a
great army of sturdy, honest, well-to-do, and well-disposed citizens': England
would be spared the catastrophe of violent revolution.[21]

Tories and peasant proprietors

From the later 1880s onwards Liberal interest in promoting social stability
by means of peasant proprietorship began to decline. There were a number
of reasons for this. Waning confidence in the capacity of Free Trade in Land
to effect a 'natural' redistribution of landed property played a part, as did
Gladstone's conversion to home rule, which caused Collings and Chamberlain to leave the party. So too did practical considerations. Liberals
reasoned that the agricultural labourer was unlikely ever to posses enough
money to become a landowner and in any case the alternative of secure local
authority tenancy appeared to provide him with the advantages of proprietorship while leaving him in possession of capital to invest in improvements. Furthermore, though some Liberals still thought that increasing the
number of property-owning peasants might help prevent social unrest, many
now felt that the political costs of doing so were too high. They believed
that creating numerous peasant proprietors would only strengthen the forces
of reactionary 'landlordism' to which their party was implacably opposed.
Others still came round to the idea that land nationalisation did not actually
represent a revolutionary threat to English constitutional traditions, which
would be harmed not by radical land reforms, but by a lack of such measures.
This belief was reinforced by changes in the Conservatives' own attitudes to
peasant proprietorship.

Until the end of the 1880s Conservatives generally regarded the legislative encouragement of small ownership as inadmissible on economic
grounds. To be sure, Tories had long praised the sturdy smallholder, whose
political instincts they assumed tended in an anti-revolutionary direction;
Salisbury himself had harboured such views for some time.[22] But Conservative appreciation of 'primitive Hodge' (Salisbury's term) had usually been

[21] *Hansard*, 3rd ser., 1883, cclxxxii. 100, 113.
[22] M. Bentley, *Lord Salisbury's world: Conservative environments in late-Victorian Britain*,
Cambridge 2001, 104.

overridden by a belief that large-scale peasant proprietorship was unsuited to the English land system – a system which, as J. A. Froude had famously argued, was the product of 'economic laws as absolute as the law of gravity'.[23] Faced with 'three acres and a cow' in the mid-1880s, mainstream Conservatism adopted a posture of principled hostility. While prepared to accept that a wider distribution of property in land could have a 'pre-eminently Conservative' effect in theory, Tories rejected legislation to revive a 'yeoman' class as 'economically mischievous' in practice. In their interpretation, the threat posed by land nationalisers and socialists was insufficient to justify the drastic measures advocated by Chamberlain and Collings, which risked undermining the security of real property, so discouraging capital investment. But a still more fundamental Conservative objection was that parliament had no business attempting the 'artificial' creation of smallholdings in defiance of Froude's 'economic laws' which, over the years, had acted to replace them with larger and more profitable units of land ownership.[24] As Salisbury explained by asking a rhetorical question of his audience in a speech at Newport in October 1885, 'Supposing you saw a hillside upon which the larch had grown and the beech had died, what would you think of any man who said, "I will cut down that larch and plant that beech – that the beech is the right thing and that the larch ought not to exist"?'[25]

Even as Salisbury posed this question, however, the conviction that the economic objections to peasant proprietorship were insurmountable was beginning to lose its unchallenged hold over Conservative political discourse. This was a function of Tories' increasing anxiety about social and constitutional stability. Over the course of the 1880s their fears about the spread of radical ideas and the possibility of serious unrest intensified. In the context of growing labour problems in the towns and increasingly virulent attacks on the land system from the LNS and others, many Tories came to see the active defence of property rights as a priority. Thanks to the work of E. H. H. Green in particular, historians are now much better informed about this development, which saw the late nineteenth-century Conservative party transform itself from the champion of aristocratic property into the champion of the property of the nation as a whole.[26] From the late 1880s on, Conservatives were prepared to promote legislation expressly designed to enhance the security of private property, seeing this as part of their patriotic mission as the 'constitutional party'. For example, proposals for facilitating working-class house purchase were advocated largely for this reason; secure

---

[23] J. A. Froude, 'On the uses of a landed gentry', in *Short studies on great subjects*, ed. D. Ogg (1867–83), London 1963, 255–77, quotation at p. 255.

[24] P. Greg, 'The new radicals', *NR* v (1885), 166; Chaplin on Collings's peasant proprietorship resolution, *Hansard*, 3rd ser., 1883, cclxxxii. 110; Prothero, *Pioneers*, 128, 137–40.

[25] *The Times*, 8 Oct. 1885, 7.

[26] Green, *Crisis*.

in the possession of his home, the English workingman would be less inclined to support confiscatory projects. It was an argument that found favour among rank-and-file MPs, who were keen to support legislative action to increase the number of proletarian homeowners. At the 1895 general election nearly one in three Unionist candidates mentioned the issue in their addresses.[27]

There was, then, a growing concern among Conservatives to bolster property rights in the face of radical and socialist challenges, and this formed the backdrop to their changing attitudes to peasant proprietorship. In the years after the perceived advent of democracy in 1884–5, the advocacy of small ownership emerged as a usefully populist and electorally attractive means of presenting themselves as patriotic upholders of the institutional and social cohesion of the nation. By 1888 the staunchly Tory *Quarterly Review* could carry an article that spoke of how 'nothing tends to keep a country together and free it from revolutionary and socialistic bonds, than the fact of a large number of freeholders'.[28] It was a view that soon found expression in the public declarations of prominent politicians, including those of Chaplin, installed at the new Board of Agriculture in 1889. In speeches at Swindon and Ely in the winter of 1891–2 Chaplin averred that legislation to create peasant proprietors was a 'Conservative measure, in the best sense of the word', as it would help 'bridge over the gulf that now existed between the farmer and the labourer and to bring all classes of the agricultural interest together'.[29] This was presented as a patriotic project: the wider distribution of property in land would inculcate rural social harmony and help prevent that class conflict which fed extremism, and which could divide the nation into warring factions.

This 'national' agenda came out strongly in the language of Salisbury. At the annual party conference in Nottingham in November 1889, Salisbury signalled that the traditional economic objections to small ownership were now vitiated by the need to 'anchor the institutions of the state' in response to the rising tide of extremist ideas and the socially destructive effects of rural depopulation.[30] Two years later, at the same event, Salisbury went still further. While acknowledging the necessarily 'experimental' nature of the forthcoming smallholdings bill, he stressed his government's belief in the

> Extreme importance ... of riveting the yeoman to the soil ... We believe the greatness of this country has risen from its yeomanry, and deeply regret that its yeomanry tends to disappear (hear, hear); and ... if by the use of the public credit we are able to increase the number of small proprietors in this country, I think it to be an enormous gain, in the first instance, to our country, and, in the second instance, to the Conservative Party (cheers) ... I

---

27 Readman, '1895', 493.
28 [H. C. K. Petty-Fitzmaurice and H. H. Smith], 'Landed incomes and landed estates', *QR* clxvi (1888), 236.
29 *The Times*, 3 Dec. 1891, 10; 30 Jan. 1892, 6.
30 *The Times*, 27 Nov. 1889, 6.

thoroughly believe that the more the peasantry of this country can be brought into connexion with the land the more safe your institutions are and the more the fibre of the English people will be preserved.[31]

His message was clear: the creation of a class of loyal freeholders, rooted to the soil of their homeland, would not only be of political benefit to the Conservative party; it would also broaden the social base of the constitution, so affording it protection against revolutionary threats. It might be the case, as Salisbury explained in another speech a few months later, that smallholdings were not the most economical form of agricultural organisation. 'But', he told his audience, 'there are things of more importance than economy. I believe that a small proprietary constitutes the strongest bulwark against revolutionary change, and affords the strongest support for the Conservative feeling and institutions of the country (cheers).'[32]

A few weeks after Salisbury had made this statement, his government introduced its Small Agricultural Holdings Bill, which received the royal assent in June 1892. In terms of its form, the bill was largely a product of the Select Committee on Small Holdings, which had been appointed under Chamberlain's chairmanship in 1888. The committee's *Report*, which appeared in the summer of 1890, concluded that it was in the 'national interest' that legislation be enacted for the encouragement of peasant proprietorship. Indeed, both in the text of the *Report* and the speeches made during the parliamentary debates following its publication, the 'national' and the 'nation' loomed large. 'Increasing the number of persons directly interested in the soil' was presented by the government and its Liberal Unionist allies as a patriotic objective. It was commended as a means of combating the 'national danger' of rural depopulation, while at the same time bolstering the security of private property – which for Tories was itself an important 'national' goal, connected in their minds with the preservation of constitutional stability. Even those Conservatives who were unimpressed by the Bill accepted the argument of its promoters that 'increasing the number of [owner] occupiers ... tends to make men more satisfied and less disposed to follow revolutionary methods', and they were also susceptible to the claim that the measure would strengthen the party's popularity among working-class voters. Those more enthusiastic asserted that the measure was 'calculated to add to the security of property' and hence to remove the 'national danger' of having a 'landless peasantry'. It was argued that were England to posses a 'numerous and prosperous' peasant proprietary, conditions of 'national safety' would ensue. Social stability would be preserved; an inclusive and national sense of belonging would not be supplanted by a plurality of exclusive, sectional

31 *The Times*, 25 Nov. 1891, 10.
32 *The Times*, 3 Feb., 1892, 6.

and mutually antagonistic class identities productive only of discord between the propertied few and the propertyless many.[33]

Although ultimately limited in its effects, the 1892 act was taken seriously by contemporaries, many of whom felt that it reflected government recognition that the extension of landownership was a powerful guarantor of national solidarity. Though the measure did not go far enough for Collings and the RLL, who wanted an element of compulsion, they were among those who took the act most seriously of all. Convinced that the greatness of nations – their 'solidity, resisting power, and lasting strength and prosperity' – depended on the existence of a 'powerful, contented and numerous peasantry', they regarded the measure as a 'step in the right direction'.[34] In their eyes it would do something towards creating a class of responsible small cultivating owners, who would help counteract the socially divisive and hence anti-national doctrines then being disseminated by the red and yellow van campaigns of the land nationalisers, and by socialists like the SDF. It was in this spirit that Collings commended the 1892 act to the fourth annual conference of the RLL in June 1893. Through legislation to create small proprietors, Collings told the meeting, England's rural 'proletariat' could be transformed into

> A class corresponding to that solid, responsible middle class which gave such strength to the towns, who would possess something – who would be anchored to the soil as it were, and would not be ready, as they were at a moment's notice now, to hang their things on their backs and go into the town or anywhere else. Such a state of things would create in the minds of men feelings of responsibility, and thought, and independence – all those qualities which made the social element in society, and gave the only sure protection against the thoughtless agitators, who ... had been going about preaching a disordered Socialism.[35]

Collings hoped that the 1892 act would lead to further more far-reaching measures, and lobbied relentlessly for progress in this direction. However, for some years following its passage, he found himself rather isolated. With the exception of the increasingly marginal FLL, Liberals had by this stage almost completely lost interest in the legislative promotion of landownership. Now far less concerned about unrest, revolution or 'communistic' threats and far more concerned about liberating the nation from the enervating effects of a reactionary landlordism, their energies were focused elsewhere. As for Collings's Unionist allies, the extent of their support for small proprietary

---

[33] *Report of the Select Committee on Small Holdings*, PP 1890 (223), xvii, pp. iii, v; *Hansard*, 3rd ser., 1891, ccli. 657–8, 663–4, 670; 4th ser., 1892, i. 911–14; ii. 1357, 1359, 1369–70, 1378, 1735; v. 835.

[34] *RW*, 26 Feb. 1892, 163; Collings at third annual meeting of RLL, *RW*, 26 Feb. 1892, 173.

[35] RLL, *Fourth annual report*, London 1893, 24.

should not be exaggerated. Most – not least the increasingly empire-fixated Chamberlain – saw the 'experiment' of 1892 as sufficient for the time being. And while this measure did spring from ideological conviction, it is certainly true that, at leadership level especially, conviction was bolstered by political calculation: reform would assist rural candidates at the forthcoming general election.[36]

Now and again in the years following, Unionist politicians did mention how giving the small man a chance to become a landowner was 'one of the best ways of ... attracting him to the institutions of his country', of steering him away from 'subversive' collectivism towards a conservative version of patriotism.[37] Salisbury made such pronouncements from time to time, and of course this line of argument made an appearance in his party's advocacy of working-class house purchase in the 1890s (though this was a policy largely aimed at urban areas).[38] Yet despite the occasional endorsement of peasant proprietorship as an anti-collectivist bulwark, Unionist leaders did not feel inclined to propose further smallholdings legislation. Before the Boer War drew their attention away from domestic issues almost entirely, the relief of agricultural rates appeared the most pressing of agrarian questions to be considered: peasant proprietorship could wait. For some Tories, indeed, it could wait forever. As should not be overlooked, significant opposition to small occupying ownership lingered in Conservative discourse even after the passage of the 1892 act. Some aristocrats remained extremely uneasy, as is unsurprising. But hostile attitudes also persisted in the arena of popular Toryism. A number of propagandist works recommended by the Primrose League took a very critical line, for example. Reprising the objections to the agrarian proposals of Chamberlain's 'unauthorised programme', they presented peasant proprietorship as running counter to the *telos* of England's national economic development. In a collection of essays published in 1895, the ruling councillor of the Burnley habitation of the League saw fit to describe the existing 'Manorial system' of the countryside as 'infinitely more advantageous than the radical notion of three acres and a cow, which is the financial zero'. Peasant proprietary, in his judgement, would only bring that 'misery and poverty' with which the benighted rustics of France and Germany were well acquainted, but which was as yet 'unknown to England in the worst times'.[39]

36 Ward, 'Land reform', 246.
37 *Cable*, 6 June 1896, 360; *The Times*, 27 July 1894, 3 (Sir H. James); 17 July 1895, 9 (Chamberlain).
38 *National Union Gleanings*, Nov. 1894, 301.
39 W. Peart-Robinson, *Burning questions*, London 1895.

Edwardian Unionism

Around the turn of the century Conservative attitudes to the peasant proprietor began to change decisively. The practical failure of Winchilsea's NAU
illustrated the ideological bankruptcy of traditionalist agrarian Toryism, and
mainstream party opinion once again swung round to the advocacy of peasant
proprietorship as a means of winning votes and forestalling social unrest, but
now with far more conviction than previously. In the last months of Balfour's
administration the issue re-emerged at the forefront of Unionist politics, and
gained further ground after the crushing election defeat of 1906. Provoked
by the *Report* of the 1905–6 Departmental Committee on Smallholdings,
which found much to recommend peasant proprietorship, and in particular
by the increasingly radical nature of Liberal proposals, prominent Conservatives and Liberal Unionists renewed their calls for a wider distribution of
landed property. As chairman of the departmental committee and former
President of the Board of Agriculture, Onslow was one such example, and
the shift in his attitudes since the 1880s is worth relating. In the mid-1880s
Onslow had responded to radical calls for reform by establishing his Association for the Voluntary Extension of the Allotments System. By promoting
the benevolent action of landlords, Onslow had hoped to head off demands
for compulsory legislation and prevent the emergence of destabilising class
antagonisms. As he told Salisbury in February 1886, he aimed to 'prove that
the landowners and the clergy are the real friends of the labourers'.[40] But by
the 1900s Onslow had lost faith in the effectiveness of allotments as a guarantor of social harmony. His view now was that giving wage-earning labourers
something to do in their spare time was not enough (allotment numbers
had expanded dramatically in the 1880s and 1890s, after all); they needed
the opportunity of becoming independent cultivators. With this in mind,
he advocated peasant proprietorship, both through the voluntary action of
landlords (in whom he had not quite lost hope) and also, more significantly,
through legislative action. Like the report of his committee, Onslow was
clear that compulsion could be recommended,[41] and this clarity stemmed
in large part from his perception that urgent action was now required to
defend property rights from radical attack. 'Can anyone doubt', he asked
party leaders in an internal memorandum of 23 March 1907,

> that if the wisdom of the early Victorian era had so arranged that the owners
> and occupiers of the soil had been largely but gradually multiplied the
> Conservative instincts of the nation would have been increased, property

---

[40] 'History of the Onslow family by the 5th earl of Onslow', typescript, 9 vols, iv. 1021
(Onslow papers, Surrey History Centre G173/1/4). See also W. H. Onslow, 4th earl of
Onslow, *Landlords and allotments*, London 1886.
[41] *Report of the departmental committee appointed by the Board of Agriculture on small holdings in Great Britain*, 1906 (cd. 3277), 28, 33.

would now be more secure, the position of every landowner, small or great would have been strengthened.[42]

The appeal of this argument increased exponentially in the aftermath of the 'People's Budget' of April 1909. Unionists were horrified by Lloyd George's land tax and valuation proposals, which in their eyes appeared to point towards land nationalisation and 'class war'. Responding to the Chancellor's Limehouse speech, Lord Lansdowne condemned the government's plans as amounting to 'expropriation' and 'robbery', as an unjust and destructive attack on private property.[43] This was also the message of Ernest Pretyman and his Land Union, which was organised to mobilise extra-parliamentary resistance to the Budget. Through its propaganda the Union issued something of a patriotic call to arms on behalf of property-loving, fair-dealing Englishmen. In a leaflet explaining its objects, Liberal policy was condemned as somehow un-English – influenced and financed by foreigners like Joseph Fels, the American soap manufacturer and promoter of land colonies with some links to radical Liberal and Labour politicians. 'The Land Union', the leaflet read, 'invites you to join the ranks of Englishmen, who are preparing to safeguard the rights of property honestly acquired, against the attacks of land nationalisers, or socialists subsidised by foreign coin.'[44] However, the safeguarding of these rights did not merely involve a posture of hostility to Liberal measures; negative criticism was coupled with constructive policy. Unlike the Liberty and Property Defence League of the 1880s and 1890s, the Land Union saw scope for interventionist state action in defence of property rights. In particular, as per its official statement of objectives, it sought 'to actively support the creation of small ownerships on terms fair alike to landlord, tenant farmer, and all concerned'.[45]

From 1909 on, the idea that peasant proprietorship could function as a practical and popular means of thwarting the 'socialistic' challenge of the Liberals became extremely widespread among Conservative opinion. As the Lincolnshire landlord Christopher Turnor put it to readers of the *National Review*, the concentration of landed property in so few hands 'is a great danger to the stability of the social condition and to the landowners themselves'.[46] Collings, for some time rather isolated in his enthusiasm for the socially stabilising effects of small ownership, had been joined by other enthusiasts. These included Walter Long, epitome of the Tory squire, who in a September 1910 letter to Collings indicated his conversion 'to the system of small ownerships' as 'the only way in which we can resist the march of Socialism, as exemplified, not by Snowden and Keir Hardie, but

---

42 'History of the Onslow family', v. 1325 (Onslow papers, G173/1/5).
43 *The Times*, 9 Aug. 1909, 8.
44 'The Land Union', in Land Union leaflets, BL.
45 Ibid.
46 C. Turnor, 'A constructive agricultural policy', NR liv (1909), 596.

by the present financial policy of the government'.[47] The novelist and MP for Gravesend Gilbert Parker was another prominent *arriviste* to the cause. In a slew of publications, most notably his pamphlet *The land for the people* (1909), Parker put forward his case for state action to create peasant proprietors. Using language that echoed the contentions of Liberal reformers in the 1870s and 1880s, Parker argued that

> Agriculture is the basis of the national pyramid, social, moral, economic ... the nation, fascinated by the roar of the factories and blinded by their smoke, has inverted the pyramid ... It is time that the basis of the pyramid was widened, lest the whole unwieldy superstructure topple over ... By losing the proportions between the field and the factory the national equilibrium is violently disturbed.[48]

Parker had influence with the Conservative leadership. Balfour appointed him to the chairmanship of an internal Small Ownership Committee in 1910 and he later served on the 1912–14 Milner Committee. Balfour, moreover, contributed a preface to Parker's *Land and people*, thus giving official endorsement to his views. This reflected a shift in the Tory leader's own position on peasant proprietary. It is true that he was never wholeheartedly enthusiastic, and never shed his private scepticism. But, urged on by Austen Chamberlain, Collings and others, Balfour was prepared publicly to declare his support for a policy of small ownership in opposition to the 'socialistic folly' of Liberal schemes. 'Nothing', he told an audience at Birmingham in September 1909, 'can be more desirable and important'.[49] Balfour's initiative had a major impact on rank-and-file Tories, many of whom paid homage to it in the January 1910 elections. In his address to the voters of North Buckinghamshire, for example, T. F. Fremantle associated himself with 'Mr. Balfour's proposals' to increase the number of freeholders, as 'only by giving a direct interest in the soil to a large proportion of the people can national stability be secured'.[50]

As in the past, Unionists dressed their strategy in the clothes of a conservative variety of patriotism. In promoting peasant proprietary, they portrayed themselves as upholding not only the social stability of the nation, but also those 'national institutions' which depended upon the maintenance of this stability for their existence. 'Ownership', Austen Chamberlain told Onslow in February 1910, 'will give stability to institutions as nothing else will'.[51] Unionists had in mind political institutions here – those institutions which they, as the 'Constitutional Party', were pledged to uphold. And by the end of the Edwardian period even individuals who might hitherto have been

---

[47] Cited in Fforde, 'Conservative party', 195–6.
[48] G. Parker, *The land for the people*, London 1909, 9–10, 32.
[49] *The Times*, 23 Sept. 1909, 7.
[50] *Election addresses*, Jan 1910.
[51] A. Chamberlain to Onslow, 4 Feb 1910, cited in Fforde, 'Conservative party', 195.

sceptical about the value of peasant proprietorship as a means of strengthening the constitutional bedrock had come to believe their own rhetoric,
and that of their colleagues. In a private memorandum of July 1912 Lord
Selborne explained that 'The Unionist Party is resolved to do its utmost
to increase the number of occupying and cultivating owners of the soil ...
because it believes that the greater the number the owners of the soil, the
greater the strength of the Nation and the greater the stability of the National
Institutions.'[52] At the end of that month the new Unionist leader Andrew
Bonar Law gave public expression to these private sentiments in a speech at
Blenheim, and they were to be repeated the following year, as the party grap-
pled with Lloyd George's Land Campaign.[53] In the humble peasant proprietor many Unionists had located a force for national salvation; a means of
protecting their England from expropriating and materialist doctrines that
threatened to supplant love of country with allegiance to class.

But for all the claims that legislation to create small ownerships was in
line with traditional Conservative goals of constitutional defence, there was
something new here. The Edwardian Unionist party had in fact adopted
much of the analysis of Collings and – to a lesser extent – the FLL. First
formulated at a time when franchise reform was very much in the air, their
analysis was, as we have seen, that the disjuncture between the land system
and the political system was a national danger that could lead to serious
social unrest. By the 1900s this was also the Conservatives' point of view.
As one prominent commentator claimed in a 1909 article for the *Nineteenth
Century*,

> A democratic form of government and a feudal land system are incompatible
> ... Ten thousand families could hold the bulk of the land when they held in
> their hands all political power, but they can no longer do so when political
> power is in the hands of 7,000,000 voters, the vast majority of whom are
> landless. We cannot afford to delay the reform of our land system any longer
> ... Property owners are the natural defenders of the state and its institutions.
> This historic fabric of Great Britain rests on a dangerously narrow basis – a
> basis which sufficed in the past, but which suffices no longer. The enemy is at
> the gates ... The political enfranchisement of our people should be followed
> by their economic enfranchisement. Property owners are conservative. A
> thorough reform of our land system will be the most democratic, and at the
> same time the most conservative measure of modern times.[54]

These were words that reflected an updating of Toryism. Partly thanks to
Liberal Unionist advocates of rural reform like Collings, Conservatives now

---

52 *The crisis of British Unionism: Lord Selborne's domestic political papers, 1885–1922*, ed.
G. Boyce, London 1987, 85–6.
53 *The Times*, 31 July 1912, 7–8. See also, for example, the speech of Lansdowne in
London: *The Times*, 25 July 1912, 8.
54 J. E. Barker, 'The land, the landlords and the people', *NC* lxvi (1909), 550–1, 566.

believed that the defence of the constitution could best be effected not by the defence of aristocratic property alone, but by the defence of property in general.[55] Hence their formulation of a Conservative agrarian policy focused on the common people, the centrepiece of which was the extension of small ownerships. This was presented as a popular – indeed a populist – policy, one designed to win votes and suited to the modern, democratic nation England had supposedly become. But it was also presented as an eminently conservative measure, as a means by which the anti-national doctrines of an increasingly radical Liberal party could be thwarted.

As this chapter has shown, in late nineteenth- and early twentieth-century England, legislative measures for the encouragement of peasant proprietorship were regarded as the most important means by which land reform could promote social and constitutional stability. But for some they were not the only such means to this end. After their party's enthusiasm for peasant ownership began to fade in the late-1880s, Liberals did occasionally present the provision of small tenancies as a way of forestalling serious unrest. The argument was that increased numbers of smallholdings and allotments, if let under conditions which gave a real sense of security to their tenants, would have a socially stabilising effect similar to that imparted by an enlarged peasant proprietary. Moreover, they would confer this benefit without sacrificing economic efficiency or fostering the political Conservatism small ownership was now widely held to create.

Like Onslow with his allotments association, some Liberals saw allotments as devices by which the poorly paid and ill-fed agricultural labourer could be steered away from political extremism. Moderates associated with ASHA were perhaps most inclined to advance such views. Sir Walter Foster, president of the association, thought an allotment made the farmworker less inclined to 'become a revolutionist'.[56] In common with the (now largely Unionist) supporters of peasant proprietorship, Liberals who took this view presented their advocacy of allotments as stemming from patriotic concern. Speaking at an ASHA conference in June 1889, Handel Cossham, MP for Bristol East, called for better allotment provision in order to combat the 'national danger' of a situation in which 'there were vast masses of people … to whom revolution could bring no danger because they had nothing to lose'.[57] Around the same time, an editorial note by 'John Ploughman' in Joseph Arch's English Labourers' Chronicle pointed to the 'political advantage' conferred by good allotments. These, the writer felt, could be described as 'The deep roots which attach the holder to the land of his birth, give him a love of country, and fill his breast with the fires of patriotism'. While

---

[55] On this theme see Green, Crisis. For the influence of Collings see P. Readman, 'Jesse Collings and land reform, 1886–1914', HR (2008), 292–314.
[56] LP, 1 Mar. 1890, 18.
[57] LP, July 1889, 55.

the man with such an allotment was a loyal supporter of his country and its interests – seeing them as identical to his own – the man who lacked one was 'like a fir tree which fell before the March wind ... Every time there is a social storm that man is in peril; he is a source of danger rather than strength to his country'.[58]

This point of view, however, was not typical of Liberal or radical discourse generally. Perhaps accelerated by the decline of the allotments question as a live political issue at parliamentary level, it had virtually disappeared by the Edwardian period.

Smallholdings, of course, did not disappear as an issue in the 1890s and 1900s: the Liberals expended considerable energy on the subject until 1914. But, in doing so, they only rarely advanced arguments about social stability, and such arguments that were advanced tended to be vague, brief or assertive. In his Liberal Publication Department pamphlet, A plea for smallholdings (1907), for example, the backbench MP Percy Molteno made passing reference to how granting labourers access to land functioned as a great 'outlet for discontent'.[59] Others sometimes expressed worries, shared also by Conservatives, that Britain's near-total dependency on foreign sources of food supply could lead to 'panic', 'riot' and 'insurrections of starving people' in the event of a wartime blockade.[60] But these arguments were never very well developed by Liberals. All in all, it seems clear that the anxiety of Liberal land reformers about social unrest in the 1890s and 1900s was very limited. Fears about Georgeite land nationalisation, which were prevalent in the 1880s, had largely been overcome. Not the least reason for this was the increasing popularity of land value taxation, and even outright nationalisation, within mainstream Liberal opinion. In these years, as the next chapter will demonstrate, Liberals were primarily interested in the effect their proposals would have on the character and physique of the English nation. Promoting social and constitutional stability was a secondary concern.

[58] ELC, 24 Nov. 1888, 1.
[59] P. M. Molteno, A plea for small holdings, London 1907, 14.
[60] W. B. Hodgson, 'The disease', in Masterman and others, To colonise England, 33; Village Search-Light iv (June 1897), 2.

3

Land Politics and the English National Character

'If the real object of statesmanship be the formation of character, there could be no reform of so much importance as land reform': E. F. Bulmer, 'Rural England from within', *IR* vi (1905), 176.

During the late nineteenth and early twentieth centuries, discussion of 'national character' loomed large in political debate. Perhaps surprisingly, it loomed larger for Liberals than for Conservatives. But, as Peter Mandler has shown, the discourse of national character was mostly in Liberal hands at this time. It was centred on the common people and their attributes, and chimed with long-held Liberal concerns about moral and political progress. In particular, it was bound up with ideas of native liberty – that of the 'freeborn Englishman' – which offered material rewards for individual initiative, thrift, hard work and so on. Furthermore, this liberty encompassed the Englishman's vaunted capacity for self-government, which in Liberal eyes had found its historical fulfilment in the progressive development of a democratic political system.[1]

Yet satisfaction at this achievement was tempered by anxiety. The Second and Third Reform Acts helped convince contemporaries that Britain had assumed not only a democratic system of parliamentary government, but also a democratic set of national identities. In this context, the people – whether English, Scottish or Welsh – were increasingly seen as constitutive of the 'nation', the repository of its strength (or weakness) and the embodiment of its values. In England, as the conviction that the nation was popularly defined grew, so too did solicitude for the English national character. The democratising of the constitution (arguably the central prop of Victorian national identity)[2] meant that, more than ever, the ordinary people were the nation. It followed that their welfare was an issue of patriotic statesmanship. This was the perspective of Liberal land reformers. In their analysis, the land system fostered rural decay and depopulation, and hence had decidedly negative effects on the national character. It was inimical to that freedom which was supposedly an Englishman's birthright, it inhibited the development of

---

[1] P. Mandler, 'The consciousness of modernity? Liberalism and the English "national character", 1870–1940', in M. Daunton and B. Rieger (eds), *Meanings of modernity: Britain from the late-Victorian era to World War II*, Oxford 2001, 119–44
[2] Parry, 'Impact of Napoleon', esp. p. 175.

those moral virtues which made for a happy home life and it was destructive of patriotism. Land reform, conversely, provided a potent antidote to such ills: it would sustain personal freedom, encourage moral virtue and inculcate love of country.

Landlordism, English freedoms and the English rural home

In charging the land system with having a depressive effect on rural inhabitants, there is little doubt that the Liberals had a strong case. In many places landlords exercised considerable control over the daily lives of their tenants. The rein was tightest where single individuals owned entire villages, and the total number of these 'closed' villages was very large.[3] Landlord 'tyranny' could take a variety of forms. Direct political intimidation was now rare, although there were a few reported cases of tenants being evicted after standing as candidates in local government elections.[4] However, prospective village tyrants had other means at their disposal. The squire could deny the labourer access to land, so frustrating any ambitions he might have of shaking off his dependence on the farmer's wages. Suitable land for allotments or smallholdings could be withheld, or supplied only at a high rent, or on stringent terms of tenure. In addition, the squire could stifle religious and political dissent by refusing to permit nonconformist chapels, and using his control over village buildings to prevent radical meetings.

Documented instances of landlordly repression are not hard to come by. Even individuals regarded as model landowners often subjected the dwellers on their land to fairly severe regulatory regimes. Lords Tollemache and Wantage are two examples. At Tollemache's Helmingham estate in Suffolk, labourers enjoyed the dubious benefits of a rather strict form of benevolent paternalism. While good cottages and allotments were readily available, a detailed set of rules was imposed. The numerous obligations required of residents included attendance in church on Sundays, adherence to precise instructions as to allotment cultivation (even the rows of crops had to face a particular direction), and conformity with a prescribed dress code (corduroy was *de rigueur*).[5] Similarly, in Wantage's Berkshire estate villages of Ardington and Lockinge, wages (in the early 1890s) were as low as 10s., pigs were forbidden in cottage gardens and politics was barred from the pub. As one farmworker told George Millin, the *Daily News* reporter whose *Life in*

---

3 In some counties between one-third and one-half of all villages were 'closed': P. Horn, *Labouring life in the Victorian countryside*, Dublin 1976, 8.
4 ELRL, *Among the agricultural labourers with the 'red vans'*, London 1895, 20.
5 Horn, *Labouring life*, 8.

our villages (1891) exposed these and other practices, 'they durnt blow their noses at Ard'n'ton without the bailiff's leave'.[6]

To critics of 'landlordism' like Millin, the power exerted by landlords *qua* landlords meant that many of the inhabitants of English villages were denied any real sense of citizenship, liberty or personal independence.[7] Indeed, reformers ranging from supporters of ASHA to radical advocates of land nationalisation persistently described the wage-earning inhabitants of these places as 'a class of men whom you might say were probably slaves or serfs in some distant land' rather than inhabitants of England.[8] In making this claim Liberals and radicals chose language designed to subvert the assumption that England was the island home of liberty. The character of English peasants was so debased that it was somehow foreign: their craven dependence and lack of freedom made them 'serfs', or even 'slaves' – the latter an appellation that many labourers themselves apparently endorsed.[9] For a country that boasted a proud tradition of combating oppression around the world, this was presented as a source of national shame: in the eyes of contemporaries, liberal England had, after all, done much to abolish slavery. Yet here it was, in all but name, in the shires of the old country. By the time of the 1906 general election Liberals could be found speaking of how the power exercised by the landlord was 'a blot on our fair name, on our pride in this "free England" as we love to call it'.[10] An anomalous 'feudal' relic, the land system was portrayed as antithetical to the core ideals of the modern democracy Britain was perceived to have become.

How, then, to free these slaves? Liberal reformers proposed a number of solutions over the years. In the 1880s and early 1890s rural local government reform was pushed to the fore. It had a well-established pedigree in Liberal political discourse, having long been central to the party's plan of agrarian emancipation. The transference of many of the powers wielded by unelected quarter sessions and JPs to popular local assemblies drew the support of Whigs and radicals alike. All shades of Liberal saw the measure as essential for the political education of the agricultural labourer, who received the awesome responsibility of the parliamentary vote in 1884. In their interpretation, local democracy was a means of inculcating the habits of social and political independence that marked the ideal Englishman's character. Believing that elected local government had a long if sadly broken tradition in England, reaching back to Saxon folk-moots, Liberals presented theirs as a project of

[6] Cited in F. E. Green, *A history of the English agricultural labourer, 1870–1920*, London 1920, 111.

[7] For example, Millin, *Life in our villages*, 80, 87–92, 109–10.

[8] *LP*, 1 Dec. 1888, 92 (Foster); George, *Progress and poverty*, 347–8, 353, 357; ELRL, *Special report, 1891*, London 1891, 13–15.

[9] 'The labourers themselves openly describe their condition as one of "slavery"': ELRL, *Special report, 1891*, 13–14.

[10] H. C. W. Verney: *LV* cxl (1906), 158.

national renewal. In their speeches of the 1880s, legislation for the introduction of representative county, district and parish councils was promoted
as a means of extending to the villages that which George Brodrick called
the 'old English art of local self-government'.[11] By supplanting the landlord-
dominated quarter sessions, these institutions would give the downtrodden
inhabitants of the countryside a degree of control over and responsibility for
their own affairs: free men as Englishmen should be, they would no longer
be subject to (nor would they tolerate) the tyranny of the squire.

Yet, despite much rhetoric, Gladstone's administration of 1880–5 failed to
reform rural local government. Following Liberal defeat at the 1886 general
election, county councils were created by Salisbury's Conservative government in 1888. However, Salisbury was far more interested in administrative
efficiency than in the democratisation of the countryside, and although his
party's Liberal Unionist allies thought differently, their influence was not
decisive.[12] As for the Liberals, county councils were welcome, but did not go
far enough, and they immediately mounted a vigorous campaign for further
reform. In particular, they focused attention on the establishment of parish
councils as a way of giving real power to individual rural communities, so
providing liberation from the 'tyranny' of squirearchical control. Translated
by Sir William Harcourt into the cry of 'the village for the villagers', this
proposal figured prominently in the party's appeal to rural voters and found
concrete expression in the Liberals' 1894 Local Government Act.[13] In making
their case for reform, Liberals emphasised the necessity of stimulating popular
involvement in community life, through which they hoped to generate what
A. H. D. Acland called 'local patriotism'.[14] Possessed of strengthened bonds
of attachment to their home villages, agricultural labourers, so it was argued,
would be less inclined to migrate to the towns.

In Liberal minds, local patriotism was inseparably connected to citizenship: full and free inclusion in the public life of the community was a
precondition of a wider sense of belonging to that community, which parish
councils would effect. By means of the parish council, for which he could
both vote and stand for election, the labourer would gain some control
over his own affairs as well as the responsibility that went with political
power. As a consequence, his character would be improved: habits of self-
respect, self-reliance and above all independence would be encouraged. As
Liberals from Cabinet rank downwards stressed, he would become, in short,

---

[11] G. C. Brodrick, 'Local government in England', in J. W. Probyn (ed.), *Local government and taxation in the United Kingdom*, 2nd edn, London 1882, 52–87 at p. 53.
[12] J. P. D. Dunbabin, 'The politics of the establishment of county councils', *HJ* vi (1963),
250–1; *Hansard*, 3rd ser., 1888, cccxxiii. 1640–702; cccxxiv. 1109–286.
[13] A. G. Gardiner, *The life of Sir William Harcourt*, London 1923, ii. 176.
[14] *Hansard*, 3rd ser., 1891, ccclii. 534.

an *English* citizen, worthy of the 'great, self-governing country' to which he belonged.[15]

Liberal perceptions of their country as 'self-governing' had been greatly boosted by the 1884 Reform Act, which increased the size of the electorate by 70 per cent, enfranchising hundreds of thousands of agricultural labourers. In this context the lack of popular government in the villages was regarded as anomalous. For Liberals, the 'serfdom' it perpetuated was scandalously at variance with the nation's historical path towards democracy, and with mainstream conceptions of the national character as innately fitted for self-government. This helps to explain the importance they placed on the measure, an importance readily discernible from the often high-flown language employed to describe it. For Acland it was a 'charter of self-government for the villages of this country', while Charles Roundell, MP for Skipton in Yorkshire and author of a pamphlet on the subject, called it 'a charter of liberty to the villagers ... an act of emancipation from virtual serfdom'.[16] The use of the word 'charter' is worth noting; James Bryce told the NLF in 1895 that the legislation formed 'the new Magna Charta of rural liberties'.[17] Presented in these terms, the Parish Councils Act was fitted into the long narrative of the nation's constitutional democratisation. Completing the transformation of the labourer into a free citizen, the legislation brought him into line with the *telos* of the English people.

The Liberal project of turning the English agricultural labourer into an English citizen had an important gendered dimension. As Anna Clark and others have shown, contemporary conceptions of English citizenship were explicitly masculine,[18] and this was reflected in Liberal plans for local government reform. Parish councils would transform the character of the labourer from subservient drudge into independent man, or such was the hope entertained. (Curiously enough, the effects of the proposed legislation on women, to whom the 1894 act would also give a vote, were almost entirely ignored by Liberals.) Through the powers vested in his local authority over public buildings, commons, footpaths and land use, 'Hodge' would, according to Liberals, be able to exercise control over the administration of his locality and the conditions under which he lived and laboured. As Acland told the Commons in 1890, he would grow less reliant on charity and other handouts, which were productive only of craven, forelock-tugging habits and

---

15 Acland: NLF, *Reports*, card 10 (1890), 74; Harcourt at Braintree, 26 May 1892, cited in Gardiner, *Harcourt*, ii. 176.

16 *Oxford Times*, 7 July 1894, 6 (Acland); C. S. Roundell, *Parish councils: 'the village for the villagers'*, London [1894], 43.

17 NLF, *Reports*, card 15 (1895), 69.

18 A. Clark, 'Gender, class, and the nation: franchise reform in England, 1832–1928', in J. Vernon (ed.), *Re-reading the constitution*, Cambridge 1996, 230–53.

destructive of 'manliness', and come to possess a level of responsibility 'such as will make a man a man'.[19]

One of the most important means by which Liberals envisaged the parish council transforming agricultural labourers into independent 'men' was by granting them better access to land. This was to be accomplished by giving the councils extensive powers over land use. Of most importance here was the proposal that they should have the authority to compulsorily purchase or let land for public purposes, in particular for smallholdings and allotments, which would then be made available on reasonable terms of tenure. With his local representative body empowered in this way, the labourer would be liberated from that dependence on the landlord which made him more a slave than a free Englishman. Knowing that he had a right to the soil and the means to get hold of it, the labourer could, Foster told the NLF in 1891, 'walk erect, a free man, no longer dreading the frown of the parson or the scowl of the squire'.[20]

Although toned down by Lords' amendments, the 1894 act caused satisfaction to Liberal opinion. It is true that in later years Liberals evinced some disappointment at the reform's effects: while the unchallenged hold of landlords over village life had been ended, parish councils had not inaugurated the 'rural revolution' some had anticipated.[21] Local authority powers of land acquisition were limited and labourer demands sometimes ran into the opposition of gentry or Tory councillors, as the Land Enquiry of 1913 was later to report.[22] Despite this, however, the Liberals made no further major attempts to enact rural local government reform before 1914. Broadly satisfied that levels of political participation and citizenship had been increased, they dropped the issue.

Yet this did not mean that Liberals believed that landlord 'tyranny' had come to an end: far from it. In the 1900s they became if anything more convinced that the countryside suffered under conditions intolerable to English ideals of freedom. But they no longer saw political reform as an effective solution. After all, agricultural labourers now had the vote at both local and parliamentary levels, and had long enjoyed the protection of the secret ballot; there seemed little further to do in this direction. The root problem, as Liberals now saw it, was not so much a lack of village democracy but the whole land system itself. As one writer explained in a *Contemporary Review* article of 1903, the conditions under which farmworkers were employed degraded their character as Englishmen:

19 *Hansard*, 3rd ser., 1890, cccxliv. 320–1 (Acland).
20 NLF, *Reports*, card 12 (1891), 81–3.
21 Cf. R. Heath, 'The rural revolution', CR lxvii (1895), 182–200.
22 *The land: the report of the Land Enquiry Committee*, 3rd edn, London 1913, ii. 185–8, 218–26.

'Farm-service' is still subjugation. It yokes and goads and brutalises. Men are dismissed if their acquaintances do not please their masters. Their wives, though under no legal obligation to do so, must still go out to field labour or 'give offence'... No sheep before her shearer was ever more dumb than the milkers and carters and ploughmen at the village meetings to which their masters may choose to summon them. They are cowed. It is to this that we have come, whom Froissart described as 'le plus perilleux peuple qui soit au monde, et plus outrageux et orgueilleux'. Pride is dead in their souls.[23]

Such observations formed the context in which Liberals launched a full-scale assault on 'landlordism' in the 1900s. This assault was conceptu-alised as much as a project of national liberation as it was one of social justice. Speaking at High Wycombe in February 1905 Campbell-Bannerman presented improved security of tenure and compulsory smallholdings legis-lation as measures which would confer 'freedom in land', and which were urgently required 'if we are to redeem our country'.[24] The rank-and-file of the party followed their leader's cue. Such reforms, they suggested, would turn the 'serf' of the countryside into a true Englishman, by giving him full access to land and hence allowing him to develop his full potential in condi-tions of freedom. In this way, Liberals argued, the national character would be reinvigorated.[25]

Not long after the passage of the 1906–8 reforms, however, many Liberals began to complain that the legislation had not had a sufficiently liberating effect. While the 1906 Agricultural Holdings Act was felt to have done much to address farmer grievances, those of the labourer still appeared largely unresolved. Having had some of its teeth pulled by Lords' amend-ments, the Smallholdings Act proved rather ponderous in its operation, with many people having to wait some time before getting land.[26] Although Carrington at the Board of Agriculture appointed extra land commissioners to speed up the administrative process, the problem was never fully solved. A large part of the difficulty was the opposition of landlords and big farmers, who in many places exerted a controlling influence over county councils. As a consequence, although councils were empowered to supply smallholdings under the legislation, many proved reluctant to do so. If they decided to act at all, they often preferred attempting to persuade landowners to provide smallholdings on a voluntary basis. But this top–down dispensing of land did little to free rural people from dependence, not least because non-local

---

23 Green, *English agricultural labourer*, 149.
24 Liberal Publication Department, *The case for dissolution: a speech delivered by the Right Hon. Sir H. Campbell-Bannerman*, London 1905, 11.
25 For example, National Liberal Club, *Address on land-tenure reform by James Rowlands*, MP, London 1906.
26 P. Morrell, 'The administration of the Small Holdings Act', *Nation* iv (28 Nov. 1908), 338–9.

authority smallholdings were not usually offered on secure terms of tenure.[27] Furthermore, as the Land Enquiry Report was to point out, labourers were frequently disinclined even to approach elite-dominated county councils to apply for smallholdings, as to do so, in public, 'often means becoming a marked man'.[28]

The 1906–8 reforms also failed to address an issue Liberals increasingly saw as central: rural housing. The quality and quantity of housing stock was one element of their concern (of which more later), but another was the question of tenure. To Liberal minds, the conditions under which labourers rented cottages exemplified the way in which the economic power of rural elites destroyed personal liberty. In many cases labourers enjoyed no security of tenure; in others, their homes were supplied with their employment – the house went with the job – and this system of 'tied cottages' did much to rouse Liberal ire. It seemed calculated, so they argued, to encourage habits of subservience: a man who knew that dismissal meant loss of both home and job would do little to antagonise his masters. He would be politically quiescent; he would tolerate poor standards of pay and working conditions; he would be disinclined to apply to the local authority for an allotment or smallholding; he would, in short, as the propagandist *Liberal Monthly* told its readers at the time of the Land Campaign, be prevented from being 'a free man in a free country'.[29] While the 1909 Housing and Town Planning Act aimed to improve the rural housing situation, its effects were limited. Although it empowered local authorities to conduct public enquiries into housing provision, poor people were often reluctant to come forward, largely due to fears that doing so might lead to reprisals by angry farmers and land-lords. Thus, even if an investigation took place, it did not always lead to the building of more houses. In the notorious Sir Edward Hambro case, for instance, an enquiry found in favour of a landowner whose solution to the housing shortage in his village was to evict all tenants who were not working on his estate.[30] And furthermore, the 1909 act had little impact on the tied cottage problem in particular, which came in for strong condemnation as 'a system of bondage' in the Land Enquiry report of 1913.[31]

The Liberal project of rural liberation climaxed with the Land Campaign. From the outset Lloyd George made clear that his intention was to 'break down the remnants of the feudal system'.[32] Launching the campaign at Bedford on 11 October 1913, he declared that landlordism had crushed

---

[27] See, for example, *Hansard*, 5th ser., 1912, xxxv. 277–87.

[28] *The land*, i. 163.

[29] LM, Nov 1913, 2.

[30] Hambro was landlord of the village of Winterborne Strickland in Dorset. After the enquiry had found in his favour, he bought up all the remaining property in the village, which further infuriated Liberal opinion.

[31] *The land*, i. 137, 123.

[32] Lord Riddell, *More pages from my diary, 1908–1914*, London 1934, 63, 70.

all independence out of the farmworker. With the common rights that had allowed him a self-sufficient livelihood having been stolen by landlord parliaments, the English labourer of today 'has been converted from a contented, well-fed, independent peasant to a hopeless, under-paid, landless drudge on the soil'.[33] To this rhetoric, Liberals added forensic evidence. The Land Enquiry report detailed numerous examples of landlord tyranny: in his introduction to the report Acland drew attention to one landowner who had bought up all nearby property 'because I do not want any undesirable person in the village'.[34]

As in the past, Liberals advocated smallholdings as a means of allowing labourers to break free from this tyranny. In a new departure, however, they also suggested that improved wages would inculcate independence: hence the proposal for an agricultural minimum wage as part of this policy of 'national patriotism'.[35] It is important to stress that the argument here was more about liberty than it was about redistributive social justice. In the interpretation of the Liberal Land Campaigners, low wages stifled the independence of the agricultural labourer, who – unable to properly provide for his family – was forced to fall back on charity and the uncertain benevolence of the squire.[36] As Acland fulminated, such cringing reliance on 'grandmotherly' handouts was destructive of 'manliness', words which chimed with the Liberal critique of the degradation of masculine character fostered by the 'feudal' land system.[37] This critique was a longstanding one. As we have seen, it had been employed in Liberal advocacy of local government reform in the 1880s and 1890s. But it was given a new lease of life during the Land Campaign. As F. E. Green argued in his *Tyranny of the countryside* and elsewhere, the great houses which formed the linchpins of the land system stimulated 'servility and envy' among ordinary people. Sustained by a vast retinue of servants – butlers, gardeners, chambermaids, grooms and so on – they made a virtue of demoralising, deferential, bum-sucking habits. In these bastions of snobbery and aristocratic ease, 'parasitic labour, of no use from the national standpoint' was given a higher worth than 'honest productive toil':[38] the flunky was Hodge's superior. Green's tone of moral outrage at this state of affairs was replicated in party propaganda. *The Homeland*, organ of the Land Campaign, condemned landlordism for its promotion of unproductive, character-sapping labour. By improving access to land and raising wages, *The Homeland* insisted, Liberal reforms 'will increase the number of men and women dependent on their own industry', with the

---

33 *The Times*, 13 Oct. 1913, 13.
34 Cited in H. V. Emy, 'The Land Campaign: Lloyd George as a social reformer, 1909–14', in A. J. P. Taylor (ed.), *Lloyd George*, London 1971, 50.
35 *The land*, i, pp. lix, lvii, lviii–lvix.
36 S. Rowntree, 'Rural land reform', CR civ (1913), 615–17.
37 *The land*, i, pp. xxviii, xxxiv–xxxv.
38 F. E. Green, *The awakening of England*, London 1912, 291–5.

result redounding to the benefit of the national character: 'Less dependence; more independence. Fewer "parasites"; more producers. The backbone and the wealth of the nation will both improve.'[39]

In Liberal argument, then, the land system was rigged up to deny ordinary men a self-reliant livelihood. This in itself was held to be destructive of national character, as it was inimical to that personal freedom long held to be the rightful inheritance of Englishmen, but it was also charged with further demoralising effects. It was a commonplace of contemporary opinion that liberty was the handmaiden of moral virtue generally: give a man his freedom, the chance of an independent career, and he would work hard, develop frugal habits and shun vice. The trouble was, in Liberal eyes, that the land system denied a man this freedom: unable to gain access to land and hence a self-sufficient livelihood, he had little incentive to develop virtuous habits of behaviour. Acland made this point in the Land Enquiry report,[40] but it was prominent in Liberal discourse throughout the period. Liberals ranging from moderate reformers to land nationalisers took the view that the 'manly independence' conferred by smallholdings, secure tenure and good wages would promote virtues like 'sobriety, honesty, and forethought'.[41] With proper pay and access to land, no longer would the farmworker lack any hope of social advancement or incentive to thrift, as he did under the arrangements of a pervasive paternalism designed to keep him in his place. No longer would he merit the description (accorded him by one radical agitator) of 'a shiftless, untrained, penniless sloven' – a person with no prospects who had quickly degenerated into moral turpitude by marrying early, procreating recklessly, disdaining knowledge and frittering his meagre earnings away on beer.[42]

This solicitude for the Englishman's character fed into another concern. According to many reformers, one of the main reasons why 'landlordism' destroyed virtues like self-reliance, hard work, temperance and frugality was because it prevented country people from enjoying a proper home life. Interestingly, this line of argument was probably most prominent on the left of Liberal-radical discourse – among land nationalisers, for instance. As the LNS *Programme* had it, by denying labourers any right to the soil, the land system ran counter to 'those home-feelings and interests which are... the best incentives to industry and thrift'.[43] But lack of access to land was not the only problem here. As the studies of pioneer social investigators like Seebohm Rowntree and H. H. Mann, as well as the eyewitness reports of laymen revealed, the homes of the rural poor, while often deceptively picturesque at first sight, were on examination deplorably squalid. Cottages

39 *Homeland*, 6 June 1914, 149–50.
40 *The land*, i, p. xxvi.
41 *LP*, 1 July 1892, 53.
42 W. Tuckwell, *Reminiscences of a radical parson*, London 1905, 151–6 at p. 156.
43 LNS, *Programme*, London 1890.

lacked basic sanitation; they were often in poor repair; they were usually very overcrowded – and rents for spacious, healthy houses were too costly for working people.[44] It followed from this that the agricultural labourer was very far from realising domestic felicity; indeed, in an important sense he was homeless. Lacking the secure tenure of a good cottage, unable to get a smallholding, he was condemned to a life drifting from place to place in search of wage-earnings, which themselves were often too low to support decent family life. As a consequence, so it was claimed, many an English village was 'not a living whole composed of independent homes, but merely a caravanserai for chance sojourners', somewhere with 'no vital connexion with the national life'.[45]

By means of land and housing reforms, Liberals and radicals sought to give the rootless and peripatetic inhabitants of rural England 'homes of their own in their own country'.[46] In so domesticating the agricultural labourer, they believed that he would also become imbued with a sense of belonging and local identity (parish councils, of course, would assist in this as well). For many, this local home feeling was the source of a wider national feeling. Because he would have an inalienable stake in the soil, because he would feel properly part of his local community, the self-sufficient smallholder of reformers' dreams was a person with a strong affection for his 'homeland', and by extension the nation to which he belonged.[47]

Yet Liberals did not simply want to create patriots; they wanted to create the right sort of patriots – men who would come to form the emotional and moral 'backbone of the nation'. They sought to create a large class of citizen cultivators – an English equivalent of the *petits cultivateurs* of France, as it were. Not for sturdy smallholders the mindless flag-waving by which the urban expression of national sentiment was frequently marked. Inoculated by the effects of secure tenure of a smallholding, they would be immune to the contagion of jingoism, that irrational 'mob passion' to which many (especially after the Boer War) believed English town-dwellers to be especially susceptible. These people, C. F. G. Masterman wrote in an *Independent Review* article of 1904, would live 'a life of free men, with that love of the country and its very soil never found in the "patriotism" of the cities – the random and pitiful patriotism of a landless people'.[48]

[44] H. H. Mann, 'Life in an agricultural village in England', *Sociological Papers* i (1904), 163–93; B. S. Rowntree and M. Kendall, *How the labourer lives*, London 1913.
[45] D. C. Pedder, 'Without house or home' (1902) in his *Where men decay*, London 1908, 73.
[46] F. S. Stevenson: LLRA, *Sixteenth annual meeting*, London 1903, 13.
[47] See, for example, speech of Corrie Grant, *Birmingham Daily Post*, 29 July 1907, 12.
[48] C. F. G. Masterman, 'Towards a civilisation', *IR* ii (1904), 502.

Land reform and degeneration

For many Edwardian Liberals, the bolstering of English national character did not just mean rooting the countryman to his 'homeland' – it also meant improving his physical ability to wage war. In their analysis, the land system had fostered rural-urban migration; and by the 1900s it was widely thought that the overcrowded and unsanitary conditions of working-class urban life were not conducive to the production of good fighting men (indeed, it was the long-established view of army officers that country recruits made the best soldiers).[49] In this context Liberals (even new Liberals like J. A. Hobson) saw measures such as smallholdings legislation as a way of boosting martial prowess. Such reforms, they argued, would stem the flow of migrants to the debilitating urban slums, while simultaneously preserving a body of country-dwelling men ideally suited to military service.[50] Action along these lines was often presented as a patriotic imperative, essential to avoid the devastating defeat that the setbacks during the Boer War appeared to presage. As an upcoming Liberal MP and a strong supporter of land reform, Herbert Samuel, warned readers of the *Independent Review* in 1904 that

> It is not from the city tenement that the best type of colonist is likely to come, or the best type of sailor, or the best type of soldier. Waterloo was won, not on the playing fields of Eton alone, but on the village greens of England as well; and if there are no more village greens, our Waterloos of the future, in spite of all that England can do, may have a different ending.[51]

Similar warnings were also heard during the Land Campaign. Measures like the living wage and the land taxes (which would promote the proper cultivation of the soil) were presented as means by which what Lloyd George called 'a large, strong, robust population' could be preserved in the countryside. And as the Chancellor cautioned in his Bedford speech of October 1913, every other European country had recognised that just such a population was 'the most important thing for defensive purposes'.[52]

Liberal advocacy of land reform as an engine for sustaining British armed might was one manifestation of a more general anxiety about the physical 'degeneration' supposedly wrought by rural depopulation. This anxiety was based on an assumption that country people were typically much healthier than town inhabitants (pre-eminently the 'Cockney', who by the 1900s had become synonymous with enfeebled and nervously excitable slum-dwelling

---

[49] A. R. Skelley, *The recruitment and terms of conditions of the British Regular, 1859–1899*, London 1977, 290–3.
[50] See, for example, LLRA, *Eighteenth annual meeting*, London 1905, 10; J. A. Hobson, *Imperialism* (1902), 3rd edn, London 1988, 103.
[51] H. Samuel, 'The village of the future', *IR* iii (1904), 392.
[52] *The Times*, 13 Oct. 1913, 13.

manhood).[53] It did not lack a factual basis: police records indicate that country recruits were fitter than their town counterparts, and thus help explain why the Metropolitan Police launched a major recruiting drive in the shires at this time.[54] Although present in the political discourse of the 1880s and 1890s, it intensified markedly following the outbreak of the Boer War. As is well known, the setbacks suffered by the army in South Africa and the physical unfitness of many recruits were instrumental in sparking a campaign for 'national efficiency'. Yet although historians have rightly observed how a spirit of 'patriotic earnestness' inspired this movement, they have largely overlooked its connection to political debate on the land question.[55]

For many Liberal and radical participants in this debate, the desertion of the countryside was a phenomenon that threatened apocalyptic consequences for the Englishman's physique. Given added force by the 1904 Committee on Physical Deterioration, their arguments presented nothing less than the 'actual life and vitality of the nation' as being at stake.[56] In December 1905, in his first major speech as prime minister, Campbell-Bannerman declared that 'the health and stamina of the nation are bound up with the maintenance of a large class of workers on the soil. (Cheers.) The town population redundant, the country population decimated, it is a subversion of healthy national life'.[57]

To a certain extent such statements on the part of Liberal politicians sprang from a social reformist commitment to public health. But their agenda here does not fit very easily into conventional narratives of 'new Liberal' politics and ideology. In his Swindon speech of 22 October 1913, Lloyd George was to promise that the Land Campaign would fill 'the countryside with a happy, prosperous, contented peasantry' and 'free towns from the nightmares of unemployment and sweating slums. Then we shall have a motherland (cheers), we shall have a motherland that its children can rejoice in'.[58] In this way, land reform was consonant with a radical tradition of social reformist patriotism, which – although missing from many historical accounts of Edwardian Liberalism – occupied an important place

[53] See, for example, H. A. Spurr, 'The cockneyisation of England', New Liberal Review v (1903), 273–83.

[54] H. Shpayer-Makov, 'The appeal of country workers: the case of the Metropolitan Police', HR lxiv (1991), 186–203. The Met was alarmed at the falling numbers of (healthier) recruits from rural areas: in 1889 they made up 47% of the total, by 1907 just 31%.

[55] See, for example, G. R. Searle, The quest for national efficiency, Berkeley 1971, 41–2.

[56] National Liberal Club, Address, 12. Although the Physical Deterioration Committee's Report suggested that levels of 'degeneracy' had been exaggerated, it did find that 'the collection of the majority of the population in the large towns' was 'the most evident and most considerable' of all the 'general causes in operation that are calculated to arrest and depress development': Report of the inter-departmental committee on physical deterioration, 1904 (Cd. 2175), i. 16.

[57] The Times, 22 Dec. 1905, 7.

[58] The Times, 22 Oct. 1913, 9.

in contemporary political discourse. It found expression in the arguments of opponents of the Boer War like C. P. Scott, who advanced a different conception of patriotism to that trumpeted by jingoistic supporters of the government's policy.[59] It was also much in evidence among younger radicals like Masterman, who was to play a key role in the Land Campaign. Many of these individuals were associated with the League of Young Liberals (LYL), the party's official 'youth' wing and a body animated by a belief that ameliorating the ordinary Englishman's lot was a patriotic imperative: 'poor and uncultured though he be, he is still an Englishman, and has a claim upon the wealth of the nation and the wisdom of the race'. In the League's view, the living conditions of working people were destructive of the national character, and land reform was one way of combating this problem. Urgent action was required, as 'the question of a greater share in the land of England by the people of England ... blocks the way to and concerns intimately the future of the race in its physical and moral aspect and cannot long be a question to be shelved or postponed'.[60]

As the example of the LYL makes clear, patriotic advocacy of land and other reforms was related to national efficiency ideas – and also those of race. This is further evidence of how the discourse of land reform cannot be easily reconciled with standard readings of Edwardian Liberal reformism as dominated by an enlightened progressivism. In addition, it bears upon contemporary conceptions of national character. As discussed earlier, mainstream notions of national character were dominated by an emphasis on personal freedom, and were much in evidence in Liberal policy and discussion on the land question. But this conception of national identity did not have an unchallenged hold over political debate: though dominant, it did not go uncontested, even within Liberal ranks. In the 1900s an alternative conception of national character – based on race – began to achieve some prominence. This was not informed by rigorously 'scientific' or biological racism, nor (despite the claims of a number of scholars) did it signify that the determinants of English identity were imagined as fundamentally racial.[61] The language in which it was framed was used loosely, with 'race' often being deployed as a synonym for 'people'; but its currency did betoken a change in attitudes. For some people, at least, the English national character came to be defined by physique, stamina and vitality as well as mental and moral attributes.

Liberal land reformers' concern with the racial element of national character is evident from the language in which their policies were presented.

---

59 Readman, 'Liberal party', 272.
60 J. A. Rees, *Our aims and objects* (1903), 12th edn, London 1912, 2, 4. By 1912 the League had more than 500 branches.
61 Cf., for example, C. Hall, *White, male and middle-class: explorations in feminism and history*, Oxford 1992, esp. ch. ix, and C. Hall and others, *Defining the Victorian nation: class, race, gender and the British Reform Act of 1867*, Cambridge 2000, esp. pp. 48–9.

The 1907 Smallholdings Bill is a case in point. In a number of set-piece speeches Campbell-Bannerman, Churchill and other party leaders argued that smallholdings would counter race 'degeneration' by keeping people on the land. At the April 1907 'Land and Housing Demonstration' in London, Campbell-Bannerman suggested that a large rural population provided a reservoir of national strength, upon which towns and cities depended for replenishment by 'vigorous life and energy'. But, he warned, this source of 'fresh blood from the country' was in danger of drying up due to unsustainable rates of rural depopulation, and

> If we are to be cut off from the natural sources of health physical degeneracy must set in, and the country must go irretrievably downhill ... [But] we have not gone so far yet that a manful and patriotic and united effort may succeed in arresting the descent. (Cheers). I would ask you what cause that you could imagine would make a stronger appeal to the love of country and the pride of race?[62]

In the Commons debates on the Smallholdings Bill, Liberal MPs followed their leader's example and emphasised that central to the measure's 'national' value was its potential for checking the racially degenerative effects of rural depopulation.[63]

But the idea that radical land reform was an effective means of checking 'race deterioration' reached still greater prominence during the controversies over the People's Budget and Land Campaign. A large part of the rationale behind Lloyd George's scheme of land taxation was that it would boost the cultivation of the soil by taxing it into 'productive' use (for this reason agricultural lands – but not game preserves – were exempt from the Budget land taxes). The resulting fillip given to agricultural output at the expense of sport and speculative landholding would help to stem the flow of rural-urban migration that was bleeding dry the national stock. It would lead, Churchill said in a speech of August 1909, to an 'increase in the sources from which the health and stamina on which the character of our race depends and have always depended'.[64]

But it was the issue of housing – also central to the Land Campaign – that probably provoked most Liberal concern about the agrarian causes of racial decay. Speaking at Marlborough in November 1913, Lloyd George stressed how his proposals would force land into use, so helping to relieve the shortage of decent accommodation in both town and country. For, as things stood at present, 'it was impossible to bring up a healthy, vigorous and strong

---

62 *The Times*, 22 Apr. 1907, 18. See also Campbell-Bannerman's speech at the Land Law Reform Association, *Seventeenth annual meeting*, London 1904, 6, and Churchill at Drury Lane Theatre, in *Winston S. Churchill: his complete speeches, 1897–1963*, ed. R. R. James, New York 1974, i. 779.
63 *Hansard*, 4th ser., 1907, clxxv. 1626.
64 *Churchill speeches*, ii. 1308.

race of men and women ... It was a national weakness as well as a national disgrace'.[65] There were two elements to the Liberal argument here. On the one hand, the shortage of adequate cottage homes drove healthy English countrymen into the towns, where – largely thanks to landlordism – they were compelled to live in overcrowded conditions, and their health declined as a consequence. On the other hand, the shortage and poor quality of cottage homes caused physically debilitating conditions of life in the villages themselves. There was a potential weakness in this argument: if the country-dweller was the epitome of healthy English manhood, how could it be that his living conditions were so bad? This was a point made by Conservative critics of Liberal plans.[66] Liberals, however, could reply by citing empirical evidence as to rural living conditions, drawn from the studies of social investigators and – by 1913–14 – the Land Enquiry reports. In so doing they developed an *a fortiori* argument for reform: the fact that many countrymen – the cream of English manhood – struggled to maintain basic standards of 'physical efficiency' made it all the more necessary to take action to tackle the rural housing problem.

Yet, for Edwardian Liberals, it was not simply that more and better cottages in the villages would mean less migration and hence less overcrowding in the cities; more and better houses in the cities were also envisaged as a consequence of the restructuring of the land system. According to Liberals, land value taxation would discourage the speculative holding of undeveloped land in and around urban areas, so increasing the supply of building plots and therefore bringing down the unhealthy levels of overcrowding. Lloyd George was especially keen on this argument. During a speech in October 1910 he argued for land taxes to make more land available for housing around towns, justifying his proposals on the grounds that

> The greatest asset of a country is a virile and contented population ... Every good farmer knows that if he is to produce the best class of cattle and of horses on his holding he must look after their feeding, their shelter, and, in the case of horses, their training. Why should men and women have less thought and attention given to them than cattle? Statesmanship is, after all, farming on a great scale. Mr. Rowntree points out in his great work that one result of our present system of wages and housing is that 50 per cent of the recruits that come up for service in the Army are rejected as unfit because of their physical inferiority. You apply that throughout every walk of our national life, and you see what an enormous loss is entailed by the nation by its neglect to attend to questions which affect the physical and mental vitality and efficiency of the race.[67]

[65] *The Times*, 10 Nov. 1913, 4.
[66] For example, earl of Malmesbury: *Hansard*, 5th ser., 1914, xv. 973.
[67] *The Times*, 18 Oct. 1910, 7.

This patriotic emphasis on the need to 'breed' a fit race was also apparent in Lloyd George's later speeches on the Land Campaign. In the course of publicising the government's urban land proposals in a speech at Holloway in November 1913, he drew attention to the fact that the population density in Hampstead was thirty-eight persons per acre, but over 200 in the East End, describing the disparity as 'a scandal that cries for redress' – a matter of national shame not least because of its degenerative implications for the 'blood' of the nation:

> I say to all those patriots who wave Union Jacks at Mr. Bonar Law's meetings, first of all, cleanse that stain from the flag ... Overcrowding ... depresses the vitality, it poisons the blood ... I want to know this: are the children of the workers of this land not as important to the State as the children of the opulent? There is plenty of room in England if the room is properly utilised.[68]

As illustrated by Lloyd George's language, Liberal land reform involved patriotic concern for race. If this casts further doubt on the assumption that the Conservatives had a monopoly on the language of patriotism at this time, it also shows that race bore some relation to Liberal conceptions of national character. By the Edwardian period, Liberal ideas of national character were informed by a fuzzy, unsystematic biological determinism, a conviction that the physique of the race had a significant effect on the destinies of the nation. Yet this point should not be pushed too strongly. Insofar as they were concerned with the Englishman's character, Liberals retained their central focus on the question of personal freedom and its associated moral benefits. Independence such as that of a smallholder, released from reliance on meagre wage earnings and the demoralising paternalism of the squire, would foster hard work, frugal habits and other virtues traditionally prized by Liberals. Even after the People's Budget, this moralising agenda was fully to the fore. Far from being 'socialistic', as many Tories said at the time and not a few historians have suggested since, Lloyd George's agenda was consonant with long-held Liberal-radical values. Independence and hard work he praised; idleness and privilege he excoriated. The land taxes and the Land Campaign were not so much attacks on wealth *qua* wealth as attacks on unearned wealth; or as Churchill put it, the government sought not only to ask '"How much have you got?", but "How did you get it?"'[69]

---

68 D. Lloyd George, *The urban land problem*, London 1913, 9–10.
69 *Churchill speeches*, ii. 1322.

Unionists and the national character

Before century's end, Conservative consideration of the connections between land reform and the English national character was limited at best. Indeed, until quite late on, many Conservatives were of the opinion that the existing land system 'had done more than any other institution of the country to build up the national character', as Walter Long told a meeting of the Central Chambers of Agriculture in 1899.[70] Doubtless Long's words were music to the ears of his audience; but by the time they were spoken, the trend of Unionist opinion was beginning to turn away from this position, towards one more critical of the land system and its effects on national character. This change is well illustrated by the agricultural writings of Rider Haggard. Drawing on his farming experience, Rider Haggard lamented the injurious effects of rural depopulation not only on the agricultural economy, but on the national character as well. In A farmer's year (1899), he claimed that agriculture was more than being about food production; it was also about character formation. Rider Haggard was prepared to accept that the 'pure-bred Cockney' might have a certain 'sharpness' of intellect, but his character was otherwise inferior to that of the sturdy countryman; life on the land developed 'patient, even minds in sound enduring bodies, gifts of which, after the first generation, the great towns rob those who dwell and labour in them'.[71] If the depopulation of country districts were allowed to continue, he fretted, it would mean the end for 'John Bull', who 'heretofore ... has been depicted as a countryman and nothing else ... if henceforth he is to forsake the soil that bred him, how will he be pictured by our children, drawing from a changed and shrunken model?'[72] Rider Haggard amplified his ruminations on this theme in Rural England (1902), a book replete with concern about depopulation and what this might entail. Here, a racial conception of national character is quite evident. Depopulation was a 'national question' that threatened 'the progressive deterioration of the race', perhaps even 'the ruin of the race'. This equated to the degeneration of national character: 'So the countryman chooses the town, and as a consequence the character of Englishmen appears to be changing'.[73]

Rider Haggard's views did not command immediate assent from main-stream Unionist opinion, but they represented a turning of the tide. Their publication, combined with the revelations about the physical unfitness of Boer War volunteers, made it more difficult to claim that the existing land system was wholly beneficial to John Bull. As the Edwardian period progressed, Unionists became more inclined to express concern about the deleterious effects of rural decay on the national character, and to see reform

[70] The Times, 6 Dec. 1899, 11.
[71] R. H. Rider Haggard, A farmer's year, London 1899, pp. viii–ix.
[72] Ibid. pp. xi, 466.
[73] Idem, Rural England, ii. 541–2.

as a means of dealing with this problem. Against the background of mounting anxiety, the arguments of campaigners like Collings and Parker proved influential. In his important 1908 tract, *The land for the people*, Parker felt able to present the national deterioration caused by 'loss of rural population' as no startling revelation, but 'a common truth'. His assertion that 'under present conditions we are declining, losing in wealth, in men, in national character, in personal physique' reflected the views of many in his party, and it was one with which Balfour – who supplied the preface to Parker's pamphlet – was apparently sympathetic.[74]

Indeed, following Balfour's public commitment to small ownership in 1908–9, much was heard from Conservative politicians about the benefits of land reform on the English character, and these benefits were often expressed using a patriotic language of race. At the January 1910 general election, this language formed part of candidates' appeals. In his address to the electors of North Cumberland, Claude Lowther affirmed that one of the 'blessings' of small ownership was that 'it would arrest the decay of the race by attracting people to the land'.[75] Similarly, in the Spen Valley division of Yorkshire, Fred Kelley claimed that 'getting people back to the land ... would physically improve our race'.[76]

Continued Unionist commitment to land reform into the years of the Land Campaign saw continued concern for the Englishman's character. As previously, his physical and racial attributes were the subject of most solicitude. The USRC proposal for agricultural wage boards, which was set out in *A Unionist agricultural policy* (1913), operated on the assumption that the rural population was the physical 'backbone' of the nation. Following the analysis of the Liberal Land Campaigners and certainly influenced by radical Unionists like Collings, Arthur Steel-Maitland and others associated with the USRC suggested that better wages for agricultural labourers would help preserve a healthy rural population and hence 'the physique of the nation'.[77] Although some Unionist critics of this policy felt that it involved too drastic a level of state intervention, its proponents argued that the higher, patriotic imperative of racial regeneration trumped such concerns. *Laissez-faire* in the matter of agricultural wages, the USRC argued, 'has produced results inimical to the race'.[78]

As is clear from the wage boards proposal, Unionist thinking on the land question towards the end of the Edwardian period was moving in quite radical directions. And it was radical not only in the sense that it proposed a level of state intervention hitherto ruled inadmissible. It was also radical because it implied a democratic conception of the nation's worth. In Conservative

---

[74] Parker, *Land for the people*, 32, 34.
[75] *Election addresses*, reel 5, Jan 1910.
[76] Ibid.
[77] *A Unionist agricultural policy*, London 1913, 5.
[78] Ibid. 11.

discourse, the indices of national greatness (or weakness) were changing, becoming more oriented towards the common man; increasingly defined, indeed, by the common man and his condition. This democratic agenda sometimes even shaded towards anti-landlordism; at times, moreover, it was also tinged with anti-commercial sentiment. For some Conservative advocates of land reform, national character was more important than narrowly economic considerations. Former land agent and star student at the Royal Agricultural College, Cirencester, and MP for the Horncastle division of Lincolnshire from February 1911, William Weigall was one who took this view. Defending Conservative smallholdings policy in a 1912 debate on peasant proprietors, Weigall declared that

> We hear much as to the wealth of this country in sovereigns, and as to export returns and import returns, but there are things that make for wealth that you cannot estimate in pounds, shillings and pence, and undoubtedly almost the greatest asset this country has got is its national character. We talk a great deal about getting people back to the land. I say if you can only keep the people on the land and out of the slums, which has been the product of commercialism, you will improve your national character, you will improve your national physique, you will improve the virility of the nation; and, I ask, is not that an asset worth even a half per cent in a banker's scheme for state-aided purchase?[79]

Here, the quality of the English national character was elevated above the quantity of material riches as an index of national 'wealth'. Not all Conservative land reformers did this (and certainly few did in so explicit a manner), but in general, theirs too was a qualitative perspective. In focusing on the ordinary Englishman and his character, they postulated a conception of national greatness as defined by and dependent upon the fitness of the national stock.

Land reformers against empire

This focus on a qualitative conception of national greatness was connected with contemporary attitudes to emigration, which increased rapidly after 1880, with hundreds of thousands leaving yearly for the white settler colonies. Now, it might be assumed that the Conservatives – as the self-proclaimed party of empire – saw this in unambiguously positive terms, but such was not the case. Proponents of colonial emigration were not thin on the ground, but it is important to emphasise that their arguments did not command anything like universal consent. Government took rather a dim view, and even Tory opinion was divided. Indeed, sometimes the contentions of supporters of emigration appear as voices of protest, raised against rather than in line with

---

[79] *Hansard*, 5th ser., 1912, xxxiv. 926.

prevailing attitudes. Writing in the February 1914 issue of the *Empire Review*, E. G. Pretyman declared that Unionists ought not to discourage people from emigrating to Canada and other colonies, but should instead 'try to cement Canada and this country together, so that the day may come ... when the British agricultural labourer will think no more of leaving this country and going to Canada than of leaving Devonshire to go to Yorkshire, and when *we shall view emigration from a very different standpoint from what we do to-day*'.[80]

For Pretyman, emigration to the colonies was part of the solution to the land question: rather than migrating to English urban slums, excess agricultural labour would leave for Canadian prairies, there to find remunerative employment in the service of a wider imperial mission. However, this point of view was not representative of Unionist opinion generally, especially in the Edwardian period, when levels of emigration reached their peak. In the years immediately before the First World War, Tory writers in the newspaper and periodical press were often to be found lamenting the loss of the 'young blood leaving England' – rural England in particular – for the Dominions.[81] That the most capable and ambitious men often seemed the most inclined to leave amplified the worry. This was very much the perspective of Collings, Parker, Ellis Barker and other influential figures pushing the Unionist leadership in the direction of land reform.[82] The best solution, as these individuals saw it, was the creation of small ownerships, which would allow the English countryman to make a career on the soil of his own country – an opportunity the land system at present denied him. This was a radical analysis, but it did not spill over into anti-imperialism. It reflected, rather, a growing conviction that Britain's future as an imperial power rested on adequate attention being given to the problems of 'the heart of the empire'. Without such attention, the English people would decay and the whole imperial edifice would collapse.[83]

This point of view was not confined to Unionists, of course. The 'heart of the empire' argument was very much associated with imperially-minded Liberals, Churchill being one example. Speaking on 4 September 1909 in defence of the Budget land taxes, he claimed that

> The greatest danger to the British Empire and to the British people was not to be found among the enormous fleets and armies of the European Continent or in the solemn problems of Hindustan ... It is not in the Yellow Peril or the Black Peril, or any danger in the wide circuit of colonial or foreign affairs. It

80 E. G. Pretyman, 'The land question: a reply to Mr Lloyd George', *Empire Review* xxvii (1914), 11–12.

81 *Daily Express*, 30 Dec. 1912, 6.

82 For example, J. E. Barker, 'The land, the people and the general election', *NC* lxvi (1909), 392–3, and G. Parker, 'British land and British emigration', *NC* lxxii (1912), 964–76.

83 C. Turnor, *Land problems and national welfare*, London 1911, ch. ix: 'The land and the empire'.

is here in our midst, close at home, close at hand, in the vast growing cities of England and Scotland, and in the dwindling and cramped villages of our denuded countryside. It is there you will find the seeds of Imperial ruin and national decay.[84]

A similarly inward-looking imperialism was evident in the language of Liberals more committed to land reform, such as Sir Walter Foster. Chairman of ASHA and involved in the LLRA, Foster was a firm imperialist, having strongly supported the Boer War. Like Churchill, he believed that imperial greatness was dependent on the conditions in which the English race lived at home. He thought that 'if we were to have a great Empire and be worthy of it, we must a healthy home'.[85] The establishment of this healthy national home, Foster emphasised in his speeches, would be accomplished by the multiplication of individual homes on the land in the form of small-holdings; these would root people to the soil and so secure 'our position as a great, powerful ... and ... an Imperial race'.[86] Similar views were advanced by George Lambert, MP for the South Molton division of Devon from 1891 and a determined campaigner for both land tenure reform and smallholdings legislation. Lambert believed that land reform would help preserve Britain's status as a great imperial power. As he told NLF conferences on a number of occasions, Liberals who really loved the empire knew it was better to 'spend money for our own country at home' than on vainglorious adventures overseas like the Boer War or the pursuit of Muhammad 'Abdallah Hasan, the dervish leader and so-called 'mad mullah' of Somaliland. Britain had spent 'two hundred and fifty millions in devastating South Africa' and two-and-a-half millions in hunting the fugitive mullah, and the latter sum alone 'would have settled no less than 5,000 cultivators on the land' at home. Lambert had no doubt that such a programme of domestic re-settlement 'would have strengthened the Empire far more than squandering treasure in the arid wastes of Central Africa' and elsewhere.[87]

In suggesting the redirection of resources away from 'God-forsaken enterprises all over the world' towards land reform, Lambert described himself as something of 'a Little Englander'.[88] Although he was exaggerating, it is true that the step from attacking the specific details of imperial policy to criticising imperialism more generally was a relatively short one. And, in the aftermath of the Boer War, it was a step more Liberals found themselves taking. Drawn out and hugely expensive, the war had done much to dilute imperial enthusiasm, with that of the Liberals, as might be expected, being especially watered-down. It is true that very few in the party, now

[84] P. Addison, *Churchill on the home front, 1900–1955*, London 1992, 88.

[85] *Lincoln Gazette*, 21 Oct. 1905, 6.

[86] *Hansard*, 4th ser., 1907, clxxv. 1626.

[87] NLF, *Reports*, card 27 (1905), 64; card 29 (1907), 65; *Westminster Gazette*, 3 June 1905, 4.

[88] NLF, *Reports*, card 29 (1907), 66.

as ever, explicitly rejected the idea of empire in itself.[89] However, 'imperialist' expressions of patriotism and national identity became progressively less prominent in Liberal political discourse in the 1900s, with mainstream Liberalism being animated by a growing condemnation of the conflation of national greatness with imperial bigness. 'Civilisation', as Augustine Birrell put it at the 1903 NLF conference, 'is not empire. It cannot be counted in square miles, nor can its value be estimated even in the huge figures of the Army and Navy estimates.'[90] In this interpretation, true national greatness was not determined by such factors, but by qualitative considerations: the character and general well-being of ordinary English people. Birrell's perspective was congruent with a strengthening contemporary conviction that what the nation required was not more overseas colonisation by force of arms, but 'home colonisation' by the provision of smallholdings and other agrarian reforms. This conviction, which recalled earlier Chartist ideas, was increasingly widespread in the Edwardian Liberal party. In a speech of February 1905 Campbell-Bannerman told his audience that

> We are quite willing to be reckoned 'Little Englanders' in the sense that we believe something more is to be made of this island home of ours, and that it deserves a thought now and again. We believe in our country and in our countrymen. But all is not well with England. How can it be so when for the greater part of twenty years the eyes of the Government have been on the ends of the earth, and its energies devoted to the acquisition of territory elsewhere, and other purposes of a like kind? During this time the feeling has been growing ... that the future of our country, the future of the race, is bound up with the reform of our land system ... The time has come for the invasion of England, for the effective occupation and enjoyment of this country of ours, by its own people.[91]

Following Campbell-Bannerman's lead, 'home colonisation' appeared prominently in the party's appeal at the general election of 1906, with Liberals from frontbenchers (like Churchill) to provincial fixers (like Percy Illingworth, chairman of the Yorkshire Liberal Federation) urging 'the colonisation of England' in their speeches and addresses. So too did the party press, the *Daily News* especially.[92] After the election, the idea remained a conspicuous theme in land reform discourse. In 1907 its continuing importance was underlined by the publication of a book of essays entitled *To colonise England*, among

[89] See M. Taylor, 'Imperium et libertas? Rethinking the radical critique of imperialism during the nineteenth century', *JICH* xix (1991), esp. pp. 14–16.
[90] NLF, *Reports*, card 25 (1903), 51.
[91] Liberal Publication Department, *Case for dissolution*, 11. See also *DN*, 28 Nov. 1905, 8.
[92] *Churchill speeches*, i. 541–2; *Election addresses*, reel 3 (1906); *DN*, Dec. 1905–Jan. 1906.

the contributors to which was a large number of Liberal MPs.[93] It informed the party's land reform policies, from the legislation of 1906–8 to the Land Campaign. As Carrington said in a speech given in the summer of 1911, *a propos* Liberal support for smallholdings, 'if we meant to retain our position among the nations of the world, as we were determined to hold it, we must keep the best men at home and colonise old England herself'.[94] Such language was deliberately chosen to evoke the words of Campbell-Bannerman in 1905–6, which functioned as a sort of talisman of the Liberal land reform project in the years before 1914. Speaking at the Bedford meeting which launched the Land Campaign, Sir John Simon paid explicit homage to the sentiments of his departed leader. Denying that the Liberals sought to set class against class, he emphasised that theirs was a patriotic crusade open to all, and one that aimed at doing what Campbell-Bannerman said at his first meeting as prime minister 'when he defined the great object of the Liberal party to be that of colonizing our own country'.[95]

What significance should the historian attach to this call for 'the invasion of England' by the Englishman? Some scholars have argued that the agrarian agenda of the Edwardian Liberal party was an aspect of a broader collectivist crusade, a novel development associated with the rise of class politics before 1914. For Matthew Fforde, the pledge made by Campbell-Bannerman at the Albert Hall in December 1905 to make 'the land less of a pleasure-ground for the rich and more of a treasure-house for the nation' was essentially expressive of an incipiently socialistic ideology of expropriation.[96] Though his overall thesis is overstated and reductionist, Fforde is right to note the role collectivist ideas played in Liberal thought and policy at the time – a point many other historians have made in more sophisticated fashion.[97] But in common with these writers, he overlooks the patriotic rhetoric employed by Liberal politicians. This manifested itself in their response to the Education Act of 1902 and their defence of Free Trade after 1903.[98] It also featured prominently in their advocacy of rural reforms. Indeed, the project of the 'colonisation of England' was portrayed as predominantly patriotic in its conception and aims. Its formulation reflected less a belief that the landed gentry represented (in however a diluted a form) the class enemies of modern

93 Masterman and others, *To colonise England*.
94 *LM* xix (1911), 446.
95 *The Times*, 13 Oct. 1913, 14. Simon was referring to Campbell-Bannerman's Albert Hall speech of December 1905.
96 Fforde, *Conservatism*, 50–1.
97 Ibid. 19–23, 44–9, 52–4, 103–10; Clarke, *Lancashire*, and *Liberals and social democrats*, Cambridge 1979; H. V. Emy, *Liberals, radicals and social politics, 1892–1914*, Cambridge 1973; M. Freeden, *The new Liberalism*, Oxford 1978; J. Harris, *Unemployment and politics*, Oxford 1972; S. Collini, *Liberalism and sociology: L. T. Hobhouse and political argument in England, 1880–1914*, Cambridge 1979.
98 Readman, 'Liberal party', esp. pp. 273–88.

democracy than the idea that the land system caused the 'subversion of healthy national life'.[99]

The adoption of the 'home colonisation' project was the culmination of the pre-1914 idea that the English national character could be improved – or salvaged – by means of land reform. In the late nineteenth and early twentieth centuries, Liberals came to believe, as one MP put it, that 'the future of our country depends not upon the extension of her borders beyond the seas, but upon the maintenance of a vigorous manhood and woman-hood at home'.[100] As they presented it, derring-do 'on the boundaries of the world' would do very little to maintain the physical and moral vigour of the domestic national stock. A different sort of patriotic endeavour was required. In their interpretation, national salvation depended on the enactment of reforms directed at the evil of landlordism. It was argued that under current arrangements the land system was inimical to archetypally 'English' freedoms and, in various ways, promoted the physical and moral decay of the national character. Such a state of affairs, if allowed to go uncorrected, was held to augur badly for England's future, as Liberals believed that the individual attributes of the common people were the determinants of true national greatness. This was not a view to which many Conservatives subscribed in the 1880s. But by the Edwardian period attitudes had changed somewhat. In these years a number of Tories and Liberal Unionists began to evince serious concerns about racial deterioration and presented legislation for the creation of sturdy peasant proprietors as a patriotic answer to this problem. Never-theless, we must not lose sight of the fact that solicitude for the national character in general was more prominent among Liberal land reformers, for whom it constituted a central element of their agrarian patriotism. The agrarian patriotism of Conservatives, by contrast, placed greater emphasis on the idea that agriculture was England's 'national industry', as the next chapter will demonstrate.

[99] Campbell-Bannerman, *The Times*, 22 Dec. 1905, 7.
[100] H. R. Mansfield, 'The rural exodus', in Masterman and others, *To colonise England*, 186.

4

Agriculture: 'Our Greatest National Industry'

> 'And he gave it for his opinion, that whoever could make two
> ears of corn, or two blades of grass, grow upon a spot of ground
> where only one grew before, would ... do more essential service
> to his country, than the whole race of politicians put together':
> Jonathan Swift, *Gulliver's travels*.

Since the eighteenth century, the improvement of agriculture had been invested with patriotic meaning. The man who made 'two ears of corn grow where only one grew before' was not simply making a tidy profit for himself, he was also a patriot performing a public good by increasing the nation's food supply. This was very much the official rationale behind the parliament-sanctioned enclosure movement. It was held to be in the national interest to enclose wasteland and maximise its productive capacity; any concern at the sufferings inflicted upon the rural poor through the extinction of their common rights was overpowered by invoking the wider claims of the nation. This perspective was predicated on the view that a flourishing agricultural industry was important to the nation in an existential sense: without a large domestic supply of food, the country would be vulnerable at time of war. As it was, the Napoleonic Wars had seen sufficiently serious food short-ages to spark popular protests and even riots, most notably in 1795–6 and 1800–1 – developments that strengthened the association between agricul-tural production and patriotism. Moreover, this association helped to justify the maintenance of a system of agricultural protection in the years after the conflict with France. Autarkic considerations informed the introduction of the Corn Laws in 1815: the government wanted to ensure that in the event of another major war, British farmers would be able to feed the home population.

This conceptualisation of agriculture as an industry of particular national importance received a body blow with the mid nineteenth-century triumph of free trade economics. The repeal of the Corn Laws in 1846 signalled a growing conviction that commerce and manufacture, not farming, was the quintessential national industry. From then on free trade soon acquired a patriotic language of its own, one that linked the abolition of 'artificial' tariffs with the nation's prosperity and world power. (Significantly, when the time came to defend Free Trade against Chamberlain's tariff reform campaign of the 1900s, Liberals were quick to adopt a patriotic position, arguing that it was a 'splendidly isolated and typically British' policy with a causal connection to the nation's wealth and greatness).[1] However, the ascendancy of Free Trade after mid-century did not entirely eclipse the older agriculturalist discourse. True, Protection fell into abeyance as a serious policy, but the idea that a prosperous and productive agriculture was a patriotic imperative remained alive, particularly among Tory opinion. Indeed, it gained prominence in the context of the late nineteenth-century agricultural depression, which occasioned many expressions of patriotic lament. A leaflet published at the time of the queen's Diamond Jubilee celebrations used the words of A. S. T. Griffith-Boscawen, Conservative MP for the Tunbridge division of Kent, to bemoan that 'while other classes and manufacturers and great industries of various kinds had risen and prospered upon the ruin of agriculture, the condition of the latter had been **the one black mark and the one stain upon the glorious reign of the Queen**'.[2] For some at least, agriculture was still the 'national industry' and its well-being a matter for patriotic concern.

The National Agricultural Union

For much of the period after 1880 agriculture was in a depressed state. In and out of parliament, its spokesmen urged the need for governmental intervention to tackle the economic crisis in rural England. They frequently insisted that this was necessary on patriotic grounds: agriculture was not simply an industry like any other, but 'a national industry', or even 'our greatest national industry'. As such, its largely Tory representatives claimed that it warranted urgent attention from supporters of all parties, who should set aside their differences and pull together to help avert impending national calamity. These views found expression in local Chambers of Agriculture, the speeches of agrarian backbenchers like Griffith-Boscawen and perhaps most notably in Winchilsea's NAU. Although largely overlooked by historians, the NAU was broadly representative of the strand of Conservative opinion that put a patriotic construction on the defence of agricultural interests. For this reason its activities and ideology repay closer examination.

With its membership open to 'all persons interested in agriculture', from dukes to agricultural labourers, the NAU was conceived as a mass organisation built on a network of village-level branches. It enjoyed significant popular support, which peaked in early 1896, when the number of branches and members claimed exceeded 500 and 60,000 respectively.[3] The NAU sought to mobilise its membership behind a legislative programme which it

---

[1] Readman, 'Liberal party', 286.
[2] 'The one black mark and the one stain upon the glorious reign of the queen', n.p. 1897.
[3] P. Readman, 'Conservatives and the politics of land: Lord Winchilsea's National Agricultural Union, 1893–1901', *EHR* cxxi (2006), 30.

called upon politicians of both parties to advance in parliament. From early 1894 all MPs and prospective MPs were sent circulars detailing NAU policy and inviting them to make promises of active support.[4] The policies that the NAU asked politicians to endorse comprised a six-point programme: 1) tax relief for agricultural land; 2) reduction of railway rates; 3) state-aided old-age pensions for agricultural labourers; 4) land tenure reform; 5) extension of the Merchandising Marks Act and the strengthening of food adulteration laws; and 6) state funding for landlord provision of smallholdings. However, in NAU speeches and propaganda, some items on the programme got more emphasis than others, and it was the issues that most concerned farmers and landlords – who exercised control over the day-to-day running of the union – that received top priority. First and foremost of these issues was the level of local taxes paid on agricultural land. NAU branches regarded rate relief as the most effective remedy for agricultural depression, and farmer members of the Union repeatedly brought the subject up at NAU congresses. Bolstered by this grassroots sentiment, Winchilsea pressed the issue forward in the years leading up to the Agricultural Rates Act of 1896.[5]

Railway rates and food adulteration were also issues of central concern to the NAU. Many agriculturalists complained that railway companies were not only imposing excessively high carriage rates, but also discriminating against home producers by charging lower rates on imported items. There seemed some evidence for this, and the NAU supported parliamentary demands for a select committee to examine allegations of preferential treatment. These demands were rejected, however: while it was true that rail costs for the transport of foreign agricultural goods were often lower than those of their English equivalents, this reflected economies of scale and more efficient packaging, not 'unfair' preferential treatment.[6] Recognising this, and the impossibility of any legislative action, NAU leaders then approached the railway companies. Meetings with the directors of the Great Eastern Railway in autumn 1895 resulted in the offer of cheaper rates on condition that produce was packed in standard-sized boxes, which the company undertook to supply at its stations.[7] By February 1896 similar agreements had been made with most of the other major railway companies.[8] As for the question of food adulteration, here the allegation was that foreign importers were loading their produce with dangerous additives and attempting to pass it off under false labels. Thus English farmers complained that much of what was sold as

---

4   The Times, 24 Jan. 1894, 6.
5   See, for example, The Times, 5 July 1894, 7, and M. E. Finch-Hatton, 12th earl of Winchilsea, 'The new death duties in England', North American Review clx (1895), 104–5.
6   Hansard, 4th ser., 1895, xxxiii. 1530ff.
7   E. A. Pratt, Agricultural organisation, London 1912, 93–4; Cable, 26 Oct. 1895, 264; 16 Nov. 1895, 312.
8   Cable, 22 Feb. 1896, 120.

foreign 'butter' was in fact a mixture of margarine and butter, or even pure margarine coloured to look like butter. The NAU shared these concerns, demanding tighter legislative controls on the description and content of what Winchilsea called 'the cheap and nasty stuff with which we are inundated from abroad'.[9]

Compared to the issues of local taxation, railway rates and food adulteration, the other elements of the official programme got far less attention from the landlord- and large farmer-dominated leadership. The union's call for state finance to be extended to landlords to meet the costs of providing smallholdings on their estates was aimed at labourer grievances. Yet quite apart from the landlord-centric nature of this proposal, it remained little more than a gesture throughout the NAU's existence.[10] As for old-age pensions, while this issue attracted more interest (not least because landowner and farmer members of the union saw pensions as a means of encouraging thrifty habits among rural labourers while at the same time alleviating burdens on the ratepayers), campaigning activity on this issue remained low-key, and little concrete was done or proposed.[11]

While it is comparatively easy to discern the NAU's policy priorities, it is less easy to make out the character of its overall ideological position. What values did it project? What, in general terms, did it stand for? At root, the NAU was animated by a patriotic desire to effect national renewal by agrarian means. From the outset its leaders insisted that the crisis in agriculture was a national crisis, striking not only at the material interests of those involved in the industry, but at the very foundations of England's greatness. In January 1893 Winchilsea set out his case in the Conservative *National Review*. Agricultural depression, he claimed, threatened the loss of English 'health and vigour' (through rural depopulation), as well as 'general bankruptcy' and the collapse of 'the whole edifice of national prosperity'.[12] According to Winchilsea, as cities depended upon market towns, so these towns depended upon villages and villages upon farms: hence, the farm was the bedrock of English life. Based on crude, autarkic economic assumptions, this was fairly mystic stuff. But the position it represented – that agriculture functioned as the taproot of national wealth and well-being – was strongly held, and formed a key element of the NAU's appeal. Assertions that England's greatness as a nation would end if agriculture collapsed were commonplace at union meetings, and usually cheered to the rafters. 'History

---

9 *Cable*, 14 Mar 1896, 169.
10 Smallholdings were rarely discussed in the *Cable*, let alone meetings of the Central Council or even annual congresses, and no direct pressure was exerted for legislation along the lines suggested.
11 A Labourer's Benevolent Fund was established in 1897, but its hopeless underfinancing indicated the leadership's priorities. After more than a year in existence, the fund's assets stood at just £26: *Cable*, 3 Sept. 1898, supplement, 2.
12 M. E. Finch-Hatton, 12th earl of Winchilsea, 'Agricultural union', *NR* xx (1893), 587–8.

and common sense alike assure us', Winchilsea declared at the NAU's annual congress of 1894, 'that however great an empire may be ... it will infallibly date its gradual decline and fall from the moment when it suffers agriculture, the oldest, the greatest, the noblest, and the most indispensable of all national industries to wither and decay (loud applause).'[13]

It followed that action to assist this industry in its hour of need was a patriotic duty. The NAU message was that agriculturalists of all parties and classes had to set aside their differences and rally round to avert impending national calamity. Landlords, farmers and labourers alike were enjoined to 'do away with party politics, and stand together as Englishmen for the cause of Old England'.[14] Open to Liberals as well as Conservatives, labourers as well as peers, membership of the union was presented as a means of doing this. In practice, however, the NAU was dominated by Conservative farmers and landlords, and Winchilsea was himself a strong Tory, having served as a Conservative MP for Lincolnshire before his elevation to the Lords. Hence the NAU's demand for combined action in support of 'our greatest national industry' was bound up with a determination to defend the traditional social order of the English countryside. This is evident from the union's argument that a flourishing agricultural economy organised around the old tripartite structure of landlord–farmer–labourer was in the best interests of all classes, and thus all should unite in its defence. While admitting that allotments and smallholdings had their uses as 'auxiliary' sources of income, NAU leaders were adamant that they could never replace the wages paid by the farmer: labourers were better off remaining labourers, rather than seeking to rise to any higher station.[15]

This defence of the traditional socio-economic system of rural England implied a commitment to the *quondam* mainstay of this system – arable farming. Skirting round hard economic realities, the NAU eulogised an England overspread by waving fields of corn, self-sufficient, independent and great, inhabited by a race of John Bulls whose physical and moral robustness derived from country living and the honest business of food production. The cosmopolitan world of finance capitalism had no place in this vision. At an NAU meeting in Peterborough in 1897, for example, one speaker suggested that market fluctuations caused by the practice of 'gambling' on the price of wheat, were forces that threatened John Bull – and by extension the English nation – with extinction. Invited to picture 'a good-looking, hard-working English farmer, standing ... struck with terror as he sees the furious bull [market], and filled with fear as he sees himself at the mercy of an angry bear [market]', the farmer-dominated audience was told that

13 *Cable*, 22 Dec. 1894, 389.
14 *Cable*, 21 Dec. 1895, 390.
15 *Cable*, 16 Dec. 1893, 613; 27 May 1893, 150.

It is into your ribs the bull pushes his horns, it is at your side the bear makes his savage grab, and if you ask me what I would do, my answer would be, 'Get a rifle and shoot the bull; get a spear and stab the bear', and then we might indulge in a pleasant picture, and paint John Bull looking round and with a cheerful smile saying, 'Now I can live, both my enemies are dead' (applause).[16]

Such rhetorical flights of fancy exemplified the NAU's atavistic patriotism: a nation of sturdy, country-dwelling producers, not enfeebled, slum-dwelling consumers was the ideal.

But if the NAU was an identifiably distinctive response to the late nineteenth-century agricultural crisis, questions as to its place within the wider political culture remain. It was founded by a Tory peer; the vast majority of its parliamentary supporters were Conservatives; it advanced a reactionary ruralist ideology. To what extent, then, were its views on agriculture representative of Conservative opinion generally, and how much influence did it have with the party?

There is no doubt that the NAU attracted the sympathy of a considerable section of the Tory backbenches. The first annual congresses were well attended by MPs (several of whom gave keynote speeches): over 100 came in 1895.[17] In advance of the election of that year, many more politicians pledged their support: at the polls 283 candidates backed the NAU programme in full, eighty-one in part.[18] The extent to which this reflected genuine influence is hard to determine, but it is significant that many candidates who were returned unopposed gave such pledges – a fact suggestive of more than surface-level commitment on their parts. Of the 112 Tory and Liberal Unionist candidates elected without a contest for English seats, forty-five supported the full NAU programme.[19] Furthermore, examination of a large sample of addresses reveals that numerous Conservative and Liberal Unionist candidates – especially those standing for county constituencies – advanced policies promoted by the NAU. Unionist candidates pledged to the NAU programme made more mention of agriculture generally and NAU policies in particular than those who had not promised their backing. Railway rates, for example, appeared in the addresses of 18 per cent of union-

---

[16] *Cable*, supplement, 5 June 1897, 2.

[17] *Cable*, 16 Dec. 1893, 612; 21 Dec. 1895, 389. Speeches were given by Robert Yerburgh (1893, 1894), Sir Richard Paget (1893), Walter Long (1895), Victor Milward (1896), and C. W. Radcliffe Cooke (1896).

[18] Readman, 'Conservatives and the politics of land', 30.

[19] Figures calculated by cross-referencing lists of candidates in *Cable*, 22 June 1895, 397, 6 July 1895, 7, and 13 July 1895, 21, with the details in F. W. S. Craig, *British parliamentary election results, 1885–1918*, Dartmouth 1989, and T. Lloyd, 'Uncontested seats in British general elections, 1852–1910', *HJ* viii (1965), 263.

supporting candidates, as against 6 per cent of the addresses of those who had not given their support.[20]

A correlation between election address content and approval of the NAU is not conclusive evidence of influence: some candidates who pledged their support were doubtless planning to include issues like railway rates in their addresses anyway. But the evidence is suggestive none the less. It seems likely that the NAU influenced candidates' platform appeals, if only by convincing them that it was an organisation which needed to be taken seriously. Politicians took care to give favourable responses to union circulars questioning them as to their views on its programme, with these circulars – and the replies they received – being reported in the local and national press.[21] Moreover, they did so knowing that that the NAU was prepared to take the field against candidates who opposed its policies; and as it happened the union 'interfered actively' in twenty-one contests in 1895, sending speakers and propaganda to assist the favoured side.[22] In the Ramsey division of Huntingdonshire, for example, NAU personnel were mobilised in support of A. E. Fellowes, much to the annoyance of his Liberal opponent.[23] Similarly, Raymond Greene, the Tory candidate for West Cambridgeshire, received assistance from the NAU in return for his decision – as one Liberal newspaper put it – to 'swallow whole that extraordinary mixture of sense and nonsense, the programme of the National Agricultural Union'.[24]

However, influence at elections was one thing, parliamentary influence quite another. An attempt to set up a working 'Agricultural Party' composed of MPs from both sides of the House foundered on the rock of established party loyalties.[25] That said, parliament did pass several important measures for which the NAU pressed. In its obituary note on Winchilsea, *The Times* observed that 'a large proportion of the legislative points aimed at by the Agricultural Union have been either already conceded or seem to be in fair way of realization'.[26] This was an exaggeration, notwithstanding the extra-parliamentary achievements regarding co-operation and railway rates, the legislation relieving rates on agricultural land (1896), as well as some

---

20 Readman, 'Conservatives and the politics of land', 55.
21 For example, *The Times*, 8 Jan. 1894 (Lincs, Horncastle); 16 May 1895 (Warwick and Leamington); *CIP*, 12 July 1895 (Cambs, Chesterton).
22 *The Times*, 18 Oct. 1895, 9; *Cable*, 3 Aug. 1895, 72.
23 *Peterborough Advertiser*, 13 July 1895, 7; *Cable*, 27 July 1895, 54.
24 *CIP*, 19 July 1895, 3. Greene's somewhat unsophisticated campaign speeches consisted of little more than asserting the need for all classes to unite together 'to consider the interests of agriculture before those of Party': *Cambridge Chronicle*, 5 July 1895, 7. This, of course, was exactly the NAU's message, and Greene's endorsement of it was presented by the local Conservative press as a compelling reason for voting for him (and also for other NAU-supporting candidates in the region, such as those standing for East Cambs and South Hunts): editorial, *Cambridge Chronicle*, 19 July 1895, 4.
25 *Cable*, 25 Apr. 1896, 264; 9 May 1896, 296.
26 *The Times*, 8 Sept. 1898, 6.

progress made on the marking and adulteration of imported produce. While such developments were consonant with NAU demands, the extent to which they were due to NAU pressure is another matter. Salisbury returned to power in 1895 pledged to tackle the problems of agriculture and would have taken some legislative steps in this direction with or without the NAU.[27] But Winchilsea's organisation was one of the more visible manifestations of agrarian discontent and its programme reflected the concerns of many Tory backbenchers. This being the case, ministers were obliged to take the NAU seriously, to meet its delegations and give favourable responses to its demands – as Salisbury did soon after taking office.[28]

The NAU represented a particular brand of Conservative agrarianism and as a pressure group had a significant impact. There seems little doubt that its policy objectives were in accord with those of a good many Conservative MPs: Walter Long would not have agreed to address the union's annual congress in December 1895 had this been otherwise.[29] But the items on the NAU programme were not constitutive of the organisation's ideological position and the relationship between this position and Conservatism was problematic, shedding useful light on the agriculturalist discourse of the political right. As shown above, Winchilsea's central argument was that the 'national industry' of agriculture could best be preserved by patriotic, cross-class action to uphold the traditional economic system of the countryside, and the rigidly hierarchical social relationships with which this system was associated. By the 1890s, however, this point of view was of marginal currency even within Conservative circles. Outdated and unrealistic, it took no account of the increasingly divisive and partisan nature of rural politics. *Pace* Patricia Lynch, the normative culture of rural politics after the Third Reform Act was more about partisan confrontation than communitarian togetherness. This left the NAU, with its emphasis on non-partisan action and community harmony, out in the cold – isolated from the mainstream of political discourse. Even the Primrose League, self-styled organ of 'Tory Democracy', was sceptical about the NAU's message of cross-class togetherness. As the League's Midlands secretary wrote in an article for the Conservative journal *England* soon after the NAU's foundation, 'sentiment' was no substitute for coherent policy. And 'it will take some doing', he warned, 'to explain the identity of interest between an exacting landlord, for instance, and a needy tenant, or the common ground existing between a hard task-master and his employee on 11s. a week'.[30]

The growing conviction that the interests of landlords, farmers and

---

[27] Salisbury's 'manifesto', delivered to the House of Lords before the dissolution, had stressed that agriculture 'deserves more than any other subject the deep attention of parliament': *Hansard*, 4th ser., 1895, xxxv. 266–71.

[28] *The Times*, 15 Aug. 1895, 5; 22 Aug. 1895, 6–7; *Cable*, 24 Aug. 1895, 118.

[29] *Cable*, 21 Dec. 1895, 391.

[30] J. E. Cooke in *England*, repr. *PLG*, 11 Feb. 1893, 6.

labourers were not in fact convergent fatally undermined the NAU's economic argument that facilitating the agricultural industry *qua* industry would assist all who lived by the land. It followed that boosting the prosperity of agriculture, as the NAU advocated, was no panacea for rural grievances generally – least of all those of the poor. Winchilsea's initiative was thus a desperate effort to preserve an imagined rural order and its values. In making this effort he was swimming against the tide. The NAU was conceived as a response to the general decline in the importance of the rural economy in English national life and to the increasingly divisive character of village political culture. But it was a rearguard action and doomed to fail: with good reason did one associate of Winchilsea's describe him as 'ever the knight-errant, championing forlorn or difficult causes'.[31] While large numbers of people were prepared to support the NAU's policy programme, few were drawn to Winchilsea's ideological message that bolstering the traditional, landlord-centric economic system of rural England was the means by which the 'national industry' of agriculture could best be revived. The ultimate fate of the NAU bears this out. Despite impressive membership figures, the spread of local branches was extremely uneven, and many members were reluctant to contribute time or funds to the cause. Following three years of growth, the NAU began to stagnate, and after 1896 slipped into gradual decline before finally disappearing in January 1901, not long after Winchilsea's early death in September 1898.

The Unionists and the 'national industry'

The NAU's failure reflected the democratic trend of Conservative agrarian discourse, as made evident in the growing enthusiasm for peasant proprietorship. Tories came to believe that the legislative encouragement of a numerous class of small owners (not local authority tenants, as in Liberal plans) was an effective way of preserving the character and health of Englishmen. Others followed Salisbury in emphasising its utility as a bulwark against serious social upheaval. Relatively few, however, advanced sustained economic arguments in favour of smallholdings: on the whole, proposals for peasant proprietorship were not associated with exhortations to bolster the 'national industry' of agriculture. The reason for this was the existence of a well-established Conservative economic critique of small-scale cultivation, and although this lost some of its purchase in the Edwardian period, it never entirely disappeared from Tory thinking.

The critique was predicated on the old idea that maximising agricultural production was itself a patriotic object, and assumed that the large-farm system was the best means by which this could be effected. It achieved consid-

---

[31] *Cable*, 2 Dec. 1899, 361.

erable prominence in the Conservative riposte to the proposals put forward by Chamberlain and Collings in 1884–5. To many agrarian Tories, particularly those of a traditionalist cast of mind, the Birmingham radicals seemed bent on replacing an economically effective land system with an ineffective one, unsuited to British conditions. As one Lincolnshire Conservative declaimed in a platform oration during the 1885 general election campaign, the contemplated reforms ran counter to 'common sense and patriotism'. Compulsory legislation to provide 'three acres and a cow', he had no doubt, would only serve to frighten capital from the land, leading to unpatriotic underproduction, and 'it was the province of the Conservative party to try to legislate so that the capitalists and landowners might still remain in the old country. (Loud cheers.)'.[32] In part, of course, this represented a determination to defend the material interests of staunch Tory supporters, but the longstanding association between large-scale capitalist farming, food production and patriotism was evidently influential. Privately, and publicly, agrarian Conservatives claimed that the break-up of the 'high farming' system through Chamberlainite reform would be a 'national disaster' because of its effects on agricultural output. Particular concern was reserved for the anticipated effects on arable output, which would fall – so it was assumed – as a result of any large-scale creation of smallholders. As a consequence, one Conservative farmer lamented to Onslow, national security would be threatened: reform 'would at once imperil our existence and raise the price of bread, which foreigners would scarcely be guileless enough to let us have, only at their own price'.[33]

These words were written in 1886, when the fear aroused by the 'unauthorised programme' was still very much agitating Tory minds. This fear abated somewhat with the defection of Chamberlain and Collings from the Liberal party over home rule, but the argument that small-scale cultivation offended the patriotic injunction to maximise agricultural prosperity and food production persisted. Until the end of the 1880s the view that smallholdings were simply inefficient in economic terms was largely untroubled by serious challenges. In his influential *Pioneers and progress of British farming* (1888), Rowland Prothero (land agent to the duke of Bedford) might have admitted the political value of smallholdings, but scepticism about their economic viability determined his overall attitude.[34] Into the 1890s large-scale capitalist landownership could be presented as a suitable object of admiring patriotic sentiment; a foil with which to parry the thrusts of a radical agrarian patriotism centred on the self-sufficient 'freeborn Englishman' smallholder. As one Conservative pamphleteer (himself a Yorkshire JP) argued in 1894

[32] *Lincolnshire Chronicle*, 27 Nov. 1885, 6.
[33] Correspondence and returns to the 4th earl from landowners regarding smallholdings and allotments, Onslow papers, G173/4/54.
[34] Prothero, *Pioneers*, 128–40.

Evidence proves that ... the larger the landed estate, the larger the produce from the land is, the better the cottages, the better the school-buildings, the better the churches, the better the chapels, the better off the farmers are, and the larger wages the labourers get ... And the Radical aims at doing away with large landowners *for the good of the country!*[35]

Far from doing good, the writer continued, radical land reform would only drive capital from the soil, so eating at the labourer's 'wage fund' and depriving the nation of riches necessary to fight war. From this it followed that the voter had but one choice: 'If you do not want your country to be some day invaded, and your villages filled with French and Russian soldiers, plundering your goods and insulting your wives and daughters, you will steadily and perseveringly give your votes against the Radical candidates at elections.'[36]

However, the prominence of such arguments in Tory discourse was definitely waning by the 1890s. Confidence in the economic superiority of the large-farm system had been severely dented by the long-running agricultural depression, which reached its nadir in the middle of that decade. Far from being engines of agricultural prosperity, large-scale arable holdings increasingly assumed the character of millstones around the necks of their owners, and indeed around that of the economy as a whole. As such, they became less suitable as focal points for economic nationalism: if, at century's end, the landlord who strove to maximise corn production was a patriot, his patriotism stemmed more from self-sacrifical pursuit of this goal than anything else. But in addition to the challenges posed to the existing system by depression, evidence of the practicality of *petite culture* was steadily mounting, and this served to soften Conservative attitudes somewhat. Propagandists of rural reform like Parker, Turnor, Rider Haggard and the indefatigable Collings continually insisted that smallholdings were economically viable, and adaptable to modern methods of farm production.[37] Continental practice was held up as providing examples that England could usefully emulate, with the intensive agriculture of Denmark being specially praised. Examination of agricultural techniques elsewhere in Europe led many Conservatives to support co-operative methods of production and distribution, which were widespread in the Low Countries, Scandinavia and parts of France and Germany. One Tory backbencher influenced in this direction was R. A. Yerburgh, who founded the Agricultural Organisation Society (AOS) in 1901 as a body to promote co-operation among British farmers, and small

---

[35] H. S. Constable, *Some hints for political leaflets addressed to the agricultural labourer*, London 1894, 30.

[36] Ibid. 49–52.

[37] For example, Turnor, *Land problems*, esp. pp. 78ff., 103–5, 136ff.; Collings, *Land reform*; and Rider Haggard, *Rural England*.

farmers in particular.[38] Yerburgh and other Conservative advocates of co-operation argued that it provided the means by which smallholders could utilise economies of scale (for instance labour-saving but costly machinery) hitherto regarded as the unique province of large farm units. In their view, the intensive cultivation fostered by 'the magic of property', coupled with co-operation to reduce transaction costs, was a real means of increasing agricultural productivity.[39] Thus small-scale agriculture was made amenable to the time-honoured goals of a Conservative agrarianism that associated efficient food production with patriotic service to the nation. By the time of the Liberal Land Campaign, even party grandees like Lansdowne felt able to suggest that the creation of peasant proprietors would not only confer social stability, but also give distinct economic benefits, which themselves were 'national' goods.[40]

By the Edwardian period, then, Unionists were far less inclined to view small farms as unsuited to English economic conditions, or anathema to the traditional patriotic injunction to 'make two ears of corn grow where only one grew before'. However, while recognition of the practicality of *petite culture* certainly made it easier for them to make the case for land reform, their reformism was essentially rooted in a non-economic rationale. Conservatives and Liberal Unionists rarely presented straightforwardly economic arguments as the clinching reasons why England needed more peasant proprietors. This was the case from the time of the 1892 Smallholdings Act onwards, with Unionist supporters of this measure preferring to emphasise its anticipated socially stabilising benefits, rather than claiming any economic advantages. In his evidence to the select committee from which the act resulted, Collings was quite clear that 'the social question, as distinct from the economic one' was paramount. The heavily capitalised and mechanised large-farm system might be efficient, Collings argued, but its very efficiency constituted a national danger in that it provided relatively few jobs and frustrated the emergence of more labour-intensive, small-scale agriculture, which would ensure the persistence of a large rural population.[41]

This position embodied the view that agriculture was a 'national industry' not simply because it was an important source of prosperity, but because – if rightly organised – it provided the key to the nation's survival. The arguments about social stability, national character, fitness and race were obviously germane here, but added to these there was a somewhat nebulous notion that the maintenance of agriculture as a viable (if not necessarily super-efficient) industry was essential to national existence. As an idea, this

[38] For the establishment of the AOS see *Second annual report of the Agricultural Organisation Society*, Leicester 1902.
[39] For example, J. E Barker, 'Every man his own landlord', FR lxxxvii (1910), 130, and *Hansard*, 4th ser., 1907, cxxiv. 1424–7 (Collings).
[40] *The Times*, 23 June 1913, 4.
[41] Collings: *Select Committee on Small Holdings*, 1889 (313) xii. 13.

was current across the whole spectrum of Unionist agrarian opinion, from traditionalist defenders of the *status quo* to advocates of radical reform. It shaped a variety of legislative proposals, including proposals to relieve the depressed state of agriculture, such as the Rating Bill of 1896. Effectively promised by the Conservatives at the 1895 general election, Salisbury's halving of the rates paid on agricultural land was a bold move, but it was also controversial, arousing considerable resentment among urban MPs of both parties.[42] Faced with this hostility, the government (and the bill's back-bench supporters) presented rate reduction in patriotic terms. In a speech at Brighton in November 1895, Walter Long, as the new President of the Board of Agriculture, described 'agricultural affairs' as 'affairs of national importance'. Agriculturalists, he contended, 'had in no small degree contrib-uted to the power which had enabled Great Britain to occupy her present position' in the world and as such deserved assistance.[43] Such vague rhetoric was carried over into next year's parliamentary debates on the bill, when Unionist MPs led by Chaplin (in charge of the bill as President of the Local Government Board) described the depression as 'a grave national calamity' and invested rate relief with a strong patriotic charge.[44]

Concern about the nationally disintegrative consequences of allowing agriculture to decay was not just associated with those who thought farmers and landlords were overburdened with taxation. By the 1900s Unionist advocates of small-scale cultivation were voicing similar concerns. In their perspective, the multiplication of smallholdings would help to keep agricul-ture going as a viable industry in which a fairly large section of the popula-tion was involved. Doing this, it was suggested, was essential for England's continued greatness – even existence – as a nation. Perhaps unsurprisingly, Collings and his Liberal Unionist allies in the RLL were especially keen on this line of argument, and appealed to history to make their point. In one RLL propaganda leaflet issued around the time of the 1906 election, for example, Phoenicia's destruction by the ancient Greeks was attributed to the former's 'lack of attention to agriculture' in pursuit of trade-derived riches; and a similar story was told about the Romans, whose decline was put down to their also having sacrificed agriculture on the altar of commercial money getting.[45] These, of course, were anti-free trade parables as well as agricul-turalist ones: England could escape the fate of the great nations of the past by adopting land reform in conjunction with Chamberlain's tariff reform scheme. Tariffs would afford protection to the greatest national industry –

[42] A. Offer, *Property and politics, 1870–1914*, Cambridge 1981, 209–10.
[43] *The Times*, 20 Nov. 1895, 7.
[44] *Hansard*, 4th ser., 1896, xxxix. 1274 (Chaplin), 1307 (Pretyman); xl. 133 (Yerburgh).
[45] RLL, 'Agriculture and the nation: what history teaches us about letting agriculture decay' [1906?], in NUCCA, *Specimen leaflets issued by the Rural Labourers' League*, London n.d.

now reoriented around peasant proprietorship – and thus the nation would be spared the dire consequences of untrammelled pursuit of material wealth above all else. With its anti-commercial, autarkic agenda, this view had some affinities with that of Winchilsea's NAU, though the insistence that agricultural and national salvation could be found in the extension of peasant proprietorship made it fundamentally different. Moreover, it achieved wide currency in Conservative discourse, as borne out in Parker's many publications on Tory land policy, for example.[46] That it did was largely attributable to Collings and his Liberal Unionist associates, whose influence historians have been apt to overlook.[47]

Disdain for the pursuit of rapid material gain was linked to a distinction between commodity production and commercial wealth. In this interpretation, increasing the aggregate wealth of the nation was held to be of less importance than increasing the aggregate production of food – indeed, in certain circumstances, it would be legitimate to sacrifice the former to the latter. Hence, buoyed up by their faith in the maxim that the possession of property 'turns sand into gold', Unionist land reformers felt able to brush aside Liberal objections to peasant proprietorship as financially unsound compared to small tenancies. Speaking on the third reading of the 1907 Smallholdings Bill, Collings displayed Olympian disregard for his opponents' bean-counting arguments in favour of tenancy, laying it 'down as an axiom that money was not the wealth of the country; it was the producing power of the country which gave it safety in time of stress'.[48] This was a line of thinking that meshed nicely with tariff reformers' deployment of a rhetoric of economic sacrifice for the greater national good.[49] But if Chamberlain's rhetoric stressed the objective of holding the empire together at all costs ('I am a fiscal reformer mainly because I am an Imperialist'),[50] that of his supporters was decidedly more inward-looking in orientation. This was particularly so for agrarian tariff reformers, many of whom did not share Chamberlain's imperial enthusiasm. In response to the powerful free trade argument that tariffs would wreak serious damage to trade, they offered a productionist, anti-materialist perspective on the national interest. For people like Collings, tariffs were the logical corollary to a revitalised agriculture based on the small man: they would offer him protection from foreign competition, so allowing his business to flourish, and with that the volume of home-produced food would increase. If one of the consequences of this was a rise in food prices, that was a sacrifice worth making, and one patriotic

---

[46] See, for example, G. Parker, 'Small ownership, land banks, and co-operation', *FR* lxxxvi (1909), 1079.

[47] Readman, 'Collings'.

[48] *Hansard*, 4th ser., 1907, clxxx. 1831.

[49] A. Sykes, *Tariff reform in British politics, 1903–1913*, Oxford 1979, 60.

[50] Cited in R. Quinault, 'Joseph Chamberlain: a reassessment', in T. R. Gourvish and A. O'Day (eds), *Later Victorian Britain, 1867–1900*, Basingstoke 1988, 88.

sentiment would enable the nation to bear. As Collings explained to the Commons in February 1909

> There must be one principle observed in dealing with this question, and that is that the producer must be put in the front rank. I have talked to scores of producers in the rural districts of France. I have said to them, 'Why do you spend a little more on your loaf?' What was the reply? 'It is the French loaf. It is raised on our soil; it is ground in our mills; and we keep the offal. Yours is the foreign loaf'. Production must go before consumption.[51]

The prioritising of production over consumption was sustained by a somewhat naïve belief that the English consumer would be willing to pay higher prices in patriotic support of home produce. In fact, considerations of price and quality weighed more heavily in the minds of consumers than the provenance of produce – value for money trumped any patriotic prejudice in favour of 'buying British'.[52] However, the production-oriented perspective of many Unionist land reformers was also sustained by the belief that the cultivation of foodstuffs was crucial to national survival. This was a development from the older languages of productionist patriotism with which this chapter began, but it cast the small proprietor and not the large farmer or landlord in the role of national hero. Reformist tracts like Turnor's *Land problems* damned the excessive enclosure of land for game preservation as wasteful of the nation's resources. After all, as Turnor put it, 'The first function of the land is to feed the people of the country … The test of true patriotism for the farmer is the amount of foodstuff he can raise. His duty to the country is to feed the people.'[53] This was a familiar sentiment, perhaps, but the 'farmer' Turnor had in mind here was the smallholder *au fait* with the latest 'scientific' methods of intensive cultivation, sheltered by tariffs and aided by co-operation – an individual who would achieve greater levels of production than the high farmers of the past. While it was admitted that this prescription for agricultural renewal could well have negative effects on Britain's material prosperity (involving as it did a tariff-stimulated rise in prices for the consumer), the national imperative of increasing the supply of home-produced food more than offset any such considerations.

Levels of concern about food supply were high in large part because of mounting anxieties that, in the event of a major war, Britain could be starved into submission by means of a naval blockade. Such worries were not of course new, but they were given added force by the heightening international tensions of the 1890s and 1900s, with Germany's naval building programme being a source of particular alarm. To meet this threat, agrarian

---

[51] *Hansard*, 5th ser., 1909, i. 167.
[52] D. M. Higgins, '"Mutton dressed as lamb?" The misrepresentation of Australian and New Zealand meat in the British market, c. 1890–1914', *Australian Economic History Review* xliv (2004), 161–84.
[53] Turnor, *Land problems*, 17–18, 58.

Conservatives put forward a number of proposals to increase domestic food supply. Winchilsea's solution, supported by a handful of Tory bankbenchers, was a network of state granaries, which would avert 'starvation and humiliating defeat' in time of war.[54] However, the idea attracted little support, being literally laughed out of the Lords in June 1893.[55]

Things changed, however, after the army's reverses in the Boer War, which administered a large shock to British self-confidence. All aspects of the country's defensive arrangements, including the provision of food supplies in wartime, came under closer scrutiny as a consequence. From 1901 numerous letters on the subject appeared in *The Times*, and articles in mainstream periodicals issued dire warnings as to the possible effects of a wartime blockade.[56] In the opinion of one commentator, hunger at home would imbue latent forces of 'revolution' and 'anarchy' with irresistible strength, leading to 'an ignominious and ruinous peace; the surrender of our navy; and a crushing war-indemnity – in short, the end of English history'.[57] In April 1903, following a meeting at Strafford House attended by Chaplin and others 'to promote an official inquiry' into the matter, the agitation culminated in the appointment of a Royal Commission: its downbeat official and alarmist supplementary reports were published two years later.[58] But this was not the end of the story. As borne out by the continued flow of publications on the subject, high levels of concern persisted until 1914. Arguing for a 'constructive agricultural policy' in a 1909 article for the *National Review*, Turnor warned that there was never more than one month's supply of wheat in the UK at any one time.[59] Three years later, the prominent Conservative agriculturalist MP Charles Bathurst produced a pamphlet entitled *To avoid national starvation*, in which – aided by a preface from the naval propagandist Admiral Beresford – he issued dire warnings about the nation's heavy reliance on imported food.[60]

As Bathurst's pamphlet suggests, Unionist advocates of land (and tariff) reform used fears about food supply as a usefully dramatic means of drawing

[54] *Cable*, 10 June 1893, 184; 11 Jan. 1896, 24; 2 Oct. 1897, 2. See also, for example, *Hansard*, 4th ser., 1893, xiii. 1281–99; xlviii. 642ff; lxvi. 1128ff.

[55] On that occasion Winchilsea 'suggested that they should establish State granaries. (Laughter.) He saw that some noble Lords laughed at this idea, but it was not an original idea on his part. The idea dated back to almost prehistoric times. It was at least 3,000 years old, and this would no doubt commend it to the Conservative mind generally. (Laughter.)'; *The Times*, 20 June 1893, 6.

[56] For example, *The Times*, 25 Dec. 1901, 4; 28 Dec. 1901, 8; 14 Jan. 1902, 10; W. S. Lilly, '"Collapse of England"', *FR* lxxi (1902), 771–84; F. N. Maude, 'The internal organisation of the nation in time of war', *CR* lxxxi (1902), 36–45; and S. Wilkinson, 'Does war mean starvation?', *NR* xi (1902), 472–9.

[57] 'Our food supply in time of war', *Blackwood's Magazine* clxxiii (1903), 280.

[58] *The Times*, 5 Feb. 1903, 4; *Report of the Royal Commission on Supply of Food and Raw Material in Time of War*, PP 1905, xxxix–xl (Cd. 2643–5).

[59] Turnor, 'Conservative agricultural policy', 594.

[60] C. Bathurst, *To avoid national starvation*, London 1912.

attention to their campaign. In doing so, many expressed their conviction that a numerous small proprietary – protected by a system of imperial preference – would help remedy the situation. Collings, predictably, was well to the fore here,[61] but other Unionists voiced similar arguments. Among the most prominent were Robert Yerburgh and Henry Seton Karr, MPs for Chester and St Helens respectively. Significantly, both men were actively involved in the Navy League, an organisation whose propaganda combined concern for the maintenance of British sea power with concern for the nation's food supply. In the analysis of the League (of which Yerburgh became president in 1900), over-reliance on imports threatened wartime defeat through the discontent, riots and even revolution that a shortage of food might bring in its train.[62] Yerburgh and Seton-Karr had long been concerned with the issue of food supply, having been strong supporters of Winchilsea's state granaries proposal in the 1890s. However, given the hostile reception accorded the state granary scheme, they – like other Unionist land reformers – moved towards the promotion of small-scale, co-operative agriculture as a practicable alternative. As founder of the AOS, Yerburgh was an especially energetic advocate of co-operation, which he felt was the natural corollary to a Tory policy of peasant proprietorship.

Liberals, agriculture and national renewal

It should not be assumed that Unionists had a monopoly on patriotic conceptualisations of agriculture as England's 'national industry'. For all their emphasis on the rights of downtrodden Hodge and the wrongs of landlordism, Liberals too had recourse to the idea that a flourishing agriculture was important to England's self-image and existential well-being. This perspective informed their politics throughout the period; indeed, if anything its influence gained strength over time, making its presence felt most strongly during Lloyd George's Land Campaign. But let us begin in the 1880s, when advocates of Free Trade in Land incorporated concern about agriculture as a 'national industry' into their arguments. According to their analysis, encouraging the break-up of great estates by removing restrictions on the sale and subdivision of land would actually boost domestic food production. In part this belief stemmed from a conviction – drawn from the earlier writings of Mill, Thornton and others – that small, independent proprietors were not necessarily less productive than the large tenant farmers associated with mid-century 'high farming' practice. But faith in spade husbandry did not form the whole of their economic case. Pointing to the under-cultivated

---

61 *Hansard*, 4th ser., 1907, clxix. 778–84; clxx. 823; J. Collings, '"An island fortress"', *NR* lvi (1910), 48–58.
62 F. Coetzee, *For party or country: nationalism and the dilemmas of popular Conservatism in Edwardian England*, Oxford 1990, 23–4.

aspect of much land in Britain, individuals like Arnold highlighted what they regarded as the overall economic inefficiency of the existing system, which concentrated land in the hands of a few.[63] This under-use of the soil was not just ascribed to the aristocratic passion for sport, though this was certainly part of the problem. Rather, as Arnold and his associates saw it, strict settlement ran counter to effective cultivation as it prevented financially embarrassed landlords from disposing of property to meet their debts, leaving them with insufficient capital to invest in production-maximising improvements.[64] Similarly, agriculturally incompetent landlords were unable to transfer their resources into some branch of industry to which their talents might be more suited. As a consequence, the land did not yield the produce of which it was capable and the whole country suffered the loss. It followed, as Arnold put it, that reform was required in 'the interests of the nation'.[65]

But this was not the only way in which Liberals felt that the system of great estates ran counter to the national interest in agricultural production. Campaigners for land tenure reform pointed to a further problem, arguing that the lack of rights and freedoms accorded many tenant farmers by landlords militated against proper cultivation. According to this argument, insecurity of tenure and inability to claim adequate compensation for improvements discouraged farmers from making capital investments in the land they farmed, to the detriment of agriculture and the nation at large. As James Rowlands, honorary secretary of the LLRA, told the National Liberal Club in advance of the 1906 Agricultural Holdings Bill, current arrangements 'put a premium on bad farming', with the result that 'the State is the loser'.[66] And for Liberals like Rowlands this loss was an occasion for patriotic as well as pecuniary lamentation, particularly insofar as it affected food supply. From the 1890s on, supporters of land tenure reform laid increased stress on this point, those of a 'Liberal Imperialist' mindset in particular. MP for East Norfolk from 1892, R. J. Price combined strong support for land tenure reform to help secure the nation's 'home food supply' with strong support for the empire.[67] Indeed, there might well have been a direct connection between his and other Liberals' imperialism and a patriotic desire to promote agricultural productivity at the 'heart of the empire' (a favourite concept of Liberal Imperialists). In a letter to *The Times* published in September 1906, the ardently imperialist F. P. Fletcher-Vane, who had stood as a Liberal candidate in the general election of that year, declared it to be unacceptable from an 'imperial standpoint' that so many thousands of acres were allowed to stand uncultivated. 'The Imperialist wonders', he continued, 'why

---

63 A. Arnold, *The land and the people*, Manchester 1887, 7–8.
64 Idem, *Free land*, 105.
65 Idem, *Land and the people*, 21.
66 National Liberal Club, *Address*, 8–12.
67 *Hansard*, 4th ser., 1896, xxxix. 1448.

we have to obtain so much foodstuffs from abroad while possessing some of the best grain-growing land in the world'.[68]

Yet, notwithstanding the arguments of supporters of Free Trade in Land and land tenure reform, economic considerations were of secondary importance in Liberals' patriotic engagement with the land question for most of the pre-1914 period. This was especially true for supporters of smallholdings legislation: while they were certainly prepared to make claims for the economic viability of small-scale agriculture, such claims were neither informed by, nor did they address, patriotic conceptions of agriculture as the 'national' industry. Things changed towards the end of the Edwardian period. The Liberal attack on landlordism in the People's Budget and Land Campaign made use of a patriotically-charged economic critique of the existing system. In part, this involved the targeting of old enemies, long subject to Liberal opprobrium: idle landlords. These individuals, who monopolised the land for selfish and frequently unproductive purposes and lived indolently off rental income, were presented as preventing the proper use of the nation's soil. Their wealth was not the problem; the complaint was rather that their monopolisation of real property denied English people generally the opportunity to apply effort and skill to the service of national prosperity. In their speeches on the 1909 Budget, Liberals stressed how in cities the speculative holding of undeveloped property stifled the enterprise of tradesmen and entrepreneurs by preventing them from gaining access to land needed for business expansion. Similarly, they contended, the unavailability of land in many rural areas frustrated capable would-be farmers, who were instead forced to find employment (for which they were not best suited) in already-overcrowded towns and cities.[69]

This was an argument that positioned the Liberals as champions of the national economic interest in the land, fighting against the 'un-businesslike' system of 'landlordism'. Moreover, like much Edwardian Liberal discourse, it was an argument that embodied continuity with the party's ideological traditions in that it postulated a broad, cross-class – and hence patriotic – coalition in opposition to selfish and sectional interests.[70] In his Budget speeches at Newcastle and Limehouse in July and October 1909, Lloyd George expressed this point of view, contrasting landlords unfavourably with the industrious of all classes. Thus he lamented the plight of a Mr Gorringe, a successful London businessman, who had requested the renewal of his lease from the duke of Westminster only to be told that the annual ground rent had been increased from a few hundred pounds to £4,000. It was not, Lloyd George explained, that the Liberals were opposed to property ownership *per se*, rather that they supported all those who accumulated it through

[68] *The Times*, 14 Sept. 1906, 4.
[69] For example, D. Lloyd George, *Better times*, London 1910, 251–3, and W. Churchill, *The people's rights* (1909), London 1970, 120–1.
[70] Readman, 'Liberal party'.

hard work.[71] In this analysis, unproductive landlords, whose incomes were based on others' labour, were parasites on the economic body of the nation. For many Liberals, land reform – and, increasingly, land value taxation – provided a means by which the land system could be placed on not only a more equitable, but also a more 'businesslike' footing.

Historians' emphasis on the 'collectivist' dimension to Edwardian Liberal policy has perhaps caused them to overlook the economic aspects of the party's land proposals at this time. It is significant that these economic arguments – what might be called an enterprise agenda – are hard to square with 'new' Liberal politics as conventionally understood. Indeed, they appear more compatible with the still-persisting traditions of nineteenth-century Liberalism. The proposals to break the land monopoly by imposing taxes on the 'unearned increment' harked back to the mid-Victorian crusade against 'artificial' constraints on the operation of the national economy – a crusade that had of course been revived in response to Chamberlain's tariff reform campaign. For Liberals, the removal of the land monopoly would release the energy and productive capacities of the nation, so completing the economic liberation of the English people that had begun with the repeal of the Corn Laws. This was the same view that had been taken by exponents of Free Trade in Land in the 1870s and 1880s, but it persisted in the arguments of Edwardian Liberals. Land value taxation, leasehold enfranchisement and other measures could be justified on the basis that they gave Englishmen the freedom to achieve economic self-fulfilment.[72] Alongside the more obviously patriotic aspects of Liberals' agrarian agenda ('home colonisation', for example), this argument formed part of their case for national regeneration through land reform. In an essay of 1912, significantly entitled 'The re-making of England', the radical writer and secretary of the Cobden Club, John F. Shaw, put the case with some force. The popular demand for land, Shaw argued, was simply 'the aspiration of a great people for self-realisation'. Its energies and talents frustrated by the land monopoly, England had not yet achieved its true potential as a nation, and would only do so once 'free play for the growth of every available thing in the national life' was provided through land value taxation and other reforms.[73]

Land reform as a means of encouraging national renewal through the release of the people's frustrated entrepreneurial energies was particularly important to Lloyd George. Before launching the Land Campaign in autumn 1913, he repeatedly claimed that land needed to be 'put on a business footing'.[74] By tying land up in few hands, Lloyd George felt sure that

---

[71] J. Grigg, Lloyd George: the people's champion, 1902–1911 (1978) London 2002, 213, 223.

[72] See, for example, Churchill speeches, i. 781.

[73] B. Villiers [J. F. Shaw], 'The re-making of England', in Mrs [J.] Cobden Unwin, The land hunger, London 1913, 200–1, 208.

[74] For example, The Times, 1 Feb. 1913, 8; 7 July 1913, 5.

the existing system discouraged economic development and enterprise in both town and country. Aware that the maximisation of production was the original justification for the existence of private property in land, he was also aware that a good deal of privately owned land was not used to its full agricultural potential. This he largely put down to the 'un-businesslike' practices of landlords, in particular their use of hundreds of thousands of acres for social and sporting purposes, rather than the legitimate business of food cultivation. Lloyd George's passion on this subject ran high. Immediately before his speech at Bedford, which inaugurated the Land Campaign, he expostulated to Riddell, 'I shall give them snuff. I shall smash the whole thing. Agricultural landlords have made an awful mess of things. What sort of business would you have if you allowed your pleasure to come first and your business second? But this is what they have done and are doing. Sport always comes first.'[75]

On the platform at Bedford, Lloyd George drove this point home. Land was under-cultivated, he told his audience, and agricultural productivity was low. But he denied that these and associated rural ills were due to Free Trade, or to disadvantages of nature – the British soil, climate and market were all favourable to agriculture. Instead, he placed the blame on 'the fatuous and unbusinesslike system upon which the ownership of land has been conducted in this country'. This system, he contended, involved sacrificing productive capacity for the selfish pursuit of pleasure and social status: landlords were neglecting their national duty by the land, and their increasing pre-occupation with game preservation epitomised this neglect. To Lloyd George's mind the proposed reforms were not simply measures of justice designed to remove the last vestiges of 'feudalism', they were also measures for the promotion of economic efficiency. If they seemed drastic, they were no more drastic than those taken by successful entrepreneurs: the Liberals simply sought to 'do as businessmen do. When a business gets into a thoroughly bad condition through long years of mismanagement it is no use tinkering here and mending there. You must recast it; you must put it on a sound basis; you must deal boldly with it (cheers)'.[76]

This enterprise agenda was elaborated upon as the Land Campaign progressed, providing a useful riposte to Conservative allegations of 'socialism'. By emphasising economic efficiency, Liberals could deny that they were bent on sweeping schemes of social engineering or wealth redistribution. Churchill, who was not privately enthusiastic about the Land Campaign, made frequent recourse to this argument.[77] Even the proposal to introduce an agricultural minimum wage could be made amenable to this line of thinking. As Asquith told the National Liberal Club in December 1913, the minimum wage would bring gains in agricultural productivity:

75 Riddell, *More pages*, 178.
76 *The Times*, 13 Oct. 1913, 13.
77 For example, *Churchill speeches*, ii. 2159.

better-paid labourers would be more efficient than those that were poorly remunerated.[78] But such arguments were not confined to the Liberals' rural proposals. The Urban Land Campaign was also justified in 'enterprise' terms. Leasehold enfranchisement was a case in point. At present, Liberals argued, businesses on leases were placed at the mercy of landlords when their leases expired. Entrepreneurs – like the unfortunate Mr Gorringe – often found it difficult to secure renewal on affordable terms, and in the event of being forced to give up their premises, their landlords effectively confiscated any improvements. In Liberal eyes this state of affairs was wholly contrary to the national interest in economic prosperity and so justified state intervention, as Churchill spelled out in a speech of November 1913.[79] Hence the proposal to invest land commissioners with powers to protect leaseholders – and particularly long leaseholders, who would be virtually guaranteed permanency of occupation.[80]

Stress on the wider economic benefits of land reform thus nicely complemented Liberal disavowal of sectional or 'class' legislation. Sectionalism and selfish interest – in the form of the land monopoly – was after all what Liberals sought to combat through the Land Campaign, which was presented as a crusade in support of popular, national interests; and the economic argument gave added support to this crusade. In line with older conceptions of agriculture as the 'national industry', Liberals regarded under-use of the soil as more than simply wasteful. In Lloyd George's words, it was also 'a national loss'.[81] This explains why Land Campaign propaganda on the issue of withholding land for sporting purposes described 'unchecked game preserving' as 'a serious injury to national interests': preventing the land from 'producing as much food as it might otherwise do', it was a luxury that cost the nation dear.[82] Similarly, farmers' lack of complete security of tenure was presented as detrimental to maximal levels of agricultural productivity, and hence a 'national loss' as it discouraged investment and improvements.[83] The Land Campaign, which promised a Ministry of Land to ensure full security for tenant farmers once and for all, addressed this question head on, with the Rural Enquiry Report promising to replace existing 'unbusinesslike' tenancy arrangements – which relied overmuch on landlord goodwill – with those

---

[78] MG, 10 Dec. 1913, 4.

[79] *Churchill speeches*, ii. 2193–4.

[80] Where a lease had been held for fewer than twenty-one years, the land commissioners could award compensation on its termination, and prevent any rent increase due to improvements or business success. For leases held in excess of twenty-one years, all leaseholders could apply to the commissioners for renewal, which would only be refused if the property was required for public purposes: CLHC leaflets, no. 4, 'The Liberal land policy and the shopkeeper', and no. 12, 'Leaseholds'.

[81] *The Times*, 13 Oct. 1913, 13.

[82] CLHC leaflets, no. 5, 'Hard facts about game', 4.

[83] *The land*, i, p. li; [C. E. Hobhouse], 'The problems of land and labour', MG, 9 Oct. 1913, 8.

which rewarded independent enterprise and effort.[84] The aim here was to restructure the land system such that it promoted hard work and industry on the part of the entire population, and doing this was conceptualised as part of a patriotic project in the service of the wider, national good. As Lloyd George explained in his second great Land Campaign speech, at Swindon on 22 October 1913, 'We want to make the best of this country for the sake of the labourer, the landlord, the people, the nation as a whole. In order to do that you have got to stimulate, to encourage, to strengthen, every instinct in the man that makes for the best work he can give to the nation.'[85]

This chapter began by discussing the connection between patriotism and food production. The link between the two was of long standing, and persisted throughout the late nineteenth and early twentieth centuries. Politicians from both main parties argued that increasing agricultural productivity was worthy of patriotic commendation and indeed ought to be encouraged by government policy. This argument was especially popular with Conservatives, many of whom felt the best policy was one that aimed to reinforce the *status quo*: the tripartite system of landlord, large farmer and wage labourer, which they regarded as a product of economic forces as immutable as that of gravity. Winchilsea's NAU presented a particularly forthright expression of this argument, which it combined with a patriotic rhetoric of social harmony in urging the need for government action to protect the 'national industry' of agriculture. However, by the end of the Victorian period Conservatives were moving away from the position represented by Winchilsea, as the failure of his union illustrates. Increasingly anxious about socialism and collectivism, desirous of formulating a popular appeal to rural voters and influenced by their Liberal Unionist allies, Edwardian Tories embraced the peasant proprietor. And while their decision to do so was primarily a function of patriotic concerns about social stability, national character, racial health, food supply and the like, economic considerations played an important part. In the context of agricultural depression, which hit large arable farms especially hard, Conservatives gradually came to accept the idea that small-scale cultivation was economically viable. Having long recognised the national (and political) merits of the yeoman proprietor, they now saw his encouragement by legislative means as within the pale of practical politics, and any lingering economic reservations were usually trumped by the heightened perception of dangers to which all Conservative patriots were beholden to respond.

Things were rather different for the Liberals. Owing to the writings of Mill, Thornton and others, many Liberals had long been convinced of the economic viability of *petite culture*; the passage of time, and the onset of agricultural depression, only served to deepen this conviction and extend its

84 *The land*, i, pp. xlviii–xlix.
85 *The Times*, 13 Oct. 1913, 13.

hold over all sections of Liberal opinion (with the exception of a few Whigs). That said, however, Liberal agrarian patriotism was not widely associated with the economics of agriculture until the 1900s. Although advocates of Free Trade in Land and land tenure reform did occasionally make reference to the idea that the maximisation of production was a patriotic imperative, the language of late nineteenth-century Liberal land reformism paid much more attention to arguing for the elevation of the national character, as described in the previous chapter. However, economic arguments did come to play a greater part in patriotic rhetoric in the Edwardian period, and particularly in Lloyd George's People's Budget and Land Campaign, which was animated by the 'business agenda' of taxing or otherwise forcing the land into productive use. Such interventionism was informed by certain attitudes towards property rights, and these form the main focus of the next chapter.

5

Property Rights and Land Reform

'The high value placed by Englishmen on testamentary freedom
has, indeed, an intimate connexion with English individualism. It
is an extension of the power of an individual to carry out his own
wishes. It enables him to give effect to them even after his death.
It is in reality the most artificial, and yet to the English public it
seems the most natural of rights and powers': A. V. Dicey, 'The
paradox of the land law', *Law Quarterly Review* xxi (1905), 224.

In late nineteenth- and early twentieth-century France, there were strict
limits on the distribution of property at death. French law required that
at least one half of a parent's estate should be left to the children, with
this property being divided equally between them. No such legal restrictions
existed in England and for some Englishmen this was a matter of national
pride – proof of the persistence of native freedoms and standing in marked
contrast to authoritarian continental practices. In an essay on land law
published in 1905, the prominent Liberal Unionist jurist A. V. Dicey gave
expression to the idea that, in England, a man was at liberty to do what he
liked with his own, and linked it to his view of the national character as
animated by an 'English individualism'. In free England, according to Dicey,
a man could dispose of his property as he so wished, and this was a function of the strength of private ownership rights, which were under normal
circumstances absolute.

This view would have found considerable contemporary support, particularly from Liberal Unionist and Conservative opinion, but it would not
have commanded anything like universal assent by the first decade of the
twentieth century. For a start, it paid scant regard to the practical restrictions imposed on the sale and transfer of land, about which many reformers
had long complained. And in any case, as Dicey himself recognised, its
influence had been waning for some time, as evidenced by the growth of
socialism and the passage of such interventionist legislation as the Irish land
purchase, agricultural holdings, and allotments and smallholdings acts.[1] But
there were other indicators of its diminishing purchase. In the same year as
Dicey published his essay, Rudyard Kipling wrote a short story, *An habitation
enforced*, in which he tells of how an American couple (George and Sophie)
came to England for a rest cure holiday in the countryside. They end up

[1] Dicey, 'Paradox', 229.

deciding to stay, and having become the local lord of the manor, George finds himself discussing with his wife the nature of their rights in the land they had acquired:

> 'D'you see that track by Gate Anstey?' They looked down from the edge of the hanger over a cup-like hollow. People by twos and threes in their Sunday best filed slowly along the paths that connected farm to farm. 'I've never seen so many people on our land before', said Sophie, 'why is it?'
> 'To show us we mustn't shut up their rights of way'.
> 'Those cow-tracks we've been using cross – lots?' said Sophie forcibly.
> 'Yes. And any one of 'em would cost us two thousand pounds each in legal expenses to close'.
> 'But we don't want to', she said.
> 'The whole community would fight if we did'.
> 'But it's our land. We can do what we like'.
> 'It's *not* our land. We've only paid for it. We belong to it, and it belongs to the people – our people, they call 'em.'[2]

A fictional exchange, to be sure, but it was one the author (a landowner himself) evidently thought plausible. It was also one that touched on the idea that the rights of landownership were to an important extent limited: Americans might think otherwise, but in England at least, a man did not always have the freedom to do what he liked with his own. This idea was at least as deep-rooted as that to which Dicey appealed, and from the 1880s had been moving into the mainstream of political discourse. Its central premise was that the nation – now meaning the English people as a whole rather than the crown – had a stake in the soil of their native land and in the use to which it was put, and that it was the duty of responsible politicians to acknowledge this.

This sense of 'the soil of England [being] the inheritance of the English people'[3] constituted another dimension to the patriotic crusade of land reformers and had an important influence on a range of policy proposals, from Free Trade in Land to land nationalisation. But before discussing this influence, it is necessary to explain the ideological underpinnings of this current of thought: what accounted for the challenge posed to notions of individualistic *meum* and *tuum* by this growing sense of national rights in the land? One answer – favoured by Dicey – was the rising tide of socialist ideology, which he saw as blossoming both within and without the Liberal party. But this is only partly right. It is true that socialism played some role in the radicalisation of land reform discourse, as will be discussed in chapter 8. However, Liberals' growing tendency to invoke 'national' claims on the land had less to do with socialist ideas than many Conservatives asserted at

---

2 Cited in K. Taplin, *The English path*, Ipswich 1979, 63.
3 Arnold, *Land and the people*, 3.

the time and some scholars have subsequently suggested.[4] In fact, Liberal arguments that the interests of 'the nation' limited individual property rights in land were informed by three key developments, all of them largely independent of contemporary socialism. These developments, which will be discussed in the first section of this chapter, comprised the emergence of a distinctly democratic sense of nationhood; the strengthening of a popular proprietorial stake in the land of England; and the increasing weight of jurisprudential discourse denying the existence of absolute rights in real property. None of these bore any necessary connection to socialism, but all were central influences on Liberal land reform policies from the 1880s on.

Landed property and the claims of democracy

There is an important causal relationship between the growth of popular sovereignty and modern conceptions of national belonging.[5] In late nineteenth-century Britain the idea that the people rather than property or 'selfish' sectional interests represented the ultimate source of political authority began to gain wide currency. Its growing acceptance was reflected by the passage of the Second Reform Act of 1867, as well as the popular politics of the 1870s – notably the Bulgarian Agitation of 1876 and Gladstone's Midlothian Campaigns of 1879–80. But perhaps the most significant moment in Britain's 'democratic' self-perception came in 1884–5, with the further extension of the parliamentary franchise. Despite the fact that the reform legislation of those years left one-third of adult males without the vote, contemporaries of all political persuasions were of the opinion that Britain now possessed an essentially democratic constitution. In the judgement of Sir Henry Maine, the Third Reform Act had promulgated 'unmoderated democracy', and other less Conservative commentators agreed.[6]

For all that it was an over-exuberant one, the pervasive view that 1884–5 had ushered in an era of mass democracy implied a conviction that the 'nation' had come to be defined by the mass of its inhabitants. This accords with much recent scholarship on national identity: Benedict Anderson, Anthony D. Smith, John Hutchinson and others have emphasised the popular and communitarian dimension to national identity and nationalist ideologies.[7] As Anderson has written, 'the nation is imagined ... as a

---

4   Cf. Fforde, Conservatism; Emy, 'Land campaign', 35–68; B. Short, Land and society in Edwardian Britain, Cambridge 1997, 338–9.
5   D. Miller, On nationality, Oxford 1995, 29–31, 89–90.
6   H. Maine, Popular government, 2nd edn, London 1886, 92. See also, for example, J. Chamberlain and others, The radical programme (London 1885), ed. D. A. Hamer, Brighton 1971, p. v; J. Keir Hardie, 'The Independent Labour party', in A. Reid (ed.), The new party, London 1895, 258, and H. Samuel, Liberalism, London 1902, 225–8.
7   B. Anderson, Imagined communities, rev. edn, London 1991; A. D. Smith, Nationalism and modernism, London 1998, esp. pp. 43–4, 129–30, 198; J. Hutchinson, The dynamics of

community ... [and] is always conceived as a deep, horizontal comradeship'.[8] This dimension was also present in the language of English nationhood.[9] Arguably, its presence had been felt even in the Middle Ages, in such texts as the prologue to the *Canterbury Tales* or – to take a still earlier example – the Anglo-Saxon war poem *The battle of Maldon*.[10] It was certainly present in the modern period. As Smith has observed, 'powerful ... elements of a *popular* English national consciousness' could readily be identified in twentieth-century culture.[11] These remarks are suggestive. As this chapter will show, many ideas prominent in the land reform discourse of our period were predicated on conceptions of a popular – and hence national – stake in landed property. Because the political nation was now seen in democratic terms, radical land reform could be presented as both beneficial to ordinary people and animated by patriotic sentiment. At a time when the Conservatives made strenuous efforts to monopolise the language of patriotism,[12] land reform provided an outlet for the articulation of a radical patriotism centred on the English people and their rights.

Much of the radicalism of this patriotic discourse stemmed from its claims regarding landownership. Reformers contended that the English people had an inalienable stake in the soil of the nation; in some way extraneous to the rights claimed by individual property-owners, the land – the whole country – belonged to all its inhabitants. This vague sense of popular 'ownership' was the second underlying development informing Liberal attitudes towards the rights of landed property. Accounting for its emergence is not easy, but it would seem that the late nineteenth-century growth of the landscape preservation movement played a significant role. Drawing support mainly from individuals of Liberal or radical political sympathies, preservationists appealed to the interests of the nation against those of the privileged few.[13] Prominent among their enemies were mining and railway speculators prepared to ruin picturesque landscape and its recreational amenity value in selfish pursuit of pecuniary gain, and – more tellingly – landlords who restricted access to land by shutting up footpaths and enclosing the few remaining tracts of common land.

Established in 1865, the Commons Preservation Society (CPS) played a key role in the emergent preservationist dispensation, laying the groundwork for the later foundation of the National Trust in 1894. Initially, its work focused on the London area, with the society mounting a series of successful

---

cultural nationalism, London 1987; A. Hastings, *The construction of nationhood*, Cambridge 1997.
8 Anderson, *Imagined communities*, 7.
9 Hastings, *Construction of nationhood*, 35–65.
10 Ibid. 41–2, 47.
11 A. D. Smith, 'National identity and myths of ethnic descent', in J. Hutchinson and A. D. Smith (eds), *Nationalism*, London 2000, iv. 1409.
12 Cunningham, 'Language of patriotism', and 'Conservative party and patriotism'.
13 Readman, 'Landscape preservation'.

campaigns against the enclosure of metropolitan commons, including Hampstead Heath. In later years the CPS extended the range of its activities and by the 1890s the preservation of rural landscape – and public access to it – had become the society's main concern. Headed by Sir Robert Hunter, a leading Liberal-supporting lawyer, and G. J. Shaw Lefevre, a prominent Liberal politician, the CPS maintained a prodigiously high and ever-increasing work rate until the First World War. Its well-connected members (many of whom were MPs) promoted protective legislation in parliament, acted to prevent the passage of bills injuriously affecting scenery, public footpaths and open spaces, supported legal action in defence of common rights, and kept up a relentless propaganda campaign. In the mid 1890s the CPS was dealing with about 100 cases per year; by the turn of the century, about 300; by the later Edwardian period, 500 to 600.[14]

Much of the CPS's attention was directed against landlords, whom it charged with threatening the popular heritage in the soil as embodied in commons and footpaths. Drawing support from the Liberal political establishment, including Shaw Lefevre, Sir Charles Dilke and James Bryce (all of whom acted as chairmen), as well as Henry Fawcett, E. N. Buxton and Sir John Brunner, the society achieved considerable success in establishing the nation's rights in respect of common land.[15] Among its parliamentary triumphs were the Commons Acts of 1866, 1876 and 1899, and the insertion of clauses for the preservation of footpaths and commons into the Local Government Act of 1894. The society was also largely responsible for the passage of many other more specific pieces of protective legislation, including bills to protect the New Forest and the renowned view from Richmond Hill. But, perhaps most significantly, the CPS defeated or amended a huge mass of legislation that threatened commons, open spaces and rights of way. Some of this legislation took the form of government measures; most, however, were Private Members' Bills – water bills and railway bills in particular. Two examples were the Braithwaite and Buttermere and Ennerdale Railway Bills of 1883–4; both were thrown out, as were all subsequent attempts to build new railways in the Lake District before 1914.

The parliamentary success of the CPS indicated the extent to which, as the *Spectator* commented in 1885, there had been an acceptance of the view that 'beside the landowner, the public, and not only the local public, but even the nation at large, had an interest in the land'.[16] This conception of the national interest as a public, popular stake was of a piece with the democratic turn taken by British political culture in the era of the Second and Third Reform Acts. In the past, of course, enclosure had been justified by

[14] CPS, *Reports of proceedings*, 1898–1901, pp. 1–2; 1904–5, p. 1; 1908–10, p. 2; 1911–12, p. 2.
[15] G. Shaw Lefevre, *English commons and forests*, London 1894, 40–1; CPS, *Reports*, passim.
[16] *Spectator*, 16 May 1885, 637.

reference to the national interest in landlords' maximisation of agricultural productivity, but the late nineteenth century saw the rise of the view that the amenity value of commons (and other open spaces) provided an alternative and superior 'national' justification for their preservation. Consciousness of the amenity value of landscape and its increasing appeal to the population at large led to a conclusion that the public interest in preservation trumped considerations of purely private gain. This did much to underpin the view that common land should no longer be seen as the exclusive possession of lords of manors. In the past, as Hunter and others argued, there had been good reasons to sanction enclosures, as it was in the national interest to increase domestic food production. However, in the context of a democratic, free trade political economy, such considerations no longer applied: Britain now imported much of its food, and the amenity value of preserving a 'communal interest in the land' was acknowledged as a national imperative. This being the case, common land 'ought properly to be regarded as a "common possession for the whole country", a "national domain" for the use and enjoyment of the people'.[17]

On top of the amenity argument, however, there was the powerful idea that commons and footpaths represented ordinary people's historic rights in the land – rights that had been disrespected during the enclosure movement but now, in a democratic age, could not so easily be ignored. The preservation of these historic rights was a central aim of the CPS and its Liberal-minded supporters. It was one, moreover, that could be presented in a patriotic light. Reviewers of Shaw Lefevre's *Commons, forests and footpaths*, which chronicled the CPS's activities, praised him as a 'staunch defender of public rights against the rapacious aggressions of powerful individuals', whose actions on behalf of the people marked him out more clearly as a man of 'patriotism' than those who served on the bench or in the armed forces, or in other capacities considered synonymous with 'the public spirit of Englishmen'.[18] Such accolades were in keeping with the language used by the CPS and other preservationists to describe the motivation behind their campaigns. For example, defenders of 'our real old English footpaths' frequently portrayed themselves as patriotic defenders of the 'birthright' of the common people, which had been handed down from generation to generation.[19] One of these defenders was Octavia Hill, a prominent member of the CPS and co-founder of the National Trust. In a speech of June 1888, which was instrumental in persuading the CPS to extend its activities to the

[17] R. Hunter, 'Communal occupation and enjoyment of land', NC lxii (1907), 494–508; C. L. Lewes, 'How to secure breathing spaces', NC xxi (May 1887), 677.
[18] *The Nation*, 4 Feb. 1911; Commons and Footpaths Preservation Society, *Reviews of* [Shaw Lefevre], *Commons, forests and footpaths*, 34 (Centre for Rural History, University of Reading).
[19] See, for example, R. Hunter, *Footpaths and commons and parish and district councils*, London 1895, 6, and O. Hill, 'Footpath preservation', *Nature Notes* iii (1892), 196.

protection of footpaths, Hill gave expression to preservationists' patriotic crusade on behalf of the people and against the selfish action of landlords. It was 'incumbent on us all', she declared, 'to preserve for our countrymen ... the great common inheritances to which, as English citizens they are born, the footpaths of their native country'. These, she warned, were 'vanishing ... closed by Quarter Sessions, the poor witnesses hardly daring to speak, the richer dividing the spoil; the public from a larger area hardly knowing of the decision which has for ever closed to them some lovely walk'.[20]

Hill's words gave powerful expression to the sense of a popular proprietorial stake in the countryside that was so important a part of preservationists' thinking. Unsurprisingly, their opponents charged them with harbouring a desire to undermine private property rights, even of professing an innovative and unwelcome agenda akin to 'communist' doctrine. But such accusations were unfounded. Preservationists and their mainly Liberal supporters did not seek to attack the institution of private property: animated by patriotic regard for popular rights, they aimed to prevent landowners from disregarding the nation's stake in English land and landscape. This aim was informed partly by a sense that certain distinctive landscapes – such as the Lake District, the New Forest or the White Cliffs of Dover – were national treasures to which all Englishmen and women had a right of access, and a right to see preserved inviolate for future generations. In these and other 'more noteworthy features of the country', the CPS and also the National Trust both perceived and stimulated a steady 'growth of ... collective ownership'. For Hunter, this felt sense of a public proprietorial stake in such 'grand natural features' justified their compulsory purchase by the state in order to ensure that they were protected from despoliation.[21]

But preservationists' protection of the national stake in land and landscape was also informed by political economy, the teachings of which made clear that rights of ownership in land were limited by considerations of national good. It had long been an established principle that the state was ultimately the sole owner of land in the country: what was termed 'private property' was simply an estate in the land – an entitlement to its exclusive or near-exclusive use. Because land was different from other forms of property, being necessary for the very existence of life, this entitlement was granted to individuals on the understanding that their 'ownership' of the soil would be of public benefit. Private property in land – originally a means by which its production could be maximised – was therefore limited by considerations of public or national interest: in principle this interest was in all cases prior.[22]

---

20 'Miss Octavia Hill on the duty of supporting footpath preservation societies [report of CPS meeting, 13 June 1888]': Kendal Records Office, WDX/422/2/4.
21 R. Hunter, *The preservation of places or interest or beauty*, Manchester 1907, 29; 'Places of interest and things of beauty', *NC* xliii (1898), 570; and 'Communal occupation', 507–8.
22 See, for example, J. S. Mill, *Principles of political economy*, 7th edn, London 1877,

Preservationists were quick to see the implications of this point for their cause, bringing it into play in cases where the selfish interest of landowners threatened the nation's stake in the land. For example, at a protest meeting following the closure of a popular footpath up Latrigg in the Lake District in 1887, the veteran Liberal politician Samuel Plimsoll flatly denied that the offending landowner's property was his own to deal with as he so wished:

> Property in land never was, is not now, and never can be, so absolute as it is in property [that is] the work of men's hands. You might put your money in a bag, row on to the lake and sink it there. You injure nobody but yourself; but the landlord can say whether he will grow crop or not. This is the *reductio ad absurdum* of their argument. If the whole of the landlords were to say, 'We will grow no food,' you would soon bring them to their senses and show them it was never their land except as trustees for the nation, and for the good of the people. (Applause.) This statement of mine is illustrated in the case of railways. Parliament gave railways powers to take land from all and sundry, whether the owners of the land desired it or not, affirming the principle that the public interest is the predominant and under-lying interest. [23]

Plimsoll's argument was as applicable to the cause of land reform as it was to that of landscape preservation (it was surely no coincidence that Hunter saw landscape preservation as a key part of the answer to the 'land question', even drafting a book-length manuscript on the subject).[24] Indeed, the idea that there was no such thing as absolute rights in landed property formed a further underlying influence on Liberal agrarian policy. That this was so does not indicate the contamination of Liberal ideology by 'socialistic' doctrine: as we have just seen, the idea that private property rights were limited by considerations of public good was a commonplace of political economy. Moreover, it was also a commonplace of jurisprudence. The late nineteenth and early twentieth centuries witnessed the sight of many establishment legal figures denying that landowners had total control of their property in all circumstances. Thomas Edward Scrutton, Professor of Constitutional Law and History at University College London and a future Appeal Court judge is a good case in point. According to Scrutton, the ownership of land was subject to 'the condition that the use a man makes of his property shall not be prejudicial to the State'.[25] It followed, therefore, that state interference on the grounds of public interest was justified in law, should the national interest in the soil be violated. This conclusion, which many

226–7, 230–2; H. Sidgwick, *The elements of politics*, 2nd edn, London 1897, 67, 73–5, 147; T. E. Scrutton, *Commons and common fields*, Cambridge 1887, 174–5; and H. Greenwood, *Our land laws as they are*, 2nd edn, London [1891], 7–8.

[23] *English Lakes Visitor and Keswick Guardian*, 8 Oct. 1887 (cutting in Kendal Records Office, WDX/422/2/4).

[24] R. Hunter, 'One phase of the land question' (manuscript, 142pp.), Robert Hunter papers, Surrey History Centre, 1621/10/3.

[25] T. E. Scrutton, *Land in fetters*, Cambridge 1886, 156.

lawyers endorsed, would give strength to land reformers and their claims throughout the years leading up to the First World War.

Free Trade in Land and land tenure reform

Many Liberals and radicals took this belief that there existed a national interest in the land beyond recognising the public's stake in quintessentially English landscapes like the Lake District, or in ancient commons and footpaths. In their eyes this stake extended over the entire land area of the country, of which the crown – representing the nation as a whole, now that England was perceived to be a democracy – was ultimately the sole owner. Let us begin with those who called for Free Trade in Land, many of whose arguments drew on the principle that the national interest in the land was prior. In the 1880s campaigners like Arnold and Brodrick claimed that land was a special type of property, qualitatively different from personalty insofar as it was rightfully subject to the power of the state, and always had been. When private ownership interfered with the public interest, the state was entitled to intervene on behalf of the nation, as it routinely did through the compulsory purchase of land for railways and canals.[26] For advocates of Free Trade in Land, that the state was entitled to do this signified a key jurisprudential truth, which few could deny (Blackstone and even Gladstone could be cited in support): in England there was no absolute rights in real property. It followed, as Arnold put it, that 'the land belongs to the nation, to the State, to the people'.[27] The claim that national property in land was a legal reality in late nineteenth-century England is a startling one, but it was not difficult to justify. As Arnold explained, the starting assumption was that because 'land is one of the elementary necessities of life', its 'absolute ownership ... is, and must be, vested in the sovereign authority, whether it be named king or parliament, people or nation'. To this authority private property rights were subordinate; with its interests they should not conflict. Hence the system by which it was divided into individual estates should therefore conduce to the public and national good.[28]

According to Arnold, his associates in the FLL and other Liberal reformers active in the 1880s, the problem with the land system was that this was precisely what it did not do. Primogeniture and strict settlement contravened the nation's rightful stake in the land of England. Artificial mechanisms for the perpetuation of great territorial dynasties and the concomitant preservation of an aristocratic ruling class, they served no public benefit. Although in the past it might have benefited the nation to possess a land system designed to maintain the great estates of an hereditary peerage, this

26 Brodrick, *Reform of the English land system*, 16.
27 Arnold, *Free land*, 185–9.
28 Ibid. 189, and *Land and the people*, 3.

was no longer true. In the context of the perceived democratisation of the political nation in the 1870s and 1880s, Liberals argued that the national disadvantages of primogeniture and entail made their elimination a patriotic necessity. Indeed, the campaign for their abolition was presented as symbolic of how 'England', in the words of one MP, was 'day by day becoming more and more the country of her people, and less and less the country of territorial despotism'.[29] Urging the removal of these 'artificial laws' which 'blasted and withered' the countryside, reformers associated with the FLL, as well as those more radical who saw Free Trade in Land as a necessary first step, presented themselves – in Joseph Arch's words – as 'the truest patriots in England today'.[30]

This patriotic crusade was thus founded on a popular conception of nationhood and the national interest: the nation as opposed to the selfish interests of land monopolists. But Free Trade in Land was not simply about standing up for the people's rightful stake in their native land, it was additionally about meeting the challenge of democracy, and fear played a role here. This was especially the case for the core exponents of Free Trade in Land clustered around the FLL, who were by and large moderate Liberals. For these individuals, the co-existence of 'feudal' land laws with a democratic political nation was not just an anachronistic and unjust absurdity; it was also a dangerous combination that could lead to national ruin. This gave an additional edge to their contention that the concentration of landed property in the hands of a few created conditions of social instability. For some, indeed, the fate of ancient Rome provided a template onto which could be mapped the catastrophically downward trajectory of the nation's fortunes, were not Free Trade in Land to be enacted. In his *English land question* of 1883, the barrister and Fellow of All Souls Arthur F. Leach painted an especially lurid picture of how Roman democracy came to be corrupted by its land system:

> [I]f something be not done … we may look on indeed with dread to the spread of democracy – a democracy without hope, without faith, without patriotism, whose sole aim will be to make the upper classes contribute to its support in idleness and yet in misery … [B]y perpetuating the present system, we take the broad and easy way that leads to destruction. We follow in the steps that led the Empire of Rome to ruin. We shall see the large landowners swallowing up the smaller owners, and the large farmers swallowing up the small farmers, while all the active and intelligent labourers emigrate to freer and happier lands. The country of England will become like Italy in the days of the Empire, a vast solitude, except for here and there a few brutish labourers, reduced almost to the condition of slaves, languidly tilling the uncared-for soil; and a few vast cities filled with smoke and dirt, and a degraded prole-

---

[29] Moss, *English land laws*, 64.
[30] ELC, 28 Feb. 1885, 2.

tariat, whose only cry is 'panem et circenses' – 'food and fireworks'. The end of that is despotism and death.[31]

Such prognostications of doom rather obscured the fact that the campaign for Free Trade in Land had achieved at least a partial success by the early 1880s, with the passage of the Settled Land Act (1882). Under the terms of this measure the tenant for life was empowered to sell land for any reason, and while exemption of mansion and park from its provisions disappointed campaigners like Arnold, the act represented a real shift in opinion regarding landed property. Its practical significance was illustrated in a key test case of 1892, where the courts found in favour of the public rather than the familial interest in a particular estate.

The estate in question was Savernake Forest in Wiltshire, the 40,000-acre seat of the spectacularly dissolute fourth marquess of Ailesbury, who after succeeding his grandfather in 1886 at the tender age of twenty-three, proceeded to accumulate a £230,000 debt by 1891, mainly through gambling and drinking.[32] The marquess's proposed solution to this dire state of affairs was to sell Savernake to Lord Iveagh, of the Guinness family (a nobleman selling his home to a beer baron to pay debts caused by alcoholism presents a nice irony, but one apparently lost on contemporary commentators). Ailesbury's heir and family, however, objected to this course of action and, citing the 1882 Settled Lands Act, the Chancery Court blocked the sale.[33] But the Appeal Court, to which Ailesbury subsequently turned, interpreted the act in a rather different way. Citing section 53 of the act, which instructed judges, in cases where the sale of the house was proposed, 'to have regard to the interests of all parties entitled under the settlement', the court ruled in favour of the sale, and on the grounds of public interest. Its argument was that under current arrangements, the tenants and labourers of Savernake suffered through the inadequate stewardship of the estate and the nation at large suffered through the resultant low levels of agricultural productivity.[34] This judgement stood, later being upheld by the House of Lords.[35]

In the event Iveagh never bought Savernake, even though the law had found decisively in his favour.[36] However, the judgements of the Appeal Court and House of Lords had made it clear that the public interest in the proper stewardship and cultivation of the land trumped private, dynastic considerations. This amounted to an explicit acknowledgement of a public

[31] A. F. Leach, The English land question, London 1883, 31–2.
[32] C. S. C. Brudenell-Bruce [7th marquess of Ailesbury], The wardens of Savernake Forest, London 1949, 315ff.
[33] Law reports, chancery division, 1892, i. 506–48.
[34] Ibid. i. 539–45.
[35] Law reports, House of Lords, 1892, 356–66.
[36] Administrative delays over arranging the sale caused him to withdraw his offer in May 1893. Ailesbury was left to live out the rest of his short life in dissipation in East London, where he died in April 1894.

locus standi in the disposal of real property – precisely the position of advocates of Free Trade in Land. Legal and Liberal opinion were converging, a development nicely embodied in the person of Scrutton, who stood as Liberal party candidate for Limehouse in the 1886 general election. As he argued in his prize-winning *Land in fetters* (Cambridge 1886), it 'injure[d] the nation' to tie men unfit to be landlords to land: 'to preserve worthless but ancient families is hardly a sufficient justification for checking the development of English lands, and hampering the agriculture of English tenants'.[37] Such a remark was entirely consistent with the judicial readings of the Settled Land Act in the Ailesbury case.

This is not to say that the 1882 act was a resounding success: after all, it abolished neither strict settlement nor primogeniture. However, it did do something to diminish the clamour for reform, despite the best efforts of Arnold and the FLL. There were other contributing factors too, of course. From the mid-1880s on, many Liberal reformers saw Free Trade in Land as an insufficiently moderate answer to the land question. Furthermore, the legislative creation of smallholdings – the reform favoured by many – could be made to seem incompatible with Free Trade in Land, as the latter would only facilitate the absorption of newly-created small properties into larger ones. In their rejection of an 1894 Liberal proposal to abolish primogeniture in cases where owners died intestate, Tory peers made deft use of this argument. Led by Salisbury, they claimed that if the Liberal plans went ahead, small proprietors would be hit hardest. Their argument was a simple one: small 'yeoman' farmers, of whose personal virtues and national utility reformers said so much, were more likely than larger owners to die intestate (legal fees acted as a disincentive to will-making). Hence it followed that the abolition of primogeniture would only serve to split up their property, which would then be 'lapped up by the great estates near them'.[38]

While the campaign for Free Trade in Land lost momentum, the same cannot be said of the similarly long-running campaign for land tenure reform. From the time of the agitation of the Farmers' Alliance in the early 1880s, supporters of land tenure reform also asserted their patriotism by upholding the nation's interest in the land. In their analysis, this interest justified state intervention in landlord-tenant relations to ensure the proper cultivation of the soil. As the Alliance's co-founder William Bear pointed out in a *Contemporary Review* article of 1882, many landlords found it was 'not to their interests or to the interest of their families ... that they should do their duty as stewards of the nation's land', being too burdened with debt to provide adequate investment in agriculture on their estates.[39] Yet the conditions under which landlords let out their land often compounded the dereliction of duty committed by putting family before country. As many farmers did

---

[37] Scrutton, *Land in fetters*, 157–8.
[38] *Hansard*, 4th ser., 1894, xxiii. 1392, 1396.
[39] W. E. Bear, 'The true principle of tenant-right', CR xli (1882), 654.

not enjoy sufficient security of tenure or rights to compensation for improvements, they were discouraged from sinking their own capital in the soil to effect the improvement in productivity that the national interest demanded. Liberals argued that this state of affairs warranted legislative action by 'the nation' – acting through parliament – 'to insist that the land shall be held under conditions of the greatest public advantage'. Unionist landlords like the duke of Argyll objected that such intervention by the state constituted an unacceptable breach of private property rights,[40] but Liberals responded by asserting the antecedent and superior rights of the nation. Such was the line taken by Bear, for whom the 'true principle of tenant-right' was based on the national stake in the soil:

> The land of the country really belongs to the nation, and it is held in trust by the Crown, which delegates it to persons called 'landowners', who, in their turn, let it to capitalists to farm. Now, the interest of the nation is in favour of the utmost profitable development of the resources of the national soil, and this end is only to be secured by giving full security to the capital of those who actually have the soil to deal with.[41]

The Liberal position on land tenure reform was presented as unacceptably extremist and even 'socialist' by its detractors, but its supporters did not rely on any novel collectivist ideology for justification of their claims. Bolstered by established tenets of British jurisprudence, in particular that which stipulated that there was no absolute private property in land, their perspective was that in an increasingly democratic political culture it appeared unjust to deny the existence of a popular stake in the land of England. The advance of 'democracy' had brought a widening of the definition of the national interest in the soil, and had thrown into sharper relief the constitutionally novel dissonance between the land system and political representation. A creation of landlord-dominated parliaments, the land system had to be brought into line with political arrangements and this meant recognising the limitations that national prerogatives imposed on the rights of private property. This was the logic behind the Liberal party's campaign for land tenure reform – a campaign that culminated in the 1906 Agricultural Holdings Act. For moderate reformers like James Rowlands, MP for the Dartford division of Kent and honorary secretary of the LLRA, the measure represented a great triumph. Speaking at the National Liberal Club on the occasion of the bill's introduction into parliament, Rowlands claimed that 'the day of a democratic national land-system has dawned ... The nation will, ere long, enter into the heritage of which it has been despoiled by measures passed by the spoliators themselves. Confiscation either of the nation's lands or tenants'

---

40 C. D. Campbell, 8th duke of Argyll, 'Agricultural depression: II', CR xli (1882), 381–403.
41 Bear, 'True principle', 654.

improvement[s] is a game which is near its close'.[42] Such sentiments were echoed by Lord Carrington, as President of the Board of Agriculture and the man responsible for the legislation.[43]

Recognition of the national stake in the land and the implications that this had for property rights could lead to more radical proposals than either Free Trade in Land or land tenure reform, however. Starting in the mid-1880s, a groundswell of opinion that drew alternative and far less moderate policy conclusions began to arise. Chamberlain's 'unauthorised programme' acted as the catalyst here, coinciding as it did with the extension of the parliamentary franchise through the Third Reform Act. Chamberlain's speeches stimulated reflection about landed property and its relationship to a democratic political nation. His demand that property be called on to pay a 'ransom' for the privileges it enjoyed was certainly controversial, not least within his own party, but it did strengthen a growing perception that the extent of these privileges was somehow anomalous, out of kilter with contemporary modernity, and thus ought to be curtailed. Some radicals suggested that the 'ransom' payable to the state in lieu of the nation's interest in the land should take the form of sweeping compulsory purchase legislation. Convinced that landlords made too little productive use of their estates, allotting large tracts to sporting purposes, and that such under-use of the soil was 'unpatriotic and disloyal' as it neglected the duty of cultivation which went with the right to own property, Arch and Charles Bradlaugh urged the need for legislation to compel landlords 'to cultivate it in the best interests of the people'.[44] Under their proposals, those who failed to 'do their duty by the country' would have property they did not farm or make available for public enjoyment compulsorily purchased by the state, to be divided up into smallholdings and allotments for letting to labourers.[45] Accusations of injustice were met by referring to the state's legal entitlement to ensure the best use of the land for the benefit of the nation as a whole.

Although the campaign for a 'compulsory cultivation bill' was relatively short-lived (it had petered out by the early 1890s), the rationale upon which it was founded informed much of Liberal-radical thinking on the land question throughout our period. Bradlaugh and Arch had justified compulsory purchase on the basis of the non-existence of absolute rights of private property and the national interest in the land; other reformers would do similarly. Campaigners for smallholdings legislation provide a case in point. In 1885, prompted by the agitation of Chamberlain and Collings, many Liberals presented the multiplication of small tenancies as a public good *tout court*, arguing that the expropriation of landlords for this purpose was justified even

---

[42] National Liberal Club, *Address*, 8.
[43] *The Times*, 17 Oct. 1906, 4.
[44] Bradlaugh, *Hansard*, 3rd ser., 1886, ccciv. 1584; Arch at Oxford, *ELC*, 21 Feb. 1885, 2.
[45] *ELC*, 9 May 1885, 3.

in cases where they might be cultivating the soil to its utmost.[46] Unsurprisingly, this provoked Conservative accusations of leftist collectivism run rampant, but Liberals insisted that their proposals did not spring from class prejudice against landlords. By no means the most enthusiastic of reformers, Harcourt saw compulsory purchase of land for smallholdings as defensible insofar as it conduced to the public interest. As he reassured a Winchester audience in November 1885, 'nothing need be acquired except at a fair price' and 'if acquisition were for the public good there was no socialism or confiscation'.[47]

Despite their later defection from the Liberal party over Irish home rule, Chamberlain and Collings's agrarian campaign of 1884–5 did much to establish the acceptability of compulsory purchase among Liberal opinion. In the years before 1914 it would be a key component of many of the party's policy proposals, from smallholdings and allotments legislation to Lloyd George's Land Campaign. In justifying the need for compulsory purchase, Liberals repeatedly fell back on the argument used by Harcourt in 1885: acquisition was in the public interest and hence legitimate and a reasonable price would be paid in any case. The analogy with railways was frequently invoked. In a speech at South Lynn in May 1890, Arch pointed to a time

> when Wisbech, March, Ely, Cambridge, or Swaffham had no railways. The railway companies went to Parliament for an Act. Whether his lordship liked it or not, whether it frightened his rabbits into fits – (laughter) – the people wanted the land, and Parliament said 'you have got to dub it up, my lord' (laughter). If a law could be made like that when a new line was to be constructed, why could it not be made when Englishmen wanted the land? (Hear, hear).[48]

Of course, one answer to Arch's question was that granting Englishmen access to land in the form of cottages, allotments or smallholdings served no public purpose – certainly no public purpose comparable to that of a railway line. By 1890 even Chaplin was prepared to accept that compulsory purchase could be justified if it conduced to the public good, but he denied that the land reforms that the Liberals had in mind would have this effect.[49] However, this position was increasingly hard to sustain as the century drew to a close. Quite apart from anything else, there was no doubt that much agricultural land was underused. Some landowners – like the hapless Ailesbury – lacked funds for the improvement of their estates; others chose to let land lie idle, either for speculative purposes or to facilitate game preservation; others still were uninterested in the practical business of maximising

---

[46] For example, Chamberlain at Birmingham and Hull in *Chamberlain's speeches*, i. 160, 171–2.
[47] *The Times*, 4 Nov. 1885, 5.
[48] *ELC*, 17 May 1890, 2.
[49] *Hansard*, 3rd ser., 1890, cccxliv. 342–3.

agricultural production. The consequence of all this, according to Liberals, was that thousands of acres were improperly used. It followed that as the efficient use of land was the original justification for private property rights, its inefficient use justified rescinding them – a point that was fairly common currency in Liberal speeches on land reform from the late 1880s.[50] In 1890 Robert Reid – a future Lord Chancellor – moved a Commons motion calling for a measure giving local authorities the power to acquire land compulsorily for public use, and this was to become a staple element of future proposals, not least Liberal plans for local government reform. In response to such arguments, Conservatives suggested that although the misuse of land was regrettable, it was comparable to the misuse of any other asset and hence not a matter for dirigiste state action, which would only undermine the security of property. This was the line taken by William Ambrose, MP for Harrow, in the debate on Reid's motion: in his view, land was equivalent to money.[51] But this was a weak argument, one that ignored accepted jurisprudential precepts: first, land was a limited resource to which all required access in order to survive, and second, unlike other forms of property, land was not the creation of man but nature – or God. This being the case, it was not according to Liberals an asset like any other.

Yet this did not mean that Liberals were motivated by antipathy to property *qua* property (as socialists might have been); they merely sought recognition of this crucial distinction, which for too long had been ignored by landlord-controlled parliaments, jealous of their own and not the national interest. Theirs was a struggle on behalf of the nation's stake in the land. Former president of the National Liberal Federation, Robert Spence Watson summed up the case well in an article for the *Northern Echo*, published in 1905:

> So long as there is no confiscation, and so long as that which is taken is properly paid for, there is nothing unreasonable or contrary to the laws of God or man in restriction of amount held, or in requiring the sale of estates if that is for the benefit of the community. This is acknowledged every day. The law of England does not allow a man to be owner of land, but only permits him to hold an estate in it. This is not a distinction without a difference, but a very important distinction. Land is said to be held of the King – that is, really, of the nation, and for the benefit of the nation. The nation can, and constantly does, recall its right to the land by paying reasonable compensation to the man who has held it and from whom it is taken.[52]

---

[50] For example, R. C. Richards, 'Some economic and commercial aspects of the land question', *National Liberal Club Political Economy Circle Transactions* ii (1894), 160–1.
[51] *Hansard*, 3rd ser., 1890, cccxliv. 323
[52] R. S. Watson, *The reform of the land laws*, London 1905, 14.

Restoring the national interest in the soil:
land nationalisers and land campaigners

A supporter of Free Trade in Land and smallholdings legislation, Spence Watson was not a radical extremist. But his arguments bore some similarity to those of campaigners further to the left, notably land nationalisers, with whom the Liberal party had developed strong links by the Edwardian period. In fact, as early as 1892, Wallace had declared that Liberal plans to give local authorities compulsory powers to acquire and let land for smallholdings and allotments represented a *de facto* endorsement of LNS principles. Unlike Unionist schemes for the encouragement of peasant proprietorship (which would simply create more landowners jealous of their *soi-disant* exclusive rights), the Liberal proposals 'recognise[d] that the public interest in the land is paramount'.[53] Such commendation of Liberal policies by the land nationalisation movement would be repeated, still more enthusiastically, in later years (the 1907 smallholdings legislation is a case in point).[54] The affinities between the land nationalisation movement and moderate agrarian reformism were real, and help to illustrate the extent to which the former was an organic development of the latter, rather than – as some historians have suggested – a 'socialist' imposture antithetical to the traditions of Liberal-radical discourse.[55]

Like many less radical reformers, land nationalisers started from the assumption that absolute rights of private property in land were alien to longstanding legal precepts, using this as evidence of their lack of revolutionary intent. George Harwood, Liberal MP for Bolton, told the 1903 LNS annual meeting that they simply sought a return to 'the fundamental principle of English law', this being, as LNS propaganda endlessly repeated, that 'the Crown and the nation is the ultimate owner of the soil'.[56] And while the state had distributed land to individuals in order to promote good cultivation and reward public duties and military service, as guardian of the national interest in the soil it retained ultimate ownership rights and could take these up again at any time.[57]

Where land nationalisers departed from more moderate reformers, however, was in their insistence on the wholesale abolition of the existing system of private property in land. The methods by which supporters of the LNS and ELRL sought to achieve this goal differed, but their guiding rationale was the same: if land was 'a public trust instead of private property',[58] then its monopolistic ownership by individuals was an imposture that

---

53 LNS, *Eleventh annual meeting*, London 1892, 12.
54 *LL*, June 1907, 68.
55 Cf. Fforde, *Conservatism*; Short, *Land and society*; Emy, 'Lloyd George'.
56 *LL*, June 1903, 48–9; W. P. Price-Heywood, *The land monopoly*, London 1906, 18.
57 Wallace, *Land nationalisation*, 22–5.
58 LNS, 'To landless Britons', London 1895, 4.

required removal. As the ELRL argued, there were in truth no 'landowners' in England, only 'landholders', or 'tenants of the people', who could legitimately be evicted from their holdings by the people should their stewardship conflict with the national interest. From this it followed that 'every Englishman ought to understand that the soil belongs to the community and that it is the power of the Crown, on the call of the Commons, to resume every acre in the country'.[59] By taxing or buying out all property owners, land nationalisers hoped to achieve a practical reassertion of 'the ancient English principle that land is not, and cannot become the property of individuals, but belongs inalienably to the whole people, of whom all holders of land are tenants'.[60]

For land nationalisers, recognition of this 'ancient English principle', which would involve the abolition of private landownership, was not an act of socialist confiscation but one of patriotic restitution, consistent with native ideas of freedom and fair play. In a speech at the annual meeting of the LNS in 1895, J. W. Logan, Liberal MP for Harborough, declared his belief 'that Englishmen were born with certain rights, and amongst those rights he held that the right of the free use of a certain proportion of the earth was an Englishman's legacy. The private ownership of the land was unjust'.[61] However, as private ownership of land was very much a reality in modern England, it followed that the rights of Englishmen had fallen into desuetude, and this made a mockery of the conventional cries of patriotism which, in time of war, enjoined men to fight for a country that was far from being 'theirs'. Reporting to *Land and Labour* about LNS propaganda meetings in the summer of 1890s, Joseph Hyder, secretary of the LNS, wrote of how

> We often addressed the men as fellow-trespassers, and justified such a mode of greeting. We are not birds and cannot fly in the air; we are not fishes and cannot swim in the water; we must go on the land, and as we haven't a foot of land of our own, we must trespass upon somebody else's land. Then again we pointed out the miserable deception under which so many men labor in speaking of 'our' country, which they would fight and die for, when it practically belongs to a few thousand landlords, and not to them at all.[62]

In making the case for the illegitimacy of the existing land system, the advance of political democracy played a crucial role. Like the other agrarian reformers discussed earlier in this chapter, land nationalisers perceived a disjuncture between the late nineteenth-century democratisation of the political system and the persistence of a 'feudal' land system. Although they felt that the absolute ownership of land was on *a priori* and jurisprudential grounds unjustifiable, its co-existence with a self-consciously free and democratic political

---

[59] J. Wheelwright, *Landlordism*, London 1896, 4–5; Verinder, *Land question*, 18–19.
[60] ELRL, *Manifesto*, 1–2.
[61] *LL*, May 1895, 48.
[62] *LL*, Oct. 1890, 2.

nation added insult to injury. In an 1894 essay, William Jameson, onetime honorary secretary of the LNS, nicely caught this sense of outrage: 'In this nineteenth century, when the liberty of the subject is so complete, when the boast is in every man's mouth that "slaves cannot breathe in England", the bulk of the people are "landless folk"... who are denied their birthright in that national estate of which the Crown is the constitutional steward or trustee.'[63] Land nationalisation was presented as the solution to this state of affairs – a means by which, in Wallace's words, the system of landholding could be brought 'into harmony with modern ideas'.[64] After all, evidence of its incompatibility with such ideas was not hard to come by: drawing on his youthful experience as a surveyor, Wallace described how landlords in democratic England could control access to land, interfere with religious freedoms and even evict tenants for political reasons.[65]

But Wallace was not only drawing attention to the discordance between England's 'modern', democratic political culture and the realities of life imposed by the system of landownership, he was also making the point that this political culture was on its own an inadequate guarantor of individual freedom. True, as he told the annual meeting of the LNS in 1894, the advance of political democracy had brought Englishmen closer to being 'free men in a free country', but the completion of their liberation could only come once they gained their rightful inheritance in the soil.[66] With their emphasis on promoting freedoms, land nationalisers had much in common with more moderate reformers. But commonality of aims only provides a partial explanation as to why Liberal ideas converged with those of the land nationalisation movement. The more fundamental reason lies in the fact that both were based on the same assumptions about private property in land. These assumptions did not derive from any new socialistic ideology of class. Their roots lay in an older tradition stretching back through Mill and the early writings of Herbert Spencer to William Ogilvie's *Birthright in land* of 1782.[67] This tradition – to which land nationalisers openly paid homage[68] – employed arguments founded on natural right, English history and legal precept to assert the non-existence of absolute rights of private property in the soil. Its legacy was the reformers' claim that the English people as a whole had a rightfully inalienable stake in the land of their country. By the

---

[63] W. Jameson, 'Land monopoly', in Reid, *New party*, 151–2.
[64] Wallace, *Land nationalisation*, 25.
[65] Ibid. 98–104.
[66] LNS, *Thirteenth annual meeting*, London 1894, 15. See also, for example, F. W. Newman, *The land as national property*, London 1892, 4; A. J. Ogilvy, *Land nationalisation*, London 1890, 22; LNS, *Programme*; and *LL*, July 1891, 4.
[67] Mill, *Principles*; H. Spencer, *Collected writings*, III: *Social statics* (1851), London 1996; W. Ogilvie, *Birthright in land* (1792), London 1891.
[68] For example, George, *Progress and poverty*, 338; LNS, *Opinions of leading thinkers*, London 1890; Newman, *Land as national property*, 4; and Jameson, 'Land monopoly', 146–8.

Edwardian period, the Liberal leadership was also prepared to act on this principle (even if practical party policy stopped well short of land nationalisation). The limitations on private property rights imposed by the legislation of 1906–8 testified to this, but so too did the land tax clauses of Lloyd George's 'People's Budget' and ultimately the Land Campaign.

The most controversial aspects of the 1909 Budget were its proposals to impose a 20 per cent tax on the unearned increment of land values and an annual duty of a halfpenny in the £ on the capital value of undeveloped land. It has been argued that Lloyd George hoped that his land taxes and the violent rhetoric with which he advocated them would goad the Lords into rejecting the Budget, thus precipitating a looked-for constitutional crisis.[69] But the land taxes were more than simply a device to provoke a clash with the peers. They were of considerable ideological significance, representing the extent to which Liberal thinking on the land question, and more particularly landed property, had evolved since the 1880s. Informed by many of the assumptions about property discussed previously in this chapter, the land clauses of the Budget drew on the idea that private property rights in land were not absolute, being limited by considerations of national interest. In the past, Liberals argued, the nation's stake in the soil had imposed public obligations on landlords: for all its faults, the 'feudal' system had at least required the aristocracy to carry out military and administrative duties in return for their territorial privileges. But with the passage of time and the acquisition of increased political power by the landed classes, these obligations had gradually been hived off. As the *Liberal Monthly* pointed out in February 1909, 'the land-holder ha[d] become the land-owner' – an individual who claimed absolute rights of personal ownership, rather than one who held land from the state in return for the provision of public services.[70] In this interpretation, to which Lloyd George had been sympathetic long before 1909,[71] land value taxation was a means of reasserting the nation's stake in the land, which previously had been embodied in the military and judicial services attached to landholding. Such had been the position of radical supporters of land taxes for some time; it was now the position of the Liberal leadership. Speaking at Birmingham on 17 September 1909, Asquith made it clear that those who objected to the land clauses, which only sought to re-impose in a different form national obligations that had previously been shirked, were in fact deficient in patriotism – unwilling, as he put it, 'to play their part, to do their fair share, in the patriotic duty of meeting the needs of the state'.[72]

[69] Grigg, *Lloyd George: the people's champion*, 226–7.
[70] LM, Feb. 1909, 11.
[71] See, for example, speech at Newcastle, *LV* cix (June 1903), 11, and Lloyd George, *Better times*, 2–3.
[72] LM, Oct. 1909, 4.

But the land taxes were not simply a means of getting landowners to do their patriotic duty by extracting payment from them in lieu of past functions no longer performed. They were also a means by which landowners would be induced to make proper use of the soil. As has been shown, Liberal reformers had long insisted that the ownership of land imposed the obligation of effective use in the interests of the wider community. At Limehouse Lloyd George took up this argument. 'The ownership of land', he declared, 'is not merely an enjoyment, it is a stewardship. It has been reckoned as such in the past ... No country, however rich, can permanently afford to have quartered upon its revenue a class which declines to do the duty which it was called upon to perform since the beginning.'[73] By taxing the 'unearned increment' and imposing a levy on undeveloped land, Liberals sought to place a disincentive on the under-use of the soil, thereby forcing owners to do that duty they owed the nation.

Not surprisingly, this appeared unacceptably draconian to Conservatives: after all, the state did not insist on the productive use of other forms of property. But Liberals countered with another familiar argument, that which claimed that land – limited in extent and the work of nature, not man – was different from other forms of property, and thus subject to different rules. The difference rested on the idea that the nation was injured by the misuse of land far more than it was by the misuse of other forms of property. And in 1909 Liberals did not lack examples of its misuse with which to justify their proposals. Aside from the usual complaints about game preservation, a particular example that came to the fore was the speculative holding of uncultivated land in and around towns and cities. Asquith, among others, claimed that this harmed national development by constraining industrial growth and promoting overcrowded housing conditions, because it restricted the availability of reasonably priced land.[74] But there was also a strong moral dimension to this argument. As Lloyd George emphasised at Limehouse, the speculative landowner was a passive beneficiary of the energy of others: with the growth and prospering of urban areas, demand for land for housing and industry grew too. Thus the speculator could cash in by selling his (undeveloped) land, the value of which had been inflated not by his own efforts but those of the wider community.[75]

Lloyd George's perspective on speculative landholding was of a piece with a more wide-ranging moral attack on landlords, one which cast them as parasites on the nation, sapping its energies by denying men access to land, constricting urban growth, inhibiting industry, fostering poor housing conditions and so on.[76] Limehouse sounded the tocsin for this full-scale war on

[73] Lloyd George, *Better times*, 155–6.
[74] For example, Asquith at Southport, *The Times*, 3 July 1909, 7.
[75] Lloyd George, *Better times*, 146–52.
[76] See, for example, Lloyd George at Queen's Hall, 31 Dec. 1909, ibid. 249–53.

landlordism, which would continue until the outbreak of a rather different conflict in 1914. But as Liberals were at pains to stress, theirs was not a war on property *per se*. Rather, they sought to moralise the institution of landed property by bringing it into line with the public interest and the nation's rightful inheritance. Quite apart from anything else, Liberals claimed, the current system – which rewarded speculators and rentiers – was arranged to benefit an idle minority at the expense of the hardworking mass of the nation, and this only served to undermine the security of property itself.[77]

Of course, such arguments did not prevent Conservatives from condemning the Liberals' Budget proposals as 'socialist'; and these condemnations were repeated with still greater force when Lloyd George launched his Land Campaign in 1913. Were such criticisms justified? Most historians, while not necessarily sympathetic to the Conservative position, have tended to agree that the Liberals' land policies after 1909 marked a shift away from the party's traditions in a social democratic or collectivist direction. For H. V. Emy, the Land Campaign ushered in 'a socialistic form of Liberalism'.[78] Not quite all scholars, however, have taken this view. According to B. B. Gilbert, Lloyd George's land policies were not driven by a socialistic or anti-capitalist agenda – he was, after all, quite willing to value businessmen and the 'business' ethos.[79] But quite apart from this, the Budget land taxes and the Land Campaign were consistent with the long-running traditions of Liberal reformist discourse – a point made in Ian Packer's recent work.[80] They were not conceived as a punitive attack on property, but part of a longstanding crusade against privilege on behalf of the nation, and in this respect had much in common with earlier reform projects. Liberals themselves stressed this continuity. Some looked back to Mill, who had advocated an unearned increment tax in the 1860s.[81] Others emphasised links to more moderate reformist traditions, presenting the Land Campaign as the modern-day equivalent of Free Trade in Land.[82] It was a sustainable analogy. Both the Land Campaign and Free Trade in Land were directed at breaking down monopoly and privilege, and both were informed by the conviction that private property rights should be limited by the nation's stake in the soil and its proper use. MP for Cobden's old constituency of Rochdale, A. G. Harvey made this point well in a speech of September 1909. Presenting the land

---

77 See, for example, Churchill, *People's rights*, 116–17, and A. Mond, 'The increment tax', *NC* lxvi (1909), 377–80.
78 Emy, 'Land Campaign', 66.
79 B. B. Gilbert, 'David Lloyd George: the land, the Budget, and social reform', *American Historical Review* lccci (1976), 1058–9, 1061–2.
80 Packer, *Lloyd George, Liberalism and the land*.
81 'The commencement of the fulfilment of a promise which had been for nearly half a century an integral part of the Liberal programme': Masterman, in NLF, *Reports and proceedings*, 31st annual meeting, Southport, 1–2 July 1909, 61.
82 For example, Cobden-Unwin, *Land hunger*.

taxes as a modern-day answer to Cobden's 1864 call for Free Trade in Land, he declared that 'We in Rochdale ... have longed for the day when the land of this country should be recognized as the main asset and possession of the nation ... We have felt that we could so adjust matters that we could develop this great asset that belongs by common right to us all.' If the campaign for Free Trade in Land had sought to achieve this, so too – by different means – did the undeveloped land duty and the increment tax.[83]

In common with that of earlier land reform projects, the ideology of the Land Campaign denied the existence of absolute individual rights in real property, and Lloyd George made this quite explicit. As he emphasised at Bedford, landownership was about 'stewardship' in the public interest, entailing responsibilities – it could not simply be regarded as an investment like any other, or as a luxury for the enjoyment of the hunting-and-shooting plutocracy.[84] Landlords who did regard it in such a selfish manner would be subject to compulsion. In an article published just after the launch of the Land Campaign, Seebohm Rowntree made this clear. According to Rowntree, good landlords who 'look upon their land, not as their absolute property to be exploited solely for their personal profit and pleasure, but as a portion of the country which has been put into their keeping to be administered for the country's good' had nothing to fear. But those 'others who look upon the land as their absolute property, and ask: "cannot a man do what he likes with his own?"' were a different matter altogether: 'To such men the nation is justified in replying "No"'.[85] And in Liberal eyes, the existence of these bad landlords meant that the system of land ownership required more extensive control by the state, in order to ensure protection of the nation's rightful claims. This was the logic of the Land Campaign, which via the minimum wage and the powers vested in the new Ministry of Lands would ensure that labourers were afforded access to land and a good livelihood, farmers were given full compensation for improvements, sufficient land was available for housing and the soil was properly cultivated.

Liberals justified such interventionism not by appealing to any doctrines of equality, or by attacking capitalism as immoral; they simply repeated the familiar argument that land was different from other forms of property and hence was subject to different terms of ownership. As was the case during the Budget debates, Churchill was vociferous in making this point, and by so doing stressed the contrast between the Liberal and socialist positions. Speaking at Alexandra Palace on 15 November 1913, he provided an excellent summary of his party's thinking:

Socialism attacks wealth; Liberalism attacks monopoly. (Cheers.) Land, which is fixed in geographical position, which is strictly limited in extent,

83 F. W. Hirst, *Alexander Gordon Cummins Harvey: a memoir*, London 1926, 76.
84 *The Times*, 13 Oct. 1913, 13–14.
85 Rowntree, 'Rural land reform', 609–23.

which is a vital necessity of trade and industry, differs from all other forms of property ... The key to Liberal thought on social questions is found in the fact that we do not, and cannot, regard the land as if it were wholly or purely a private concern or a private possession. – (Cheers.) We regard it rather as a trust from the State to be used in the interests of the nation at large.[86]

In its insistence on the special nature of landed property and the 'national' inadmissibility of its absolute ownership, this was entirely consistent with longstanding Liberal and radical arguments.

The Land Campaigners' aim of bringing the system of landed property (back) into harmony with the interests of the nation was not in itself new. As this chapter has demonstrated, it had been championed in the 1880s and 1890s by advocates of Free Trade in Land, smallholdings legislation and land tenure reform; it could also claim a longer radical pedigree stretching back to Mill and the LTRA. But the Liberal party's leadership had not given its full support to any of these earlier projects, and insofar as the Land Campaign did enjoy this support, it certainly was a new departure, representing the culmination of pre-war Liberal thinking on landed property. However, culmination also implies continuity, and it was the case that the arguments used in relation to property rights were consistent with Liberal-radical ideological traditions, and indeed with the traditions of the party more generally. Given the task of writing the introduction to the Rural Land Enquiry Report, A. H .D. Acland had a good sense of these traditions and of the Land Campaign's faithfulness to them. Towards the end of his text, Acland sounded a stridently patriotic note, one that provided evidence of the survival of the nineteenth-century Liberal idea of patriotism as inclusive and opposed to sectional interests (like 'landlordism'), which were inimical to national harmony. The Liberal land policy, Acland asseverated,

> will come to be the policy of national patriotism ... We cannot afford to yield to the plea of the owner and occupier of older days in districts where the national welfare is being regulated 'I can do and will do what I like with my own'. There is a higher necessity constraining us and we owe it to posterity, without acting in haste or doing injustice, to take a broader view of the responsibility of the State in regard to this momentous problem ... It is to be hoped that we are not about to see the interest of the large owners and occupiers on the one hand set over against the interests of the labourers and Small Holders on the other. From the widest and most patriotic point of view their interests should be capable of being harmonised.[87]

In the late nineteenth and early twentieth centuries, Liberals' insistence that private property rights in land were limited by national considerations

---

[86] MG, 17 Nov. 1913, 12.
[87] *The land*, i, p. lix.

formed a key part of their language of agrarian patriotism. Even in the 1900s, however, this language steered clear of socialistic ideas; the claim that a man could not do what he liked with his own did not require recourse to any such ideas for its justification. For Liberals, the claims of the nation were quite sufficient.

PART II

LAND POLITICS AND VISIONS OF ENGLAND

6

The Liberals and Rural Englishness

> 'There can be no doubt that in late years there has been a very
> decided increase of general interest in history amongst us. The
> nature of political questions, and the tendency of thought about
> social questions, have given a decided impulse in this direction.
> In small towns and villages, historical subjects are among the most
> popular for lectures; and historical allusions are acceptable to all
> audiences': Mandell Creighton, 'The picturesque in history', in
> his *Historical lectures and addresses*, London 1903, 262.

The next three chapters deal with the patriotic visions of land and nation
that informed Liberal, Unionist and Labour responses to the land question.
These visions took various forms, ranging from idealisation of the 'good old
English squire', to the more radical myth of the sturdy yeoman proprietor,
to socialist conceptualisations of a 'merrie England' founded on equality
and personal freedom. There were marked differences between these visions
in terms of their ideological content, but one important common denominator stood out: though concerned with the future of the nation, all drew
heavily on its past. As Mandell Creighton, historian and bishop of London,
noted in his Royal Institution lecture of 1897, history played a prominent
part in contemporary political culture, and the important historical nature
of debate on the land question should be situated in this context.[1] The
language of land politics involved appeals to different versions of history
as a means of resisting or justifying reform. This was true in Ireland and
Scotland, where historicist readings of those countries' histories informed
the agitation leading to legislation like the 1886 Crofters' Act.[2] But it was
also true in England, where reformers called on the early-modern, medieval
or even Anglo-Saxon past in support of their policies, which in many cases
were presented as designed to restore lost or threatened continuities in the
English national *telos*.

In a sense, this use of history is unsurprising. In the later nineteenth
century there was what has been termed a 'historist reaction' to *a priori* modes

---

[1] For more on the importance of history in contemporary discourse see Readman, 'Place
of the past', 147–99.
[2] C. Dewey, 'Celtic agrarian legislation and the celtic revival: historicist implications of
Gladstone's Irish and Scottish land acts, 1870–1886', *P&P* lxiv (1974), 30–70.

of reasoning in political economy.[3] From the 1870s on, it was increasingly felt that many contemporary problems – how to explain the distribution of property in land for instance – could neither be understood nor solved in ways that were universally applicable: they could only be dealt with by relating them to the history of the nation under consideration.[4] Due greatly to Henry Maine's *Village communities in the east and west* (London 1871), this shift towards historicism in intellectual discourse had its analogue in practical politics. As the distinguished medieval historian Sir Paul Vinogradoff observed in his introduction to a volume of essays on *Villainage in England*, published in 1892, '[t]he influence of historical speculation on politics' was 'definite and direct':

> even the most devoted disciples of particular creeds, the most ardent advocates of reform or reaction dare not simply take up the high standing ground of abstract theory from which all political questions were discussed less than a hundred years ago: the socialist as well as the partisan of aristocracy is called on to make good his contention by historical arguments ... The facts can hardly be denied: the aspiration of our age is intensely historical; we are doing more for the relative than for the absolute, more for the study of evolution than for the elucidation of principles which do not vary.[5]

Here, Vinogradoff was responding to those politicians who drew upon the medieval past in the service of present-day politics, and, as he was probably aware, no aspect of politics provided more evidence in support of his statement than the land question. Of those politicians concerned with this issue, it was Liberals – radical Liberals especially – whose rural visions were most influenced by readings of both medieval history and the English national past more generally; and it is their visions with which this chapter starts. These visions of the rural past took two main forms. The first privileged Anglo-Saxon England, specifically its self-governing village communities and the land system that they administered. The second, and the more important, upheld a post-medieval but pre-enclosure England, a country of cottages and commons that existed before the poor were transformed from self-sufficient cultivators into a wage-receiving class of agricultural labourers.

Versions of a popular national past, I: Anglo-Saxon

Aspects of the Anglo-Saxon past had long been held in high regard in British cultural discourse. As Simon Keynes has recently shown, Alfred the Great

---

[3] A. W. Coats, 'The historist reaction in English political economy, 1870–90', *Economica* xxi (1954), 143–53.
[4] See, for example, J. E. Thorold Rogers, *The economic interpretation of history*, London 1888, ch. iii.
[5] P. Vinogradoff, *Villainage in England* (1892), Oxford 1968, 3.

had for hundreds of years been portrayed as a national hero – an example of virtue and good character for monarchs and men to follow.[6] His stock increased in value throughout the course of the nineteenth century and into the twentieth, with the thousandth anniversary (or millenary) of his death being commemorated in 1901.[7] However, while this feting of Alfred can tell us much about the significance of the English past at this time, it was largely confined to the cultural sphere. Perhaps because he functioned as such a powerful figure of patriotic consensus, being generally regarded as the 'founder of the English nation', Alfred was little invoked in late Victorian and Edwardian political debate. This was in marked contrast to the institutions of the pre-Conquest polity, pre-eminently the 'village community' with its communal system of landholding and its popular system of self-government (the 'folk-moot'). During the early and middle parts of Victoria's reign, the Anglo-Saxon village community and its appurtenances were much praised in popular history writing. Largely as a consequence of this, it was widely seen as demonstrating the antiquity of English liberty and representative government, both by upholders of the constitutional *status quo* and radical reformers who chafed at the 'Norman yoke'.[8]

Although the use made of Anglo-Saxon England in political discourse declined towards the end of the nineteenth century, this decline can be overemphasised. The medieval past in general, and the pre-Conquest past in particular, retained a significant presence in English political language in the 1880s and 1890s, and on into the Edwardian period. A key reason for this was the continuing popularity of favourable historical accounts of the Anglo-Saxon village community. Between 1880 and 1914, the books of J. R. Green, E. A. Freeman and William Stubbs, which idealised the political independence of this community, were repeatedly republished and attracted a wide readership. These works – especially those of Green and Freeman, which provided the most uncritical accounts – had a substantial impact on Liberal and radical opinion. So too did Maine's hugely influential *Village communities*, despite Maine's personal toryism and his own positively hostile attitude to the application of ancient principles of local government and landholding to present-day conditions.[9] For many reformers this body of scholarship provided a historically English vision of local government, one

---

[6] S. Keynes, 'The cult of King Alfred the Great', *Anglo-Saxon England* xxviii (1999), 225–328.
[7] In error, as it turned out: Alfred is now known to have died in 899.
[8] J. W. Burrow, *A Liberal descent: Victorian historians and the English past*, Cambridge 1981; C. Hill, 'The Norman yoke', in *Puritanism and revolution*, London 1958, 50–122, esp. pp. 109–20; E. F. Biagini, *Liberty, retrenchment and reform: popular Liberalism in the age of Gladstone, 1860–1880*, Cambridge 1996, 53–6.
[9] C. Dewey, 'Images of the village community: a study in Anglo-Indian ideology', *Modern Asian Studies* vi (1972), 303–4; J. W. Burrow, '"The village community" and the uses of history in late nineteenth-century England', in N. McKendrick (ed.), *Historical perspectives*, London 1974, 263–4.

that informed proposals for parish and district councils. For others, particularly readers of Maine and Green, the vision was societal rather than political or administrative in form, while at the same time being distinctively English in its own way. This vision centred on the communal land ownership supposedly prevalent in Anglo-Saxon times, and was upheld as an example from which modern legislators could draw inspiration.

Let us take, first of all, the question of rural local government. In the 1880s and early 1890s Liberal advocates of parish and district councils frequently made admiring reference to the Anglo-Saxon system of village administration. Drawing on the writings of Freeman and Stubbs, as well as more recent authors like Laurence Gomme,[10] they presented their proposals as inspired by this system, the spirit of which they sought to revive in modern England. By instituting elected councils, reformers sought to introduce a structure bearing some relation to what Foster called 'the old system' of popular village assemblies that had existed in the Anglo-Saxon past.[11] This system, Liberals and radicals still claimed, had been lost through the action of the Norman yoke: 'obliterated at the ... Conquest by the monarchical and aristocratic centralisation of the Feudal system', as Arch's *English Labourers' Chronicle* put it in 1889.[12] In their interpretation, an authoritarian method of rule (what Dilke called 'the French Feudal manor') had been imposed by a foreign invader and perpetuated through the centuries by the landed aristocracy. Alien to innately English conceptions of liberty, it depressed the spirit of local independence first embodied in the 'free institutions' of Anglo-Saxon England.[13] The Parish Councils Bill, H. H. Fowler explained in a speech to the Commons in 1893, 'was not a creation, it was a restoration of those principles of local self-government which are at the root of all free institutions, and which ... existed in this country in great force and freedom and efficiency many centuries ago'.[14] However, after the 1894 act, Liberal interest in local government reform faded away. The issue disappeared from the party's popular appeal, playing no significant role in the election campaigns of the Edwardian period.[15] A belief that continuity with the Anglo-Saxon spirit of local government had been restored to the nation was undoubtedly a factor in this. But the Anglo-Saxon past did not only enter political discourse through debates on parish and district councils: it was also present in the language of those who sought radical reform to the system of landholding.

---

[10] See G. L. Gomme, *Primitive folk-moots*, London 1880, and *The village community*, London 1890.
[11] *Hansard*, 3rd ser., 1891, ccclii. 567.
[12] *ELC*, 26 Jan. 1889, 1.
[13] Dilke at Chelsea and Halifax, *The Times*, 7 Oct. 1885, 10; 14 Oct. 1885, 7.
[14] *Hansard*, 4th ser., 1893, xviii. 1166.
[15] Readman, 'Patriotism and the general election of 1900', 98; Russell, *Landslide*, 65; Blewett, *Peers*, 317, 326.

Advocates of land tenure reform paid scant attention to the national past, Anglo-Saxon or otherwise. Rather, the patriotic dimension to their proposals took the form of a legitimating argument, largely based on legalistic precepts, that there existed a national interest in the soil that was superior to purely private considerations. On the whole, the same was also true of campaigners for Free Trade in Land, who as exponents of the virtues of proprietorship were understandably chary of endorsing the Anglo-Saxon system, which in its original form was apparently based on communal rather than individual ownership of land. It was a different story, however, for land nationalisers. While it is true that the LNS and the ELRL did justify their policies with reference to natural rights and legal concepts, they also turned to history for support. This was particularly true of the LNS's campaign in the 1890s, which invoked the Anglo-Saxon past to demonstrate that land was originally held in common and ideally should be in the future. In making this claim, Maine was often pressed into service. *Land and Labour* and LNS tracts printed extracts from his *Village communities*, quoting, for instance, a passage that dated the onset of 'the terrible problem of pauperism' from the time when 'the old English cultivating groups (in which land was collectively, and not privately, owned) began distinctly to fall to pieces'.[16] References to Maine also featured in the speeches of land nationalisers. Stepdaughter of John Stuart Mill and a leading figure in the LNS, Helen Taylor was one of those especially given to citing the writer. In a speech in 1891 she quoted Maine in support of her argument that

> The majority of the people of this country, from their birth to the grave, were [today] always in the position of trespassers on somebody else's land. There were some old towns of England in which the high roads and streets were still the property of the people, but it was not generally so. They had to buy the land on which those roads and streets from men who called themselves the owners of the land. This had not been so in their dear native land ... In old times England was scattered over with village communities who owned the land. These communities met periodically to decide how much these families could cultivate ... Round about the villages was the common land upon which the sheep and cattle grazed. No one had to pay for pasture in those days. Outside the village was the forest land, which also belonged to the people.[17]

However, while such evocations of the agrarian system of the ancient village community were certainly notable aspects of the language of radical land reform in the 1890s, their importance should not be exaggerated. Views like those of Taylor were largely confined to the political argument of land nationalisers; only occasionally did they crop up in statements of official Liberal party policy. Moreover, what influence they had had faded out by

16 LNS, *Opinions*, 7; *LL*, Jan. 1891, 4–5.
17 *LL*, May 1891, 9. See also *LL*, July 1891, 5.

the Edwardian period. Although such events as the King Alfred Millenary illustrated the continuing resonance of Anglo-Saxon England in the cultural life of the nation, the idealisation of its institutions had by this time almost entirely disappeared from the language of English politics. There were a number of reasons for this. It has already been noted that the introduction of parish and district councils was perceived to have realised the pre-Conquest ideal of local self-government: after 1894 this ideal necessarily served little purpose as inspiration for reform. A second reason was the demolition of the argument that the communal proprietorship of land, which allegedly prevailed in Anglo-Saxon England, had preceded its ownership by individuals. In his *Domesday Book and beyond* (1901), F. W. Maitland made a sustained claim for the existence of a 'core of individualism' in the ancient village community, arguing that it was absurd to assert the historical priority of group, or corporate, ownership of land: individual ownership by individual men obviously came first.[18] Widely accepted by contemporaries, Maitland's 'image of the village community', as Clive Dewey has written, 'rendered it unfit for use as radical propaganda': in the 1900s land reformers had to look elsewhere for inspirational visions.[19]

Versions of a popular national past, II: the pre-enclosure vision

One place that they looked, or rather continued to look, was at pre-enclosure England. Throughout the period, Liberal-radical political discourse drew upon an idealised vision of the early-modern countryside. A landscape of cottages and commons, it represented an alternative historical locus of the *quondam* village community. Democratic in character, this was a vision that celebrated the 'full, abundant, and self-sufficient' lifestyle enjoyed by ordinary rural people before the descent, in more recent times, of 'the paralysing and desolating hand of the landlord'.[20] The villagers in this imagined 'old England' had considerable control over their own affairs, and although this independence did not take the form of outright self-government it fostered a vigorously popular community life. A crucial driver of this community vitality was popular access to the soil, either by way of common rights, the possession of a plot of land, or both. As Harcourt told parliament in a debate on the Parish Councils Bill, even the cottagers of Elizabethan England benefited from a law entitling them to allotments, and he read out the text of the original statute to prove his point.[21] Indeed, reformers frequently portrayed the pre-enclosure past as a time when the man without land was an aberration, a deviation from the norm – 'outside the universal system of English

---

[18] Burrow, '"Village community"', 282–3; Dewey, 'Images', 324–6.
[19] Dewey, 'Images', 327.
[20] R. Russell, *First conditions of human prosperity*, London 1904, 116.
[21] *Hansard*, 4th ser., 1894, xx. 1055.

life', as James Thorold Rogers, professor of political economy and Liberal MP, described them in one of his Oxford lectures of 1887–8.[22]

For many critics of the modern system of landholding, the access to land that had existed in the past, when soil was held in common, was a positive social good. In their eyes, the pre-enclosure past was genuinely representative of that time idealised by Goldsmith (whom they were fond of quoting) as one 'ere England's griefs began, / When every rood of ground maintained its man'. A nation of self-sufficient smallholders, the English people had then been happily prosperous in their unsophisticated independence. The comparatively modern problems of pauperism and unemployment were as yet unknown to this 'race of freemen'.[23] The primary reason for this, reformers believed, was the existence of commons. These expanses of heath and forest were essential to the survival of smallholders and cottagers, who supplemented the production of their own plots of land by making use of their ancient rights to gather fuel and pasture their livestock. 'In the old days', Chamberlain explained in one of his speeches before the 1885 election,

> There were immense tracts of waste and common land all over the country ... The poor people had rights over these commons – they were able to get fuel, they were able to cut turf, they were able to support sometimes a cow, sometimes it was geese or poultry, and in that way they were able to add to their small increases, and they made altogether a tolerable livelihood.[24]

However, as Chamberlain was at pains to stress in his 1885 campaign, the eighteenth- and early nineteenth-century enclosure movement had extinguished these common rights and the independent if simple livelihood they supported, with disastrous effects on the nation.[25]

Many other reformers shared this perspective, giving voice to it both during the tumultuous debates of 1885 and in later years. In doing so, they presented a narrative of national dispossession: sanctioned by the acts of aristocratic parliaments, millions of acres had been enclosed, allegedly in the name of agriculture and the public interest, but actually the sole beneficiaries were the great landowners themselves. In one of his impassioned speeches, made at the height of the 'three acres and a cow' agitation of the mid-1880s, the radical Liberal clergyman and champion of rural reform William Tuckwell vividly summarised this sad story of national dispossession:

> There was a time in England ... when two-thirds of the people owned land. Then there was no pauperage, no vagabondage, and no unemployed. But the aristocracy got into their hands the making of the laws, and they crushed out

22 Thorold Rogers, *Economic interpretation*, 295.
23 For example, Tuckwell, *Reminiscences*, 9–10; *LM*, July 1907, 74; *LP*, Nov. 1888, 82; and F. Impey, *Small holdings in England*, London 1909, 11–12.
24 *The Times*, 10 Nov. 1885, 10.
25 *Chamberlain's speeches*, i. 142.

the small holder by manorial rights, and threw the small farms into big ones; and eight million acres of common land, on which the poor man could feed his cow and pig, and grow and dig his potatoes, and cut his fuel, were swept, without compensation, into the high landowners' hands, and now the land of England was in the hands of 360,000 men.[26]

This narrative of disinheritance was often taken up by Liberal propaganda as a stick with which to beat the Conservatives, whom it naturally cast in the guise of the landlords' party. Publications ranging from ASHA's *Land and People* to the official *Liberal Magazine* drew their readers' attention to 'the miserable story of enclosures', the clear moral of which was the need for land reform. It was a story that Liberal politicians themselves also retailed, often with considerable brio. In the Harborough division of Lincolnshire, J. W. Logan described the robbery of commons over the centuries by 'Baron Privilege' in the political literature he aimed at his constituents.[27] Herbert Samuel, a keen land reformer in the 1890s and 1900s, did similarly.[28] As candidate for Henley at the Khaki election of October 1900, Samuel set forth an alternative brand of patriotism to the imperial bluster of the Tories, who had been seeking to exploit the Boer War (then thought to be drawing to a victorious conclusion) for their electoral benefit. As demonstrated by one of his election leaflets, Samuel's patriotism could be described as one of agrarian little Englandism, with one of its focal points being the 'lost common':

> Vote for RED – the bright British scarlet,
>   The red that the Tories abhor,
> For SAMUEL will help keep our Empire,
>   Tho' he's not always mad for a war.
>
> Look at home at the barbed wire fences,
>   Enclosing both path and field!
> Think of Commons now lost to your children,
>   These are crops that the Tories yield.
>
> Then Hurrah for the RED and for SAMUEL!
>   Hurrah for the freedom we boast!
> We'll get SAMUEL in, and we don't care a pin,
>   For the Blues and the landlord host.[29]

---

26 *ELC*, 30 June 1885, 5.
27 *LL*, Feb. 1901, 20–2.
28 *Henley and South Oxfordshire Standard*, 28 May 1897, 8.
29 'A tip for Friday, Oct. 5, 1900: the general election stakes', political papers of Herbert, first viscount Samuel, HLRO, A/13/3.

The long shadow of enclosure

In their speeches, writings and propaganda, many reformers presented an unrealistically roseate picture of village life under the common field system, and many also indulged in a good deal of rhetorical posturing when it came to describing the negative effects of enclosure. But while certainly over-blown, their rhetoric was far from empty; it addressed a deep-seated sense of injustice that was felt by intellectual, middle-class Liberal opinion, but also by the ordinary people of rural England, who nurtured their own historical grievances. In short, the appeal to the history and pre-history of enclosure resonated with a wide section of English public opinion, which did much to contribute to its strength as political language. How can this be explained?

First of all, it is important to understand that the enclosure of commons was still continuing in the late nineteenth and early twentieth centuries – albeit on a vastly reduced scale compared to what had gone before. For Liberals convinced of the iniquity of stealing the 'people's land', or simply of the wisdom of preserving open spaces that might provide opportunities for healthful recreation, enclosure was seen as a threat to be faced in the here-and-now, not just an episode in the nation's history. The measures passed to protect commons from enclosure such as the 1876 Commons Act and the Repeal of the Statute of Merton in 1893 effectively put a stop to proposals for large-scale enclosures, but attempts on a small scale continued, many taking the form of illegal encroachments by landlords. In 1910 Shaw Lefevre estimated that the CPS typically received about a hundred complaints regarding such cases each year.[30]

The complaints thus received reflected local-level grievances. Although it is difficult to determine exactly what ordinary rural people actually thought, it is evident that in mobilising grass-roots opposition to enclosure, preservationists drew on a well of popular feeling that reached down deep into local communities. Eli Hamshire, a carrier turned village agitator from Ewhurst, near Guildford, gave voice to this feeling in his populist tract, *The source of England's greatness*, an authentic statement of working-class rural radicalism. In it he railed against recent encroachments and attempted encroachments on commons in his locality, contrasting this with the difficulty ordinary people had in gaining any access to land for their own use:

> One man has enclosed the church tow-path in our little parish; and at Cran-leigh one man who owns thousands of acres enclosed the Goose-green, and an old farm labourer chopped the posts and rails down. In the parish of Wonersh there is a large piece of land added to the park, and there were a few working men who applied for a piece of land, and they were told the land was in chancery. The parishes, Cranleigh and Wonersh, belong to the same lord of

---

[30] Shaw Lefevre, *Commons*, 214–15.

the manor. You see, these men who have abundance of land could enclose it if it was in chancery, but the working man can't get a rod of ground.[31]

But leaving aside such testimonies of popular grievance, it is in any case clear that disputes over commons frequently arose when ordinary people sought to assert or protect their traditional rights over the land, so drawing the attention and support of the nationwide commons preservation campaign. In 1889, for example, a series of 'stormy public meetings' prompted the CPS to intervene in the case of Great Torrington Commons, Devonshire, upon which local people felt illegitimate encroachments had been made. The intervention of the society led to the passage of an act to protect the commons, under which the land was vested in a body of fifteen locally elected conservators. Of the thirty-one individuals who stood for election to the office of conservator, at least twenty were working-class.[32]

The extent of local hostility to modern-day threats to common land had much to do with the folk-memory of enclosure, which retained a strong presence in the collective consciousness of many rural localities. Touring Suffolk in 1891, ELRL 'red van' activists discovered that those of their lectures which drew on local grievances regarding the enclosure of particular commons proved notably effective, even though the commons in question had been lost many years ago. As the League's official report observed, despite the passage of time, '[t]he tradition still however survives that these lands once belonged to the people, but by some trick they have been filched away'.[33] This 'tradition' of popular dispossession was remarked upon by other Liberal and radical commentators, who were doubtless happy to see that their political agenda resonated with the viewpoint of ordinary country people, and not just idealistic intellectuals and the public-spirited middle class. There was also no doubt that the popular tale of disinheritance through enclosure was subject to some romantic embellishment in its telling.[34] But recourse to purple prose should not lead us to underestimate the level of grass-roots grievance at past injustices. As two men of letters with some claim of access to the authentic voice of contemporary rural England, George Sturt and Edward Thomas provide further evidence of the long shadow cast by enclosure. Describing an encounter with one of his rustic interlocutors, Sturt (a wheelwright, whose own village was enclosed in 1861) related how the old labourer 'point[ed] to the woods, which could be seen from the valley', and '[s]aid spitefully, while his eyes blazed: "I can remember when all that was open common, and you could go where you mind to. Now 'tis all fenced in,

---

[31] A carrier's boy [Eli Hamshire], *The source of England's greatness and the source of England's poverty*, 4th edn, Ewhurst 1892, in D. Stemp (ed.), *Three acres and a cow: the life and works of Eli Hamshire*, Cheam 1995, 89.
[32] G. M. Roe, 'Great Torrington Commons', *Report and Transactions of the Devonshire Association for the Advancement of Science, Literature, and Art* xxxi (1899), 162–3, 169.
[33] ELRL, *Special Report, 1891*, 12.
[34] See, for example, J. T. K. Tarpey, cited in Cobden Unwin, *Land hunger*, 77–8.

and if you look over the fence they'll lock ye up. And they en't got no more *right* to it ... than you and me have! I should *like* to see they woods all go up in flames!"[35] In *The heart of England*, Thomas recounted a similar conversation with an elderly wayside tramp, who also felt cut off from his native country and its landscape – indeed he considered himself an Englishman possessed of as little liberty as the subjugated natives of the empire. As Thomas reported him saying,

> There are not enough sticks in this wood to warm the only man that wants them. I suppose they use all the firing to keep the pheasants warm. Hark at them! If I were a rich man I wouldn't keep such birds ... England is not such a place it was when I was a young man. It is not half the size for one thing. Why, when I was a young man, you could go up a lane with a long dog or two and pick up a bit of supper and firing and nothing said. The country seemed to belong to me in those days, but now I might as well be in Africa.[36]

By playing on this popular sense of loss, Liberals and radicals could forge strong populist appeals, and there is little doubt that these redounded to their benefit in election campaigns. But while useful as ammunition for rhetorical assaults on 'the landlord's party', the heritage of dispossession bequeathed to the English rural poor by enclosure also served a more specific function. In the interpretation of many reformers, it was compelling evidence of an historical wrong that modern legislators were beholden to right. For Frederic Impey, honorary secretary of AHSA and an influential voice throughout the period, the fact that the poor had been given so little compensation for the loss of their commons established 'an unanswerable reason for the interference with our land system, on behalf of the class who have suffered most from its effects'.[37] Measures for the provision of allotments and smallholdings, which Impey and others advocated, were conceived not as class legislation in any socialistic sense but restitution for the past crime of enclosure, which greedy landlords had perpetrated on an innocent nation. Their promulgation was thus a patriotic act – something that should be 'the highest privilege of all who love their country to help in bringing about'.[38]

This rhetoric of national restitution emerged as a major element of land reform discourse in the mid-1880s, around the time of Chamberlain and Collings's 'Radical programme'. A key reason for this was franchise reform. Radicals had long connected the crime of enclosure to the incompleteness of British democracy. Lacking representation in a House of Commons consisting largely of landlords, the people of the countryside had been powerless to prevent the abrogation of their ancient rights. In a debate on the 1884

---

[35] Cited in K. D. M. Snell, *Annals of the labouring poor: social change and agrarian England, 1660–1900*, Cambridge 1985, 227.
[36] E. Thomas and H. L. Richardson, *The heart of England*, London 1906, 36.
[37] F. Impey, *Three acres and a cow*, new edn, London 1887, 6–8.
[38] Ibid. 24.

Reform Bill, Chamberlain thrust this argument before parliament, causing uproar on the Tory benches:

> What has happened in consequence of the agricultural labourers not having a voice in this House? They have been robbed of their land. (Cries of 'No, no!', and 'Withdraw!') I repeat that they have been robbed of their land ('Prove it!') They have been robbed of their rights in the commons. ('No, no!') They have been robbed of their open spaces – ('No, no!') ... The agricultural labourers are still being robbed ('No, no!').[39]

The widespread post-Third Reform Act belief that Britain was a democracy gave agrarian radicals an opening to exploit. That the national good could now be defined in far more popular terms added force to the case for restitution. Because parliament would in future be elected on a 'democratic' franchise, it was much harder to equate the interests of landlords with those of the nation, as had apparently been done when the commons were enclosed. Conservatives alleged that the measures radicals proposed amounted to expropriation, but their objections drew the response – from Arch, Chamberlain and others – that it was the great landowners who were the original expropriators. Well might the Tories raise the cry of 'confiscation', Arch told a Suffolk audience in 1884, but they forgot that

> The landlord had stolen eight millions of acres of ... common lands – (hear, hear, and cheering) – that was not confiscation; oh, no! (Laughter and cheers.) They [the landlords] made laws for themselves when the people could not alter them ... Under this *regime* no less than 3,784 Commons Enclosure Bills were passed, and they could see, when the democracy of England wielded the helm of the ship instead of the aristocracy, whether the democracy would not demand that these eight million acres should not be disgorged and given to the people again. (Hear, hear, and cheering.)[40]

If he believed in his own rhetoric, Arch was to be disappointed: although it gave the vote to the agricultural labourer, the 1884 Reform Act was not immediately followed by the popular reappropriation of enclosed commons, or indeed any measures of restitution for their loss.

Despite this, the conception of land reform as restitution for enclosure survived. Initially, it was sustained by the fact that most Liberal land reformers remained loyal to Gladstone after the Home Rule split of 1886. Chamberlain and Collings might have left the party, but other prominent figures remained, among them Arch, Impey, Carrington, Channing and Foster. Most had strong connections with the Allotments Extension Association, which played an important role at a time when the agricultural trade unionism of the ALU was slowly dying out. Through the association's newspaper and the periodic conferences it organised, much was done to keep the rhetoric of restitution

---

39 *Hansard*, 3rd ser., 1884, cclxxxvi. 956.
40 *ELC*, 12 Apr. 1884, 2.

alive.[41] Aside from these relatively moderate Liberal reformers, there were the land nationalisers, whose evocation of a pre-enclosure golden age went hand in hand with a clearly restitutive agenda. This agenda is obvious from the declared aims of the land nationalisation organisations. While one made its goal evident in its title ('The English Land *Restoration* League'), the other (the LNS) enshrined the commitment 'to restore the Land to the People, and the People to the Land' as its official object. The propaganda of both groups, and particularly that of the LNS, put forward the idea that landlords had robbed the people in the past, very often by means of enclosures sanctioned by a self-serving parliament. In his 1892 tract, *The land as national property*, Francis William Newman – classical scholar, vice-president of the LNS and Cardinal Newman's brother – indicted 'the class of English landlords' as one which had grievously abused its power of legislation, using that power to commit enormous fraud on the *nation* – fraud for which it is high time to call it to account'.[42] Many other pamphlets and leaflets followed a similar line, relating in stirring language how the 'national heritage' in the land had been unjustly appropriated and insisting that it now needed to be 'restored' to its rightful owners.[43]

As Wallace argued in an 1894 essay, the restoration of this heritage through land nationalisation would be 'just and merciful restitution' for past wrongs inflicted upon the poor and hence an important work of social justice.[44] This was an image of social justice strongly coloured by patriotic feeling. While there was certainly an *a priori* rationale for nationalisation, in which it was presented as a societal good in itself, there was also a more emotively nationalist rationale at play too, centring on historic rights. In this interpretation, many of the time-honoured liberties enjoyed by ordinary people had been lost, and their reassertion in modern form was a patriotic imperative. Once the common had been stolen, one LNS pamphleteer explained, 'the sunshine of the labourer's life' was eclipsed. As a result, 'A dark cloud now hangs over him; and an almost joyless life of hopeless toil, poverty and dependence, ending in a pauper's grave, is only too often his fate. Men of England, as you love your country, as you love your homes, as you wish your name to be for ever blessed by future generations, you must regain your birthright.'[45] The enclosures that had taken place in years past were held to have violated the national interest in the land. 'Simple robbery ... done ... under false pretences', they amounted to unpatriotic impositions on truly English

---

[41] See, for example, speech of Foster in ASHA, *Public meeting at Bridgwater*, London 1890, 4.

[42] Newman, *Land as national property*, 16 [emphasis in original].

[43] For example, LNS, *Property and the land question*, London 1892, 2; *Programme*; and *To landless Britons*, 2–3; and Price-Heywood, *Land monopoly*, 16–18.

[44] A. R. Wallace, 'Economic and social justice', in A. Reid (ed.), *Vox clamantium*, London 1894, 188–9.

[45] C. Wicksteed, *Village politics and cottage farms*, London n.d., 8.

traditions, 'innovations upon the national heritage in the soil ... which a spirit of true conservatism should lead patriotic men to attack'.[46]

Edwardian apotheosis

Tirelessly propounded by Liberal reformers and land nationalisers throughout the 1890s, the rhetoric of restitution achieved its apotheosis in the Edwardian period, more particularly in the years between the Conservative party's landslide election defeat in 1906 and the outbreak of the First World War. Liberals now agreed, as Carrington put it in advance of the passage of the 1907 Smallholdings Bill, that 'the present state of affairs was less favourable in many respects than in the 18th century before the commons were enclosed'.[47] Although enclosure might have increased agricultural productivity, they believed that it had done so at unacceptable cost: the system of large farms worked by degraded, demoralised wage-labourers – which enclosure had facilitated – represented a departure from national traditions, being 'foreign to the habits and genius of the people in the past'.[48]

Thus the land legislation of the new Liberal government was presented as an attempt to correct the mistakes of history, to restore to the nation 'something of the England of yore' (in Campbell-Bannerman's phrase).[49] In his preface to the Liberal party's handbook to the workings of the 1907 Smallholdings Act, Carrington articulated the official line when he described the measure as a 'remedy' for the effects of enclosure.[50] As previously, this language of restitution served an important rhetorical purpose in providing Liberals with a useful tool for rebutting Conservative claims that they were wedded to an expropriating socialistic agenda. In an important speech in April 1907, Campbell-Bannerman indicated that far from being 'confiscatory' revolutionaries heedless of English history or traditions, Liberals were patriots alive to the necessity of rebuilding a lost sense of continuity with the national past. Far from being 'destroyers', the prime minister explained, the government were in fact 'restorers' whose goal it was to undo 'the crystallized evils of generations' by returning to the people their right to cultivate the soil of their country. In any case, he told his audience, landlords would receive a fair price for land acquired from them under the terms of the Smallholdings Act. Explicitly invoking the idea of a heritage of dispossession bequeathed

---

46 A. R. Wallace, My life, new edn, London 1908, 80, 83; LNS, A parliamentary candidate's catechism, London 1892, 1; Jameson, 'Land monopoly', 154–71 at p. 171.
47 The Times, 22 Apr. 1907, 13.
48 Impey, Small holdings, 11–12. See also, for example, LM xv (1907), 322–3, and C. R. Buxton, 'Small holdings: the English bill', Albany Review i (1907), 368.
49 Liberal Publication Department, Case for dissolution, 12.
50 Carrington, preface to C. Grant, The small holdings and allotments handbook, Bristol 1908, pp. vi–vii.

to the nation by the enclosure movement, he joked that it was not as if his party proposed 'to steal anybody's belongings, not even a goose from off the common, still less the common from under the goose'.[51]

But Liberals did not simply deploy this sort of language as a rhetorical device, an effective means of disavowing expropriatory intent. Neither did their use of it merely reflect a desire to shore up mass support in the shires. It can be argued that its use also reflected policy on the land question: party members' reading of the history of enclosure gave ideological impetus to proposed reforms, not least those of the Land Campaign. Not all historians would agree with this, however. In the interpretation of Avner Offer, the Land Campaign was informed by a Benthamite agenda, with Lloyd George seeking to improve the operation of the market through government intervention.[52] But while Offer has a point insofar as the Liberals had no desire radically to increase government spending, and certainly regarded their proposals as conducive to 'business' and economic efficiency, the description is a misleading one. To be sure, Edwardian Liberals had not abandoned economic liberalism for socialistic collectivism, but their agrarian reform programme drew more heavily on history than it did on abstract political economy.

As in the 1880s and 1890s, when scholarly commentary on the Anglo-Saxon past had exerted considerable influence, the historical dimension to Liberal thinking on the land question owed much to history writing. Towards the end of the nineteenth century historians began to move away from chronicling the constitutional development of the country, the course of wars and the deeds of monarchs, instead paying more attention to the history of the 'common people'. This shift in emphasis was initiated by J. R. Green, whose popular focus proved especially congenial to Liberal and radical opinion. Of those historians who followed Green's example, many advanced new interpretations of the enclosure movement and its societal effects. In the light of the well-documented evidence of the hardship it caused to the rural poor, they drew conclusions at variance with the older assumption that enclosure had been necessary for 'progress'. Three books were of particular significance here: Gilbert Slater's *English peasantry and the enclosure of common fields*, W. Hasbach's *History of the English agricultural labourer*, and J. L. and Barbara Hammond's *Village labourer*.[53] All these books portrayed enclosure in an unambiguously negative light and all exerted considerable influence over Liberal policy.

A future president of Ruskin College, Slater had strong connections to Liberal and radical circles and in 1912 became a leading member of Lloyd

---

[51] *The Times*, 22 Apr. 1907, 13.
[52] Offer, *Property*, 376.
[53] G. Slater, *The English peasantry and the enclosure of common fields*, London 1907; W. Hasbach, *A history of the English agricultural labourer*, London 1908 [1894]; J. L. Hammond and B. Hammond, *The village labourer*, London 1911.

George's Land Enquiry Committee, contributing a twenty-page 'Historical outline of land ownership in England' to its report. His 1907 book, which he hoped would inspire land policy, carried an admiring introduction by Carrington which suggested that this hope was not misplaced. 'The enclosure of common fields, and the passing away of the English Village Community to make room for the agricultural organisation prevailing today', Carrington averred, 'is a subject not merely of historical interest, but one which touches very closely some of the most vital national problems of the twentieth century.'[54] Slater's work was supplemented by Hasbach's *History*, which was first published in English in 1908 (having originally appeared in German in 1894). An erudite volume, the book provided plentiful evidence of the harm wrought by enclosure, as well as detailed treatment of life in the pre-enclosure village, which was described in favourable terms.[55] Liberals were particularly drawn to Hasbach's view that there was a greater level of community and less rigid divisions between social classes before the commons were lost. This claim was taken on board in the Land Enquiry's *Rural report*, which called on Hasbach's authority to argue for the need to re-institute the social gradation in rural society that had existed before enclosure, so as to provide 'a ladder' by which a labourer 'may have a chance of rising'.[56]

Of the three books, however, it was the Hammonds's *Village labourer* that had most impact. Published in 1911, it described the growth of the territorial control of the landed elite, paying special attention to enclosure and its effects. Like Slater and Hasbach, the Hammonds described enclosure as destructive of the socially harmonious and self-sufficient village community, and provided plenty of documentary evidence in support of their claims. Unlike them, however, their argument was put forward in stirringly passionate language that drew a strong emotional response from Liberal readers, among them leading land reformers like C. R. Buxton and Charles Trevelyan.[57] The following passage, dealing with the effects of enclosure, is a typical example:

> The governing class killed by this policy [enclosure] the spirit of a race. The petitions that are buried with their brief and unavailing pathos in the *Journals* of the House of Commons are the last voice of village independence, and the unnamed commoners who braved the dangers of resistance to send their protests to the House of Commons that obeyed their lords, were the last of the English peasants. These were the men, it is not unreasonable to believe, whom Gray had in mind when he wrote:- 'Some village Hampden that with dauntless breast / The little tyrant of his fields withstood.'[58]

---

54 Carrington, preface to Slater, *English peasantry*, p. xi.
55 See esp. Hasbach, *History*, 107–16.
56 *The land*, i. 154–61; cf. Hasbach, *History*, esp. p. 76.
57 Clarke, *Liberals*, 158.
58 Hammond and Hammond, *Village labourer*, 104.

Recognising the potential appeal of this sort of thing, Liberal and radical land reformers made much use of extracts from the *Village labourer* in their propaganda. The book was cited and quoted in leaflets distributed by the Committee for the Taxation of Land Values and the Central Land and Housing Council, in articles published in the *Liberal Monthly* and elsewhere, and in the Land Enquiry Report, to mention just some examples.

Schooled by Slater, Hasbach and the Hammonds, Liberals made extensive reference to enclosure during the Land Campaign. The agricultural minimum wage, improved access to land, better housing provision and so on were all presented as making amends for historical injustice. In his introduction to the Land Enquiry Report, Acland leaned heavily on history to justify the Liberal proposals. Drawing on Arthur Young and other historical sources, he claimed that before the maelstrom of enclosure, 'two of the most characteristic features of English village life ... were the large numbers of small men with rights of their own, and the gradation of village life from cottager to small holder, and small holder to farmer'.[59] Reiterated by Slater in his 'Historical outline',[60] this view held that the commons had supported a cohesive social structure, which in its turn fostered both independence and community belonging; and it was their loss that had led to social fragmentation, the economic and moral degradation of the poor and the accretion of tyrannical power in the hands of landlords, the effect of which was to deepen the miasma of dependence and drudgery in which the English countryside was sunk. At Bedford, Lloyd George painted this picture of historical injustice in vivid colours:

> The workman is worse off than he used to be. There was a time when he had an interest of his own in the land – a freehold interest. The labourer was a freeholder in the land. He had his common (cheers); there he could graze a cow that would give him milk and butter for himself and his children. There was a little patch where he could raise corn to feed them. There he had his poultry, his geese, his pigs; a patch of land where he could raise green produce for the table. He was a gentleman; he was independent. He had a stake in the country. His title was as ancient and apparently as indefensible as that as the lord of the manor. Where had it gone to? Stolen. Landlord Parliaments have annexed Naboth's vineyard. There is now occasionally a little garden. Sometimes as a matter of grace there is a little row of potatoes. But he has no longer a right in the soil, as his fathers had. He has been converted from a contented, well-fed, independent peasant to a hopeless, under-paid, landless drudge on the soil. His wages are less to-day in proportion to their purchasing capacity than they were in the reign of Henry VII.[61]

Here, the moral of Lloyd George's story was that the proposed minimum

---

[59] *The land*, i, pp. xxvi–xxviii.
[60] Ibid. i, pp. lxi–lxxxiii.
[61] *The Times*, 13 Oct. 1913, 13.

wage and the other measures of the Land Campaign were at least some recompense for the theft of the commons. It was a moral that was endlessly repeated by Liberal propagandists throughout 1913–14, who made much of the 'crime' of enclosure (to the extent of preparing lists of enclosures made in each county in England, cheaply published in pamphlet form).[62]

Reform, modernity and the English past

In a typically impassioned speech to his Battersea constituents during the 1906 general election campaign, the 'Lib-Lab' MP John Burns contrasted what he saw as the debased, modern-day imperial patriotism of the Conservatives with his own patriotic vision of an older, pastoral England. 'He was no frothy Imperialist, or pot-house Jingo', Burns told the cheering crowd; rather,

> He would go to Parliament ... for the England that Chaucer exalted in song, that Milton ennobled in verse, and that Shakespeare glorified in immortal play, for an England of green fields and healthy peasants, for an England that would care more about the peasant than the pheasant – (laughter) – for an England with more cottages in the country and less slums in the city, for an England the citadel of labour and the centre of freedom, for the England that King Arthur inspired and that King Alfred consecrated with his life, for the England of the old yeomen farmers who loved their country because she provided them with fields out of which they could get short hours and good remuneration – the England of the golden age before Imperialism had wasted its substance and prostituted its strength.[63]

At one level, this was mere electioneering rhetoric, designed to rally popular support with high-sounding phrases. Indeed, despite his references to 'green fields', 'healthy peasants' and 'yeomen farmers', Burns was to disappoint land reformers during his time at the Local Government Board between 1905 and 1914 when he proved notably hostile to 'land colonisation' schemes for unemployed workmen and their families.[64] That said, his words did illustrate how Liberals called on a ruralised conception of the national past, one by which they often suggested their land reform proposals were inspired. This raises questions about Liberal attitudes to modernity. Was their frequent recourse to idealised visions of *quondam* rural England a function of a backward-looking, reactionary mindset at odds with the increasingly urban-industrial present? If so, it might well be argued that the language of Liberal land reformers provided a political counterpart to the retrogressive ruralism that some say dominated English cultural discourse at this time.

---

[62] For example, *Homeland*, 6 June 1914, 142; CLHC leaflets; and 'The story of the enclosures', *LM*, June 1914, 16.

[63] *DN*, 8 Jan. 1906, 8.

[64] Harris, *Unemployment*, 142, 191–3, 197.

Now, leaving aside the question of ruralism in English culture (which was probably less retrogressive than has been claimed),[65] Liberal invocation of the rural past did not denote hostility to modernity, or any desire to effect a return to the conditions of life that existed in the pre-industrial past. While it is undeniable that many reformers admired certain aspects of the pre-industrial past (the common-field system, for instance), very few promoted the physical resumption of old-fashioned agricultural techniques. Campaigners for Free Trade in Land to advocates of land nationalisation insisted that small-scale agriculture was economically viable, being as compatible with modern methods of efficient production, like automated machinery and chemical fertilisers, as a system based on large farms.[66] This was a claim made with good reason, as the assessments of non-partisan contemporary experts and a number of modern-day economic historians would suggest.[67] It was also borne out by the simple fact that fairly sizeable numbers of small farms still existed: as Mick Reed has shown, in seventeen agricultural counties in 1885 over two-thirds of holdings were less than fifty acres in extent, and even by 1911 in only two of these counties did the average holding exceed one hundred acres.[68] Although small-scale cultivation was far less extensive than on the continent, 'peasant' farming had not died out in Britain by the late nineteenth century; and its renewal through reform was thus by no means a necessarily impracticable suggestion.

In common with Unionist reformers, Liberals and radicals backed their arguments up by referring to contemporary practice in other European countries. The veteran backbencher F. A. Channing is a case in point. While Channing looked to the past for inspiration, he also looked outwards to the continent, feeling – like Collings – that the modern agricultural methods adopted by small farmers elsewhere in Europe had much to recommend them. As he observed in 1907, the smallholders of Denmark employed the latest agricultural innovations, ranging from scientific methods of farm stock selection to co-operative systems of supply and distribution. At a time when Danish ham was appearing in ever-increasing quantities in British shops, Channing's admiration verged on awe: 'every invention is brought into play [by the Danes]', he affirmed. 'Your little Dane with his forty acres, actually has his own telephone at 56s. a year, and thus has his finger at any minute on

[65] Cf. Wiener, English culture; Mandler, '"Against Englishness"'; Readman, 'Landscape preservation'.

[66] For example, A. Arnold, 'Free land and peasant proprietary', NC vii (1880), 304–6, 311–16; Samuel, 'Village of the future', 394–5; and Pedder, 'Without house or home', 78.

[67] J. Thirsk, Alternative agriculture, Oxford 1997, 209–10; H. Levy, Large and small holdings (1904), Cambridge 1911, 102–13; J. L. Van Zanden, 'The first green revolution: the growth of production and productivity in European agriculture, 1870–1914', EcHR xliv (1991), 228–38.

[68] M. Reed, 'Nineteenth-century rural England: a case for "peasant studies"', Journal of Peasant Studies xiv (1986), 85.

the pulse of the market in his own capital, and in London too! He nicks in with his produce at the right minute and scores his modest and continuous profit.'[69]

Within the Liberal party, support for agricultural innovation was not confined to advocates of smallholdings, of course. It also extended to proponents of land tenure reform. Founder member of the Farmers' Alliance, William E. Bear, was one such individual. The modernity of Bear's agricultural vision is nicely illustrated by his *Agricultural Rip Van Winkle* (1893), a Utopian description of a rural England of the future. Disappointed with the inadequate progress of land reform, its protagonist is put to sleep by a fairy queen. When he awakes, he sees a boy sitting on a gate to a freshly sown field, upon which a large flock of rooks are swarming. He ticks the boy off for neglecting his bird-scaring duties. But the boy replies that because the seeds are soaked in a 'patent rook-disguster' the birds now help the farmer by eating insect pests. Released by technological advance from the tedious chore of chasing rooks, the child is reading a book on physiology, so that he will be able to become a stock manager on a co-operative farm. Like other budding farmers, he has to pass a technical examination in this and other subjects, such as agricultural chemistry and mechanics. Agriculture, in Bear's utopia, is a technological industry: as his protagonist discovers later in the book, inventions like electric threshing machines and manure-spreaders are commonplace.[70]

Channing's and Bear's endorsement of modern methods of agriculture illustrates how Liberals did not desire any wholesale return to the conditions of former times. Rather, they sought to restore and maintain valued continuities with the English past, an aim that they presented in nationalistic terms. Liberal proposals for local government and land reform were conceived in similar terms. In advocating the reform of local administration in the counties, Liberals described their plans as 'follow[ing] the ancient historical lines of free local government in this country', as Dilke put it in 1885.[71] However, they did not envisage reincarnating pre-Conquest structures of local government and imposing them incongruously on modern England. Liberal dedication to what one MP called 'building up our new system of national local government upon the lines of our Saxon forefathers'[72] did not imply anything like a desire for a return to this system as was; it was a question of preserving essential principles rather than prosaic substance. As one writer explained, '[t]he machinery of local government in Saxon times would of course be as unfitted for the present day as Saxon clothes or Saxon arms; but a return in rural districts to something like the old three fold

---

69 F. A. Channing, 'Latest lights on small holdings', *Monthly Review* xxvii (1907), 32–3.
70 W. E. Bear, *An agricultural Rip Van Winkle*, London 1893, esp. pp. 11–24.
71 *The Times*, 7 Oct. 1885, 10.
72 Roundell, *Parish councils*, 7–8.

division into county, hundred, and township seems highly desirable'.[73] Such would restore the institutional continuities of the 'old English constitution' – a goal Liberals felt had been accomplished with the passage of the 1894 Parish Councils Act. Shortly after the enactment of this measure, the MP for Skipton sketched these continuities when he told a Liberal meeting in Bradford that the

> Township, or tithing, which, in the aggregate, formed the old Saxon Hundred, ... which again in the aggregate formed the Shire – this hierarchy of territorial divisions of local government, corresponds almost exactly with the Parish Council, the District Council, the County Council, of our own day. And thus we have brought home to us what Bishop Stubbs describes as 'the progressive persistent development of English constitutional history from the primeval polity of the common fatherland'.[74]

The idea that a spirit of local self-government and freedom constituted a crucial determinant of English national identity was a strong one, persisting long after the decline of interest in the Anglo-Saxon past as inspiration for reform. In the 1900s, with local government reform having largely run its course, Liberals presented land reform as the primary means of resuscitating the independent spirit of village identity that did much to animate national life. By seeking to revive 'the desire for the soil', in particular through small-holdings legislation, Liberals aimed to recreate the sense of local community that historians like Slater and the Hammonds told them had prevailed before enclosure. As Carrington wrote in an official 'handbook' to the 1907 Smallholdings Act, such legislation would restore 'in a form adapted to modern conditions ... the free life of the old village community, which was so effectually destroyed by the Inclosure Acts of the eighteenth and nineteenth centuries'.[75]

Carrington's *caveat* about 'modern conditions' indicates how his party's restorative project did not involve any indiscriminate reversion to past conditions. Liberals sought not the reinstitution of the pre-enclosure village, rather the renewal of certain principles of its community life, specifically those relating to landholding. This was an important theme in Liberal argument during the Land Campaign. Presented as something that would improve agricultural productivity, relieve urban entrepreneurs from excessive rent burdens and so put landholding on a 'business footing', the Land Campaign was a 'modern', progressive crusade against antiquated 'feudalism'. But while this indicated disdain for the 'feudal' aspect of the rural past, it did not imply blanket condemnation of that past *tout court*. As the Land Enquiry Report made clear, the pre-enclosure village community – though it was gone forever – provided inspiration for modern-day reform:

---

73 M. D. Chalmers, *Local government*, London 1883, 24.
74 Roundell, *Parish councils*, 8–9.
75 Carrington, preface to Grant, *Small holdings and allotments handbook*, p. vi.

The completion of the work of enclosure destroyed the inherited traditions of the peasantry, their ideals, their customs, their habits, their ancestral solutions to the problems of life – all, in fact, that made up the native homeland civilization of rural England. With the disappearance of the primitive framework of village life, vanished – for a time, at any rate – many of the virtues of the class, their independence, pride, frugality, self control ... Without a return to an extinct social and industrial system, the old conditions cannot be entirely rebuilt for them, any more than they can be for other classes. The most that can be done is to *revive as far as possible the best features* of a form of life which has passed away and cannot be completely restored.[76]

This selectively historicist agenda was emphatically forward-looking: it was not the political expression of a futile agrarian antiquarianism. Moreover, it was clearly influenced by the views of the politically-engaged historians Liberals drew so heavily upon, who combined appreciation of the injustice of enclosure and the hardships it caused with ready acknowledgement of the inefficiency of the pre-enclosure rural economy.[77] Such a perspective implied working with the grain of modernity, updating the best ideals of the past, and infusing them into the ongoing Liberal struggle for progress. In this way, as Carrington explained in his preface to Slater's *English peasantry*, the pre-enclosure village community constituted 'a hope of the future as well as a memory of the past'.[78]

As Liberals imagined it, this future was no purely pastoral idyll, no pre-industrial paradise. While concerned to sustain the rural population and revive rural life, they did not want a nation of peasants. Neither, however, did they want a nation consisting entirely of city-dwellers. Rather, they recognised the respective benefits conferred by town and country, and advocated the maintenance of a balanced relationship between the urban and rural elements of the nation. As Herbert Samuel explained in his *Liberalism* (1902), an important statement of his party's ideology,

The city breeds active minds, but the country breeds sound bodies. The city breeds resourcefulness, the country stability. The city breeds wealth, but the country breeds men. A nation is not in a healthy state when only the town population grows and the rural population is stationary; it is in a very unhealthy state when the town population grows at the expense of the other and the rural districts decline.[79]

The message here was clear: England was in this last, deplorable, state. But in prescribing reforms like the 1907 Smallholdings Bill as remedies, Liberals like Samuel were not proposing a wholesale return to an Arcadian 'simple life'. Believing that 'the wholesome life of the farm or the garden, the daily

---

76 *The land*, i, pp. xxviii–xxix.
77 Slater, *English peasantry*, pp. vii, 5.
78 Carrington, preface, ibid. p. xiii.
79 Samuel, *Liberalism*, 103.

work in pure air, the natural life away from smoke and the din of factories, maintained an element of our population which was worth preserving',[80] as one MP put it in a debate on the 1907 bill, they merely sought to ensure the survival of a peopled countryside. This did not denote any rejection of urban in favour of rural versions of England. Indeed, Campbell-Bannerman hotly denied that 'the decay of the countryside is the price we have to pay for the prosperity of the towns, as if there was something inconsistent and incompatible in being at once a great manufacturing and a great agricultural people'.[81] Curbing the depopulation of the countryside through the enactment of land reform was presented as a means by which urban and rural England could be made to stand 'in some proper degree of size as compared one with the other'.[82]

This goal was seen as one whose fulfilment would benefit town as well as country. After all, land reform was regarded as of crucial relevance to the pressing problems of modern urban life. Popular among MPs for London and borough constituencies from the mid-1890s on, land value taxation was considered particularly applicable to one of the most pressing of these, namely the issue of housing.[83] By preventing the speculative holding of land, Liberals from Campbell-Bannerman, Lloyd George and Churchill downwards argued, it would make it easier to obtain building sites in and around towns and cities, many of which were suffering from severe shortages of housing stock and the high rents and slum conditions that they produced.[84] However, Liberals also promoted rural land reform as a method of addressing such problems. From the days of Chamberlain's Radical Programme, 'getting more people on the land', or at any rate keeping them there, attracted wide support as a solution to urban overcrowding, unemployment and the evils to which they gave rise.[85] As one candidate at the 1906 election told voters in Camberwell, smallholdings would help to 'encourage many a countryman to stay on the land, and thus relieve the citizens of London and other great centres from the incessant drifting of workless men from the country to the town'.[86]

---

80 W. Robson: *Hansard*, 4th ser., 1907, clxxv. 1706.
81 *The Times*, 22 Apr. 1907, 13.
82 J. Tomkinson, LLRA, *Sixteenth annual meeting*, 13.
83 At the 1895 general election, 65% of Liberals standing for London seats and 20% of those standing for English borough seats (outside London) mentioned TLV in their addresses. In 1900 the equivalent figures were 78% and 55% respectively: Readman, '1895', 492, and 'Patriotism and the general election of 1900', 98.
84 Campbell-Bannerman, Lloyd George, Churchill, Dr Macnamara and H. E. Kearley, reported in *LV* cv, cvii, cix (1903); *The Times*, 22 Apr. 1907, 13; *Hansard*, 4th ser., 1903, cxviii. 145, 151–2.
85 Departmental committee on small holdings: supplementary report of Sir Francis Channing, 46. See also, for example, Impey, *Three acres*, 8, and A. Acland, 'What can be done for our country villages', *New Review* iv (1891), 320.
86 D. Williamson (Camberwell, Dulwich), *Election addresses*, reel 3 (1906).

In April 1905 the Liberal politician, journalist and future secretary to Lloyd George's Land Enquiry C. R. Buxton delivered a lecture on smallholdings to the Christian Social Union. Concluding his address, Buxton called for the foundation of 'something on the lines of the Gael League [*sic*] for England', by which he meant 'an English league which will take up the whole question of country life, and the revival of old English life generally, the better and sounder and less fluctuating English life of the past'.[87] Buxton's call went unheeded. But the revivalist agenda of his proposed league was shared by many of those Liberals who were involved in the land question. Yet notwithstanding Buxton's invocation of the 'better and sounder life of the past', the rural revivalism of Liberal political discourse was a thoroughly modern phenomenon. In most of its forms it looked to the present and future as well as the past. Its proponents sought the revival of the essentials of old English country life (however defined), but not at the expense of modernity. They embraced agricultural innovations and up-to-date technologies. Furthermore, their visions of rural England were employed as part of a reformist project which sought to address key contemporary problems, such as that of urban overcrowding. At a deeper level, however, these visions reflected a patriotic agenda. Their exponents sought to preserve salutary continuities between the rural past and the predominantly urban present in order to maintain an historically-grounded sense of national identity.

[87] C. R. Buxton, 'Small holdings', *Commonwealth* x (1905), 144.

7

Conservative Agrarianism

'Therefore, chime sweet and safely, village bells,/ And, rustic chancels, woo to reverent prayer,/ And, wise and simple, to the porch repair/ Round which Death, slumbering, dreamlike heaves and swells./ Let hound and horn in wintry woods and dells/ Make jocund music though the boughs be bare,/ And whistling yokel guide his gleaming share/ Hard by the homes where gentle lordship dwells./ Therefore sit high enthroned on every hill,/ Authority! and loved in every vale;/ Nor, old Tradition falter in the tale/ Of lowly valour led by lofty will:/ And, though the throats of envy rage and rail,/ Be fair proud England proud fair England still!': from A. Austin, 'Why I am a Conservative', *NR* vi (1885), 564–5

Around the same time as Austin's poem appeared in the *National Review*, W. H. Mallock's *The old order changes* was published in instalments in the same periodical. Mallock's novel begins with a conversation in which the book's protagonist Mr Carew declares that 'If our old landed aristocracy ever came to an end, *my* England will have come to an end also; and I shall buy a chateau in some Hungarian forest. I should not be leaving my country: my country would have left me.'[1] Carew's England was that which dominated the rural vision of a particular strand of traditional agrarian Toryism, described here (in Salisbury's phrase) as 'pure squire Conservatism'. Celebrated in the poetry of Alfred Austin, poet laureate and staunch Conservative, it was a place imagined as a fertile land overspread by large arable farms and dotted with quiet picturesque villages pervaded by a spirit of placid contentment. Its lynchpin was the class of territorial magnates that for centuries had provided the nation with leadership and governance – the 'authority' which Austin idealised as being 'loved in every vale'.[2] For those, like the fictional Carew, who cherished this idea of England, it was imperative to sustain a paternal yet benevolent landlordism and the communities of deference which it supported. In their interpretation, if this benign form of landlordly rule were to disappear, the continued existence of an historic sense of English identity would be endangered. As this chapter will go on to show, however, pure squire Conservatism's prominence in Conservative discourse on the land question steadily diminished over time. By the Edwardian period, its place

[1]   W. H. Mallock, *The old order changes*, London 1886, i. 3–4.
[2]   Austin, 'Why I am a Conservative', 564–5.

had been taken by a rather different vision, one centring on the peasant or 'yeoman' proprietor.

Pure squire Conservatism and the nation

In a famous lecture of 1877 J. A. Froude had provided what was perhaps the definitive statement of pure squire Conservatism. According to him, large landowners were vital for a flourishing, healthy national life, as a glance at the continent revealed. In Spain, Froude reported, the disintegration of the old hereditary aristocracy was a direct cause of the decline of that country's greatness; while in France, the lack of an established gentry class since 1789 had conferred chronic political instability, with ongoing oscillation between anarchy and despotism. All this stood in marked contrast to England, where the territorial elite had been closely associated with national traditions for many centuries, with two of their most notable achievements being Magna Charta and the Glorious Revolution of 1688. For Froude, the continued existence of ancient landed dynasties provided 'links between the present and the past, and carr[ied] on unbroken the continuity of our national existence. In such families the old expression *Noblesse Oblige* is a genuine force'. It followed from this that Froude found radical land reform deeply uncongenial. Proposals like Free Trade in Land would in his view only lead to the replacement of the old elite with a new capitalist order; one without any ties of affection to the soil or particular localities, possessed of no inherited sense of duty and – liberated from the sense of stewardship conferred by primogeniture and entail – inclined to regard land as an investment like any other.[3]

Froude's conception of nationhood as one sustained by the old landed elite was shared by a significant if dwindling body of Conservatives and Unionists. Under increasing attack from Liberals bent on ending the 'land monopoly', these individuals placed particular emphasis on the social peace that supposedly obtained under the traditional rural order. A 'Merrie England' of class harmony was upheld in opposition to what were portrayed as the divisive schemes of reformers. In the early 1880s this stratagem even featured in the official propaganda of the Conservative party, which presented the land tenure reform proposed by the Farmers' Alliance and their Liberal allies as a 'most unpatriotic' attempt to exploit agricultural depression for political advantage by loosening 'the bonds that unite the interests of landlord and tenant'.[4] Versions of this argument recurred in later years. In 1896, during a Commons debate on a land tenure bill, one scion of a prominent aristo-

---

[3]   J. A. Froude, 'Uses of a landed gentry', in his *Short studies on great subjects* (1867–83), ed. D. Ogg, London 1963, 270–5.
[4]   National Union, 'Who are the friends of the farmer?' (1882), 5, and 'Sham friends of the farmer' (1882), 3: Archives of the British Conservative party, Bodleian Library, Oxford, pamphlets and leaflets, pt I.

cratic family asserted that the proposed legislation would reduce 'the old friendly relations between landlord and tenant ... to a commercial basis. The landlord would try to extract every possible penny from the tenant, and the tenant would be bound by hard and fast rules'.[5]

Such claims were not confined to the Unionists' response to land tenure reform schemes, however. Liberal plans for local government reform were also condemned as inimical to the tranquillity and social cohesion of traditional rural life. County councils were all very well (though some Tories had their misgivings), but parish councils, being less remote, would bring the contagion of disunity right to the heart of the village. As the well-known Tory writer P. H. Ditchfield explained in the *National Review*, if the Liberal proposal came to fruition, 'the quiet atmosphere of our hamlets will be rudely disturbed by an election ... we shall have the usual personal squabbles, electioneering promises, and fights; and, instead of a happy and contented village, we shall have a pandemonium of discord and unrest'.[6] For many Conservatives, parish councils would destroy what was left of the community life of old England. Emblematic of this life were the now largely extinct customs and pastimes like harvest homes, sheep-shearing suppers and May Day festivals – activities to which the squire and farmer had traditionally given patronage, and which were felt to have promoted 'good feeling' between classes, preventing the labourers 'from growing hard, grasping, and discontented with their lot'.[7] A revival of the 'Merrie England' spirit of such 'simple pleasures', not the imposition of parish councils or radical land reform, was what the depressed and decaying countryside required.

Some Unionists actively sought a revival of this spirit. Among them was Robert Loyd Lindsay, Baron Wantage, owner of 52,000 acres in Berkshire, Northamptonshire and elsewhere. Crimean war hero and paternalist Tory landlord *non pareil*, Wantage was a prominent advocate of the voluntary provision of allotments by landowners. His benevolent paternalism stemmed from a strong sense of *noblesse oblige* bolstered by religious convictions. Contemporaries saw him as the personification of Victorian chivalry (the VC awarded in Crimea added to this impression), and he was even compared to King Arthur.[8] Emblematic of Wantage's attitudes were the 'Lockinge Revels' of August 1885, which he staged with his wife in the grounds of their Berkshire estate. Attended by hundreds of guests attired in Tudor costumes, including Wantage's own cottagers, this three-day event featured a medieval procession, open-air theatre, a jousting tournament, a riband dance and – as its highlight – a lavish 'Festival of the Summer Queen'.[9]

Few landlords went to the effort of putting on events like the Lockinge

5 *Hansard*, 4th ser., 1896, xxxix. 1461.
6 P. H. Ditchfield, 'Parish councils', *NR* xviii (1891), 254.
7 Idem, *English villages*, London 1901, 280–1.
8 R. T. Stearn, 'Lindsay, Robert James Loyd-, Baron Wantage (1832–1901)', *ODNB*.
9 *The Times*, 27 Aug. 1885, 5; *Graphic* xxxii (1885), 289–90.

Revels. However, uniting rich and poor by means of social activities that evoked a pre-industrial 'Merrie England' of squire-centred deference communities was an idea that appealed to other Conservatives, among them – as we have seen – the earl of Winchilsea, founder of the NAU. In his view, the ideal English squire was

> The pivot on which country life revolves ... Not a cricket club can be started, not a friendly society inaugurated, not a flower show held within a dozen miles of his park without an appeal to the squire's purse, which is sure to be successful ... Has a laborer been turned off because he is too old to do a full day's work on the neighbouring farm? The squire's bailiff will have orders to employ him. Is a village dame in want of fuel? She may gather it under his oaks, and if her daughter is recovering from an illness she will have an order for a daily supply of fresh milk from the dairy and soup from the kitchen, until she is convalescent, with a bottle of port wine into the bargain from the squire's own cellar to bring back the faded roses to her cheeks.[10]

Of course, this idea of the 'good old squire' of yore was largely a myth. However, some Conservative landlords did seek through their own actions to preserve a sense of continuity with the imagined Tory past he personified. Perhaps the most telling examples of such individuals were Lord John Tollemache of Helmingham and Lord Wantage of Lockinge. Both Tollemache and Wantage presented themselves as exemplars of old-fashioned benevolent paternalism, an ethos they clearly regarded as protective of the traditional social structure of the countryside. Fiercely proud of the ancient English origins of his family, Tollemache had set himself up in the manner of a medieval baron by building a huge neo-feudal style castle in the Peckforton Hills, at the heart of his Cheshire estate. The benevolence he dispensed from its castellated ramparts took the form of a comprehensive system of large allotments, of which all labourers on his land were eligible to take advantage.[11] At Lockinge, Wantage also granted his labourers access to land in the form of garden plots and (less extensively supplied) smallholdings, while at the same time improving the wages of his labourers; in addition, he introduced co-operative stores and a savings bank paying 5 per cent interest.[12] Like Tollemache, he situated his landlordly goodwill in a pre-industrial context. The 'Revels' of 1885 illustrate this, but so too does the building work carried out on his Berkshire estate. Largely designed by Lord and Lady Wantage themselves, the cottages they constructed for their labourers were deliber-

[10] Winchilsea, 'Death duties', 99.
[11] 'Lord Tollemache's cottage farms', *Chambers's Journal* 5th ser. ii (1885), 769–72; F. Impey, 'Lord Tollemache', *New Review* ix (1893), 299–313.
[12] H. S. L. Lindsay, *Lord Wantage*, London 1907, 400; Stearn, 'Lindsay'.

ately evocative of a 'Merrie England', with many features common to Tudor vernacular architecture being included in their design.[13]

In their private activities, individuals such as Wantage and Tollemache aimed to resurrect the spirit of a Merrie England such as they imagined to have existed in the past – a socially stable, contented place founded on an enlightened landlordism. Unlike many Liberal and some Unionist reformers, but like Winchilsea's NAU, they were not prepared to see rural society radically altered or dismantled by the creation of a numerous class of small farmers. Although there were those (Wantage among them) who did practise the discretionary provision of smallholdings on their own estates, none wished to undermine the tripartite structure of landowner, tenant farmer and agricultural labourer. In allocating a sizeable allotment to each cottage on his Cheshire estate, Tollemache's object was not to set up independent cultivators but 'to save the old English labourer from extinction'.[14]

Tollemache's practice won many plaudits, and despite his socially restrictive agenda he was personally popular with his own tenants and labourers.[15] What he apparently achieved on his estates, Onslow's association of the mid-1880s sought on a national level. Supported by a large number of Conservative peers and landowners, the association aimed to institutionalise benevolent paternalism with a view to preserving the traditional social structure of the English countryside. It advocated the discretionary provision of allotments in order to promote class harmony and ensure a supply of good farmworkers, not so that labourers would have the opportunity of becoming self-sufficient farmers.[16] As Onslow explained in 1886, 'the allotment in all cases should be looked upon as the recreation of leisure time': ideally under one acre in size, its cultivation should not involve any reduction in the hours or quality of work the agricultural labourer put in for the farmer who hired him.[17]

At this point Onslow was concerned to demonstrate that compulsory allotments legislation, which he opposed, was unnecessary. Other Tory paternalists thought differently, however, including Murray Finch-Hatton, Lincolnshire MP and future earl of Winchilsea. Although Finch-Hatton supported the extension of Onslow's system as far as possible, he favoured compulsory legislation giving local authorities allotment-providing powers in cases where voluntary provision was inadequate, and indeed planned to introduce a bill to this effect. But his ideas differed markedly from those of radical reformers. For the latter, allotments were a means of liberating the labourer from total dependence on farmer and landlord, so providing the

[13] J. L. Green, *English country cottages*, London 1899, 100, 103; 73–5, 102; Lindsay, *Wantage*, 386.
[14] Lord Tollemache's cottage farms', 770–1.
[15] For example, *The Times*, 11 Aug., 1890, 3.
[16] Onslow, *Landlords and allotments*.
[17] Ibid. 58.

first rung of a ladder that could lead to a completely self-sufficient liveli-hood. Hence radical proposals often aimed at providing quite large plots of land, thereby enabling labourers to substitute allotment cultivation for wage-earning. This was certainly what Chamberlain and Collings had in mind in the mid-1880s, and it alarmed Finch-Hatton. In a Commons debate of January 1886 he criticised Collings's Allotment Bill on the grounds that it failed to define the maximum size of allotments to be created under its provi-sions. While he approved of small allotments, large ones were a different matter, as they would only deprive the farmer of 'his best labourers at the very moment he wanted them the most'.[18] This attitude reflected Finch-Hatton's commitment to the preservation of the traditional rural order, with its rigid hierarchies and the limited opportunities for social advancement that these implied. But at the same time he did not see the compulsory provision of small allotments as running counter to this reactionary goal; indeed, to his mind the two were mutually supportive. Once it appeared likely that compulsory legislation was inevitable, even under a Unionist government, his position came to be shared by Onslow, Tollemache and other exponents of pure squire Conservatism. When Finch-Hatton – now Lord Winchilsea – introduced his Allotments Bill to the Upper House in July 1887, Onslow expressed his support; and Tollemache was to give his backing to the Salisbury government's own measure, which passed into law later that year.[19] Both bills involved an element of compulsion, but both also imposed tight limits on the size of allotments, in order to ensure that the plots made available would not provide farmworkers with an alternative to wage labour.

Tory landlords' concern to preserve 'the old English labourer' *qua* labourer was in line with a specific vision of rural England as an expansive and predominantly arable country. A land of large corn-growing farms, not of insubstantial cabbage-growing smallholdings, this conception of England underlay much Unionist criticism of reform proposals in the 1880s and early 1890s. In these years traditionalist Conservatives ridiculed radical plans for the legislative creation of small cultivators as an attempt to replace the historic English land system with an alien and undesirable French one. Their cause supported by *The Times*, the *National Review* and other leading publi-cations, they portrayed the peasant proprietors of France (and other conti-nental countries) as suffering 'wretched' conditions of life no Englishman could possibly tolerate. Inhabiting squalid mud-floored cottages, they were overworked and impoverished, subsisting on a 'meagre' diet of tomatoes, lentils, salad and other such stuff which 'our people would refuse to endure'.[20]

18 *The Times*, 27 Jan. 1886, 7.
19 *The Times*, 1 Sept. 1887, 8.
20 F. P. Verney, 'Peasant properties in France', NR x (1887), 551; F. M. de Borring, 'The peasant proprietor of the south', NR vii (1885), 348–50; [H. Reeve], 'Plain truths and popular fallacies', ER clxii (1885), 578.

Moreover, even if agrarian Tories had believed that a land system based on smallholdings were beneficial, most would still have insisted that its 'artificial' imposition was inadmissible. Measures like the 'experimental' act of 1892 were just about acceptable, but fundamental changes in the overall pattern of landholding would only be deemed legitimate if they 'evolved' naturally. It was an argument that persisted as an element of Unionist political discourse until the First World War.

In particular, it permeated the ethos of the NAU, whose demand for action in defence of 'our greatest national industry' reflected a particular social vision. Unlike those reformers who advocated the transformation of rural society through the creation of a numerous class of self-sufficient peasant cultivators, NAU leaders stressed the virtues of rural society structured on the traditional lines of landowner, large tenant farmer and agricultural labourer. Their ideal was the organic, hierarchical but harmonious rural community, presided over by the benevolent squire. While Winchilsea often stressed that the NAU was equally open to all three classes, he always intended that the landed elite should play a key part in its executive direction.[21]

In calling on landlords to play a leading role in the NAU, Winchilsea appealed to the notion of a benevolent, selfless, even chivalric aristocracy, willing to make personal sacrifices for the greater good. Writing of the newly-formed NAU in the National Review, he claimed that the future fortunes of the infant organisation would

> tend to show whether, as Englishmen ... we have degenerated from our ancestors, who, when they took the field, hesitated not to commit honour, fortune and life, to the keeping of their own tenants, and would have disdained to entrust the defence of their banner to any save the stout band of yeomen who followed it from their English homes, willing to die for it in time of war, because they justly regarded it as the emblem of protection and sustenance in time of peace.[22]

At one level, such high-flown exhortations were disguised appeals for funds from the coffers of the agrarian elite, and Winchilsea certainly placed considerable importance on obtaining substantial donations from this source. But he clearly believed that the ideal of the dutiful and patriotic nobleman was one that would resonate strongly with the values of the landlords to whom he appealed. Even after the experience of the NAU's early years had somewhat disabused Winchilsea of his high hopes of aristocratic selflessness, he was quite prepared to assert that the spirit of noblesse oblige amongst the notables of the shires was such that increased taxes – as in the shape of Harcourt's death duties – were unwarranted impositions on those who already did their paternal duty by the countryside.[23]

---

21 See, for example, Cable, 26 Aug. 1893, 360.
22 Winchilsea, 'Agricultural union', 592–3.
23 Idem, 'Death duties'.

Winchilsea's faith in the continued persistence of enlightened agrarian paternalism may partly be explained by his personal practice as landlord. With some justification he was widely regarded as a 'model' landowner, being concerned to improve living conditions as well as to maximise agricultural productivity. On his Lincolnshire estate rents were kept at relatively low levels, allotments were provided for labourers and charity was very freely dispensed.[24] It seems that this helped to foster strong bonds of goodwill between Winchilsea and the people who lived on his land, many of whom evidently held him in very high regard. This was borne out on his death in 1898, which was accompanied by remarkably profuse expressions of regret.[25] So it is possible to see the NAU as Winchilsea's attempt to institutionalise, on a nationwide basis, the benevolent paternalism – and the social relations which went with it – that he sought to uphold at a local level through the stewardship of his own estates. In the context of the 1890s this was undeniably a reactionary project. Indeed, Winchilsea's ideological vision reflected a conception of England as a nation that was profoundly out-of-date, bearing little relation to contemporary reality. Most crucially of all, however, it was out of kilter with mainstream Conservative opinion.

Throughout the late nineteenth and early twentieth centuries, Conservative opposition to land reform based on a traditionalist vision of the agrarian *status quo* (or, as in Winchilsea's case, an imagined *status quo ante*) steadily lost ground to the idea of peasant or 'yeoman' proprietorship. The importance of pure squire Conservatism peaked around the time of Chamberlain's 'unauthorised programme', when it was upheld as an alternative to that exalted by radical advocates of smallholdings. Yet, despite the continuing prominence of the landed classes within the membership of the parliamentary party,[26] the traditional Tory vision of the English countryside declined in influence after the mid-1880s. Largely confined to the backbenches, its parliamentary exponents found themselves pushed ever closer to the margins of political life. To be sure, their ideals continued to find favour with the increasingly protectionist NAU until its demise in 1901. They elicited little sympathy, however, from most politicians of cabinet rank (Balfour, in particular, was notoriously hostile).[27] By the first years of the twentieth century, few leading Unionists identified with the agrarianism of Chaplin, let alone that of Wantage, Winchilsea or Tollemache. This was as true for those involved in Chamberlain's campaign for fiscal reform as it was for the party at large, Chaplin's own membership of the Tariff Reform Commission notwithstanding.

That said, however, elements of the old argument did resurface once again in the language of Tory opposition to the 1909 Budget and the Land

---

24 *Cable*, 3 Mar. 1894, 138.
25 *Lincoln Gazette*, 10 Sept. 1898, 6; *Cable*, 17 Sept. 1898, 184, 187.
26 J. P. Cornford, 'The parliamentary foundations of the Hotel Cecil', in R. Robson (ed.), *Ideas and institutions of Victorian Britain*, London 1967, 268–311.
27 D. Cannadine, *The decline and fall of the British aristocracy*, New Haven 1990, 450.

Campaign. It was perhaps most visible among that of 'diehards' like E. G. Pretyman, whose forensic assault on the People's Budget was informed by a conviction that the old ways were the best: the established system of landlord, farmer and labourer, and the social values by which it was supported, ought not to be undermined by central state action. But we should not exaggerate the importance of this perspective. Even the wing of the party to which Pretyman belonged was by no means unequivocal in its support for the ideals of pure squire Conservatism. Indeed, many diehards were in fact supporters of quite radical schemes of land reform, among them Charles Bathurst, Lord Selborne, Lord Milner, Henry Page Croft and Austen Chamberlain.[28] All of these figures endorsed smallholdings legislation in conjunction with tariff reform and other measures (such as improved agricultural education); some like Bathurst were closely connected to the USRC, an important source of radical agrarian proposals.

As demonstrated *a fortiori* by the example of the diehards, the relative weakness of the politics of pure squire Conservatism was not just apparent in the narrowly political sphere. Many literary evocations of a Tory Merrie England of benevolent landlords and deferential peasants were distinctly threnodic in character, simultaneously celebrating and lamenting the passage of this England into history. Towards the end of *The old order changes*, Mallock has the aristocratic Carew admit that he actually belongs to a world 'that is dead or dying'. This was a view evidently shared by the author himself, who in the mid-1880s had perhaps entertained hopes that such a world could be revived.[29] Other Tory writers expressed similar views in their books. Ditchfield's *Old English country squire* and Caroline Gearey's *Rural life*, to take two examples, were infused with a deep sense of permanent loss: the rural life they eulogised so fervently was indisputably 'dying out', along with the 'good old English gentleman' and his values.[30] 'The squire grows old and the squirearchy too. He has had his day, and he knows it', was Ditchfield's solemn verdict.[31]

Such judgements reflected contemporary socio-economic realities. It is true that enlightened landlordism in the old style did have its exemplars in individuals like Tollemache and Wantage, but it is also true that their benevolent practice drew attention precisely because it was the exception and not the rule. In any case, both men were dead before 1914, and none emerged to take their place as champions of *noblesse oblige*. Of course, just how extensive aristocratic paternalism had ever been is a moot point, even

---

[28] This was a point missed by G. D. Phillips, *The diehards: aristocratic society and politics in Edwardian England*, Cambridge, MA 1979.

[29] J. Lucas, 'Conservatism and revolution in the 1880s', in J. Lucas (ed.), *Literature and politics in the nineteenth century*, London 1971, 188.

[30] C. Gearey, *Rural life*, London 1899, 210.

[31] P. H. Ditchfield, *The old English country squire*, London 1912, 335.

in Tollemache's Helmingham or Wantage's Lockinge.[32] But there is no doubt that insofar as it did exist, it was dealt a severe blow by the depression in British agriculture after 1873. Hard-hit by falling capital values, many landlords were forced to economise, and benevolent community-building activities were scaled back.[33] Others still withdrew from the land altogether, their places being taken by *nouveaux riches* individuals who – while wanting to play lord of the manor – usually had little real connection with rural life, little appreciation of customary 'paternal' practice and were often non-resident for long periods. As the Tory writer Edward Dicey claimed in 1895, new men and 'wealthy traders' were supplanting the old landlords, and as many of these *arrivistes* only used their estates for shooting purposes they had 'no closer connection with the tenants than a lodger in a hotel has with the servants and waiters'.[34] Dicey was exaggerating somewhat, but his observations contained an essential truth. By the end of the nineteenth century a strict system based on contractual arrangements was inexorably taking over from the more relaxed practices of the past, which – in the eyes of its defenders at least – had been founded on mutual good feeling between classes and judicious acts of discretionary kindness on the part of the squire. This had clear implications for debate on the land question: lacking an analogue in social reality, pure squire Conservatism was a political language increasingly devoid both of meaning and appeal.

Unionists, yeomen proprietors and patriotism

Ranging from cottagers to substantial John Bull-like figures, the yeomen of England had long been held in high regard, even by those who considered their near-complete disappearance to be inevitable. Effusively praised by historians (Macaulay had called them 'an eminently manly and truehearted race'),[35] they were thought to have enjoyed their heyday in the three or four hundred years before the enclosure movement. Often described as quintessentially English in character, the sturdy yeoman was invoked by Unionist advocates of smallholdings to repudiate the charge that small-scale proprietorship ran counter to national traditions. Liberal Unionist reformers were especially fond of appealing to history in this way; and none more so, of

---

[32] In early twentieth-century Helmingham, there was 'an underlying, smouldering resentment': J. Gerard, 'Lady bountiful: women of the landed classes and rural philanthropy', *Victorian Studies* xxx (1987), 203–4. See also F. M. L. Thompson, 'Landowners and the rural community', in G. E. Mingay (ed.), *The Victorian countryside*, London 1981, ii. 469–73.

[33] Newby, *Deferential worker*, 60–3.

[34] [E. Dicey], 'The Conservatism of to-day', *QR* clxxx (1895), 553–4.

[35] T. B. Macaulay, *The history of England from the accession of James the Second*, London 1858, i. 335.

course, than Collings, whose own urban-industrial background bore eloquent testimony to the power and reach of the yeoman myth.[36]

Although historians have often downplayed Collings's political importance (for Matthew Fforde, he was 'a rather bucolic figure who lacked gravity'[37]), his influence over Unionist land policy was in fact considerable. As such, he is worth dwelling on here. Like many land reformers, Collings had a highly-developed historical sensibility. In his analysis, which he developed in his *Land reform* (1906), the English poor had suffered centuries of oppression at the hands of their rulers. Most crucially, he believed that they had been robbed of their land through enclosure, which had reduced the independent yeoman of England from archetypal 'freeborn Briton' to degraded wage-labourer, part of what Collings called the 'landless proletariat'. Deprived of their rightful inheritance in the soil, many such individuals had, according to Collings, left the countryside for the towns, there to lead toilsome and no less degraded lives in the unwholesome slums.[38] It followed from this essentially radical analysis that restitution was required to right the wrongs of enclosure, which had not only created a landless proletariat (so endangering social stability), but had also been simply unjust, as the dispossessed peasantry had never been adequately compensated by the state for the loss of their commons. Speaking on the second reading of a smallholdings bill in 1891, Collings argued along these lines, as he also did one year later when the act was passed, writing in a preface to a pamphlet explaining the legislation that it was (partial) repayment for an historical debt incurred by enclosure.[39] It was an argument he repeated throughout the years before 1914, mobilising it to justify further legislation aiming at the restoration of 'yeoman' proprietors, like his long-running Purchase of Land Bill.[40]

Collings's reading of history and the need to correct its injustices was very similar to that of many of his political opponents, including land nation-alisers and even some socialists. His was, of course, a radical position, one that he had espoused in the days of the unauthorised programme; but it remained his position after he left the Liberal party. And although he moderated his public statements to avoid undue offence to his Conservative allies, it still surfaced quite prominently – for instance in his evidence to the Select Committee on Small Holdings in 1889.[41] Indeed, this committee and the act to which it led suggests that Collings's ideas had significant purchase

---

[36] Despite being a businessman who had spent much of his life in Birmingham, and whose father had been a builder, Collings described himself as descended from a long line of 'peasant proprietors ... squeezed out of existence by the iniquitous administration of the Enclosure Acts': Ward, 'Land reform', 133.

[37] Fforde, *Conservatism*, 77.

[38] Collings, *Land reform*.

[39] *Hansard*, 3rd ser., 1891, cccli. 653; J. Collings, preface to H. E. Miller, *The Small Holdings Act, 1892*, London 1892, pp. vi–vii.

[40] See, for example, Collings, *Hansard*, 4th ser., 1907, clxx. 822.

[41] *Select Committee on Small Holdings*, 1889 (313), xii. 1–18, 44–86, 109–16.

over Unionist opinion from quite early on. While enclosure was not quite made 'the key of the inquiry', as Collings wanted, its report did conclude that 'the rural population, and especially the agricultural labourers, have a claim on Parliament for consideration, in consequence of the indirect effect on their interests and prospects of past legislation and practice with regard to inclosures'.[42] Thus in calling for legislation to create small proprietors, the committee was influenced by an appreciation of past injustices; and, to a certain extent, the resulting act of 1892 can be seen in this light also. In presenting this measure to parliament, Conservatives and Liberal Unionists alike cast themselves as looking to the restoration of the yeomanry of old, and the legislation was perceived as such even by its most hostile critics.[43] In the Commons debate on the bill, one newly-elected MP expressed his hope that the reform would 'preserve and increase the greatness of this country' by reviving 'that class of yeomen who in years gone by have been [its] backbone and strength'.[44] Such aspirations were not confined to the backbenches: the party leadership voiced similar sentiments. However insistent they were as to the 'experimental' character of the legislation – and some, like Chaplin, were very insistent – members of Salisbury's cabinet (including Salisbury himself) made it clear that the bill constituted an attempt to 'recreate' the 'sturdy yeomen' of England.[45] Even the ever-sceptical Balfour affirmed that the measure aimed at restoring the 'system of small yeomen' to the countryside.[46]

But we should be wary of assuming that the expression of such sentiments indicates any particularly deep-seated conversion to Collings's point of view. After all, a conviction that small proprietors acted as a 'bulwark' against revolutionary change figured prominently in the government's motivations, as did considerations of electoral expediency. Both these factors were more important than any sense of historic injustice. This being the case, once the 'experiment' had been made, the question of restoring the 'yeoman' proprietor fell into the background of mainstream Unionist discourse and did not re-emerge until the mid-1900s. For a time, then, Collings found himself rather isolated. Even his old ally Chamberlain, whose interests were moving away from land and towards the empire, could not be entirely counted upon. Speaking at Stratford-upon-Avon in the 1895 general election campaign, Chamberlain condemned the Liberals for what he called their 'class' legislation: 'No greater mistake was made by their opponents in past elections, and

---

[42] Ibid. 8; 1890 (223) xvii, p. xi.
[43] As *The Times* (no friend of land reformers) commented disapprovingly, the Unionist government – as well as its Liberal opponents – were now committed to 'a project for bringing back into existence the old race of yeomen and small landowners' (27 June 1892, 11).
[44] W. F. D. Smith, *Hansard*, 4th ser., 1892, ii. 1709.
[45] Ibid. i. 911–12; Salisbury at Exeter, *The Times*, 3 Feb. 1892, 6.
[46] *Hansard*, 4th ser., 1892, ii. 1722.

they were making the same mistake now, in trying to show that the interests of landlords, farmers and agricultural labourers were divided. That was an absurdity that ought to be self-evident.'[47] This sounded less like Radical Joe and more like the earl of Winchilsea.

Things changed, however, after the Boer War, when Collings's views once again found favour. It is true that some in the leadership distrusted him: Balfour had a low opinion of his political ability and Devonshire had little time for his reformist schemes.[48] Moreover, even those sympathetic to his views were often left exasperated by the flaws in the detail of his proposals (he was, for example, excessively optimistic about the ease with which cheap credit could be arranged to provide loans for land purchase).[49] Despite this, however, Collings's ideas did exert significant influence. Although Chamberlain was incapacitated by a stroke in 1906, Collings retained the ear of his son Austen, with whom he enjoyed close personal relations. Austen Chamberlain collaborated with Collings to exert pressure on the leadership, one outcome of which was Balfour's public declaration in favour of the legislative extension of small ownership in 1909; and it was surely significant that Balfour described this policy as that of 'the old Radicals'.[50] But whatever Collings's direct impact on policy, it is clear that his ideas were compatible with those of the party rank-and-file, who welcomed Balfour's 1909 announcement with enthusiasm. Well might Collings tell Joseph Chamberlain's wife, two months after this election, that smallholdings legislation 'having gone through the stages of ridicule & indifference is now a recognised plank on the Unionist platform'.[51]

Collings's influence in the Edwardian period was a function of the growing popularity of the yeoman myth in contemporary Unionist discourse. To a certain extent this myth was even propagated by aristocratic Conservatives. In the Lords, Tory peers introduced a number of bills aimed at the creation of small proprietors. One such was the earl of Dunmore's Small Ownership and Land Bank Bill, which got through its second reading on 2 May 1911. In the debate on that occasion, Carrington – as Liberal president of the Board of Agriculture – commented that only a few years previously Tory grandees had been sceptical about smallholdings, 'But now I am glad to say we are all supporters ... The Tory Party has been converted to the small holdings idea in platoons, and they are now being baptised in battalions. The landlords of England are taking up the idea not only in theory, but in practice.'[52] Carrington's remark was made with good reason: later in the same debate Lord Curzon acknowledged that that there was now much common

---

[47] *The Times*, 17 July 1895, 9. See see also speech at Rugby, *The Times*, 23 July 1895, 7.
[48] Dutton, '*His Majesty's loyal opposition*', 118.
[49] A. Chamberlain, *Politics from inside*, London 1936, 475.
[50] *The Times*, 23 Sept. 1909, 7.
[51] Collings to Mrs Chamberlain, 20 Mar. 1910, Joseph Chamberlain papers, JC22/48.
[52] *Hansard*, 5th ser., 1911, viii. 98.

ground between the parties on the question of the need for reform; that the subdivision of landownership was in itself desirable; and that, indeed, 'the old system of great landed estates is rapidly breaking up'.[53] Similar sentiments were voiced by Lansdowne, who replied to Lloyd George's radicalism with an acknowledgement that the old system, which was in decline (as evidenced by the sale of great estates), needed supplementing with a system of small ownership.[54]

All this reflected the renunciation of pure squire Conservatism. Tory landlords were more receptive to the idea of smallholdings legislation and certainly showed a keener appreciation of the socially conservative virtues of the yeoman; but for most such individuals, advocacy of reform had relatively little to do with acknowledgement of past injustices. This was true of those landlords who clustered around Onslow's Central Land Association (CLA), an organisation which combined support for radical reform with commitment to a somewhat traditionalist agrarian vision, one not unlike Winchilsea's in its emphasis on cross-class action in defence of agriculture. As Onslow himself explained at a meeting of the CLA's Central Committee in May 1909,

> The whole aim and object they had in view was to unite into one body all those interested in Agriculture, whether they were owners, farmers or labourers. They believed that the interests of the land and of agriculture would be listened to in a way that they had never been listened to before ... They wanted to interest the greatest number of people possible in the land and to bring before them the fact that the interests of the land were not confined to landlords.[55]

Yet at the same time others took up more radical positions, endorsing Collings's view of history. One such individual was Christopher Turnor, Lincolnshire landlord, co-founder of the CLA and USRC member. In his influential *Land problems and national welfare* (1911), Turnor made clear that the existing system of landholding was productive of national evils and called for reform to encourage small ownership. In doing so he drew upon a radical vision of English history, one clearly derived from that of Collings, to whom he paid tribute.[56] For Turnor, as for Collings, enclosure not only damaged the 'national welfare' by divorcing the people from the soil, it 'was of itself an unrighteous [policy], for it was the robbery of the poor legalized by Acts of Parliament', and as 'Parliament has taken away the land; it must now reverse the process'.[57] Hugh Aronson's *Our village homes* (1913) offered a similar perspective. In the preface to this book, the Conservative backbencher Lord

53 Ibid. viii. 105.
54 *The Times*, 25 July 1912, 7; 23 June 1913, 4.
55 Onslow, 'History of the Onslow family', 1333, Onslow papers, G173/1/5.
56 Turnor, *Land problems*, 116–19.
57 Ibid. 116, 234–5.

Henry Bentinck observed that 'Early in the Nineteenth Century the agricultural labourer lost most of his valuable common rights, and with them went all hope of an independent existence. In all the years that have passed since then, he has had little incentive to remain on the land' – a state of affairs, both Bentinck and Aronson felt, which warranted remedial legislation.[58]

For these radical Unionists, appreciation of the injustices of the past went hand in hand with their demands for a wholesale restructuring of the agrarian system around a 'yeoman' model. This model, which drew inspiration from the past but at the same time would be supplemented by co-operation, agricultural education and other innovations, was presented as a replacement for the pure squire Conservatism now in eclipse. Hence, as Gilbert Parker explained, landlordly paternalism was to be ditched in favour of 'self-help', as embodied in the person of the independent small proprietor:

> It is this which we propose to substitute for the landlord and that timely aid and those indulgences by which English landlords have enabled the system of tenancy to achieve its successes. At a moment when the old landlordism, and with it the fine relations which have existed between owner and cultivator, seem doomed to disappear, some substitute must be found, and none can be found more sure or stable than the bestowal on the cultivators themselves of the power of self-help.[59]

This had strong affinities with traditional Liberalism, but it was made Conservative by the conviction that the democratisation of landownership through the creation of yeoman smallholders would serve to promote social stability, thwart left-wing extremism and protect the institution of private property, while at the same time encouraging a class of men inclined to vote Tory at election time.

It would be a mistake to ascribe too much importance to the yeomen myth. By no means was it ever beloved of all Conservatives and Liberal Unionists and even those who espoused it did so with differing degrees of enthusiasm. While it is true that support for the legislative creation of 'yeomen' proprietors became widespread, even amongst Tory peers, not all Unionists gave their backing to reform for the same reasons. Some, like Collings, were animated by a sense of historic injustice; others preferred to place more emphasis on the idea, discussed in chapter 2, that small landowners would help secure social stability. Nevertheless, by the last decade of the century, the yeoman myth had established itself as the crucial element in an idealised vision of the English rural nation, one to which Conservatives and Liberal Unionist MPs had ready recourse. When faced with the increasingly radical land reform proposals of the Liberals in the 1900s, they turned to this vision rather than the traditionalist alternative. Centred on the 'good old

58 H. Aronson, *Our village homes*, London 1913, pp. v–vi, 111–12.
59 G. Parker, 'Land reform and the chancellor', NC lxxiv (1913), 281.

squire' and the social system he supported, this latter vision was ill-suited to the Unionists' own reformist response to the Liberal agrarian programme, which in policy terms was the advocacy of new measures for the promotion of peasant proprietorship. Operating in an increasingly democratic political culture, Unionists were concerned to present themselves less as the defenders of the property of landed aristocrats, and more as the defenders of the property of the nation as a whole. While the yeoman vision of Merrie England was unproblematically compatible with this shift in agenda, the same could not be said of that embodied by pure squire Conservatism.

Unionists and reactionary Englishness

The purchase of the yeoman myth tells us something important about late Victorian and Edwardian Conservatism. The political right is usually linked with the defence of an aristocratic ruralism – the world of mansions, parks and demesnes. But this ruralism had less currency in the wider culture than is often assumed.[60] Idealisations of rural England often focused on the lives of ordinary people, and if nostalgia, sentimentality and the elision of harsh social reality were undoubtedly present, the squire was conspicuous by his absence. For many Conservatives the yeoman homestead rather than the stately home represented the English countryside ideal – hence the cross-party enthusiasm for the independent smallholder. But while this vision of the rural nation was undoubtedly popular rather than aristocratic, it was also strongly bound up with conceptualisations of the English past. Therefore, in looking for national renewal through the creation of sturdy yeomen, were not Unionist reformers looking backwards, just as those of their counterparts who espoused pure squire Conservatism were also looking backwards? Might not it be said, then, that Unionist political discourse on the land question presented two different versions of reactionary Englishness, both suffused with nostalgic longing for idealised, non-recoverable pasts?

At first sight affirmative answers to these questions seem self-evident. There is little doubt that Conservative and Liberal Unionists did espouse reactionary languages of ruralism, that of Winchilsea being an obvious example. But it is important not to assume that the prizing of bygone values (like *noblesse oblige*) or modes of life (like yeoman proprietorship) necessarily involved any wholesale rejection of modernity or disengagement from contemporary social realities. To be sure, a good deal of antipathy to modern life was manifested in the language of pure squire Conservatism, which embodied a vision of organic rural communities animated by a spirit of deference to the benevolent leadership of the large farmer, the parson, and above all the landlord. In the eyes of its exponents, this was a self-sufficient,

---

[60] Readman, 'Landscape preservation'.

predominantly arable England: a great island nation whose rural landscape was covered by broad fields of corn worked by a happy peasantry. As a vision of the nation, it fitted well with the autarkic patriotism of agrarian Tories like Chaplin and those associated with the NAU. This patriotism, it will be recalled, centred on an anxiety to preserve the domestic supply of wheat and, more generally, the 'national industry' of agriculture. Translated into practical policy, it meant the advocacy of measures like the remission of railway rates, the provision of food depots and granaries, bounties on home-produced grain and the imposition of import tariffs. Pure squire Conservatism provided an important ideological dimension to this inward-looking and broadly protectionist agenda, very different in form from the urban-imperial vision of the nation around which Chamberlain's campaign for Tariff Reform coalesced.

The contrast with Chamberlain is suggestive. With it in mind, the agrarian vision of traditional Tories can easily appear implacably opposed to modernity, the reflection of a pre-Corn Law conceptualisation of nationhood alien to the industrialised England that 'Brummagem Joe' inhabited. It is certainly true that a number of Unionists, coached perhaps by the writings of Austin and Ditchfield, looked back fondly on what they imagined to be the 'good old times', some of the salutary aspects of which many such individuals sought to incorporate into their politics, or perhaps into their own daily lives. Winchilsea and his NAU provides one case in point, Wantage's building of Tudor-style cottages on his Berkshire estate another. However, not all those involved in the articulation of pure squire Conservatism wanted to turn back the clock, even supposing this were possible. Winchilsea certainly did, but it is worth re-iterating that the NAU was a failure. And, in any case, Winchilsea's undoubted atavism was tempered by his personal advocacy of the use of modern-day technology in agriculture. An automobile enthusiast, he believed that motorised transport was of great potential use to farmers.[61] And this combination of squirearchical values and pragmatic acceptance of some aspects of modernity was apparent with respect to other landed Tories of a politically reactionary cast of mind. Take Wantage, for example. The houses he constructed for his labourers deliberately evoked a Tory version of bygone Merrie England, but unlike many older cottages (not least those dating from the sixteenth century), they were relatively comfortable places in which to live. Extremely well built, Wantage's cottages were roomy, fitted with up-to-date conveniences and of a high sanitary standard.[62] Their inhabitants, moreover, did not work the soil using the methods of the past: Wantage experimented with artificial manure, irrigation and ranch-

---

[61] In one of his last speeches in the Lords, Winchilsea opposed a bill to restrict the speed of locomotives on highways on the grounds that the fast transportation offered by such vehicles was of great assistance to agriculture: *Hansard*, 4th ser., 1896, xliv. 300–2. See also 'How the motor car may help agriculture', *Cable*, 5 Dec. 1896, 361.

[62] Green, *Country cottages*, 26–8; M. A. Havinden, *Estate villages*, London 1966, 95–6.

style farming, as well as routinely employing steam-ploughs and automated mowing and reaping machines on his land.[63]

The charge of blanket anti-modernism is similarly mistaken when made against Unionists who upheld a vision of an England populated by small proprietors. In their eyes the yeoman and his pre-enclosure world were not irrelevant to contemporary problems. At the very least they provided inspiration for political action: a totem for countering what were perceived as the expropriating and socially destabilising doctrines of the Liberal party. More easily reconcilable with democracy than that of pure squire Conservatism, this vision was of considerable and growing electoral utility to Unionists, who in the late nineteenth and early twentieth centuries were increasingly preoccupied with the defence of property. To be sure, those who advocated measures for the creation of small proprietors looked back fondly on the 'good old English yeoman', but only occasionally did they aver a need for 'a restitution of things more or less on the lines of former times'.[64] While it did draw heavily on the past and (for some) was informed by appreciation of the injustices of the past, the remaking of the yeomanry was not a project that repudiated industrial modernity. Indeed, as one correspondent to the *Rural World* asserted in 1891, the small proprietors of old had produced some of the heroes of the industrial revolution. Had Collings's Smallholdings Bill of that year been passed by parliament,

> It would again have created among our intelligent labourers, mechanics, and would-be small landowners, the sturdy yeomen of whom England was once so proud, and from whose ranks sprang our Watt, Stephenson, and Arkwright – men whose energy and toil have made England great, and whose names rank foremost among our honoured sons.[65]

Finally, Unionist advocates of peasant proprietorship did not envisage a return to pre-modern methods of cultivation. Despite the jibes of detractors, they cannot be described as misty-eyed visionaries who disdained engagement with the realities of growing crops and rearing livestock in late nineteenth-century England. The existence of a growing body of evidence attesting to the practical viability of *petite culture* has already been noted. Moreover, even those who did describe the peasant lifestyle in exaggeratedly felicitous terms devoted considerable time to the technical side of contemporary small-scale agriculture. Collings read numerous technical books on farming practices in countries like Denmark and Belgium, where peasant proprietorship was widespread.[66] This study strengthened his conviction that the extension of small ownership was feasible in Britain, a conviction shared

---

[63] Lindsay, *Wantage*, 385–6; Stearn, 'Lindsay'.
[64] 'To old times again', *RW*, 17 Oct. 1890, 1220–1.
[65] *RW*, 28 Aug, 1891, 585.
[66] W. I. Wilks, 'Jesse Collings and the "back to the land" movement', unpubl. MA diss. Birmingham 1964, 101–17.

by other Unionist reformers like Rider Haggard and Gilbert Parker, to take two prominent examples.[67] Collings's RLL reflected his outlook, and gave much attention to the practical aspects of peasant farming. In the League's newspaper, articles on such down-to-earth matters as 'monster apples and how to grow them', 'injurious insects' and 'how to increase the manure pile' were commonplace. Though the value of individual 'spade cultivation' was emphasised, so too was the idea that small farming, if done well, was an 'intellectual' activity, involving skill, knowledge and the application of modern scientific methods.[68] Indeed, Collings was a keen advocate of the introduction into schools of 'scientific training' in small-scale agriculture, along the lines of that which was supplied in other European countries, and he persistently promoted legislation aimed at this end.[69]

This chapter started with Mallock's *Old order changes*, a novel in which one of the characters, Mr Carew, had spoken in support of the landed aristocracy and its values. At the time when Mallock wrote this book, Carew's sentiments had reflected his own. Indeed, *The old order changes* was of a piece with his defence of the landed elite in the 1880s, which he mounted in the context of the claims made by Henry George and other radicals. In his *Property and progress* (1884), a political tract designed to counter George's *Progress and poverty*, Mallock portrayed the great landowners of England as animated by a spirit of kindly paternalist solicitude in their relations with the toiling masses; their radical enemies, by contrast, were presented as being linked to sinister business interests and motivated by class envy. In effect, Mallock was calling for a sort of revived feudalism, and if his views were somewhat extreme they were not entirely outside the pale of contemporary Conservative discourse. Over time, however, his views changed; and they changed in line with shifts in mainstream Tory thinking, one of the features of which was a decisive turn away from pure squire Conservatism in political debate on the land question. In the 1890s Mallock's defence of the old order and its squirearchical values disappeared from his writing, to be replaced by a hard-headed anti-socialist defence of the capitalist middle class and their values. Far from upholding benevolent paternalism as the pattern to follow, Mallock denied that property ownership enjoined any obligations to help the poor, focusing instead on providing an economic justification for indus-

---

[67] Rider Haggard, *Rural England*, esp. ii. 546–50, and *Rural Denmark and its lessons*, London 1911; G. Parker, 'A word for small ownership in reply to Lord Lincolnshire', NC lxxii (1912), 430–1, and 'Small ownership: new light on old difficulties', NC lxx (1911), 583–5.
[68] See, for example, RW, 6 June 1890, 918.
[69] Collings, *Land reform*, esp. pp. 20–2, 433–4.

trial capitalism (indeed, he rather hoped that industrial capitalism would one day remove the need for charity and self-sacrifice).[70]

Mallock's changing views reflect wider shifts in Conservative argument in these years. As E. H. H. Green has shown, the late nineteenth and early twentieth centuries saw the Tories – in alliance with the Liberal Unionists – transform themselves from the party of landed property to the party of property in general.[71] In the context of the democratisation of the nation after the Third Reform Act and the electoral challenges this implied, as well as the great depression in agriculture, such a change made perfect sense; but in the sphere of land politics one of the casualties of this ideological realignment was the creed of pure squire Conservatism. Conversely, however, one of the beneficiaries of this change was the myth of the yeoman proprietor, which came to exert considerable influence over Unionist political opinion and loomed ever-larger in the party's appeal as the years passed. By the Edwardian period, Conservatives had taken cognisance of advancing democracy. Disdaining the ideal of rural communities centred on the benevolent squire (examples of which were increasingly thin on the ground), they instead focused on developing a popular language of agrarian patriotism centred on the peasant proprietor. It would seem that this language won over voters, as borne out by the party's recovery in rural constituencies at the general election of January 1910. But its use was not simply a shrewd move in party political terms; as this chapter has argued, it also reflected a sea-change in Conservative ideology.

---

[70] See D. J. Ford, 'W. H. Mallock and socialism in England, 1880–1918', in K. D. Brown (ed.), *Essays in anti-labour history*, London 1974, 317–42.
[71] Green, *Crisis*.

8

Land, the Nation, and the Left

'Socialism may ... be summed up in one line, in four words, as
really meaning ENGLAND FOR THE ENGLISH ... To-day
England does not belong to the English. It belongs to a few of the
English. There are bits of it which belong to the whole people, as
Wimbledon Common, Portland Gaol, the high roads; but most of
it is "private property"... Socialists (all Socialists) say that all the
land should belong to the English people, to the nation': Robert
Blatchford, *Real socialism*, London 1898, 13–15.

History has demonstrated the fallacy of the late nineteenth- and early twentieth-century socialist view that class consciousness would soon come to
eclipse national consciousness. In no country was this more evident than
in England – the country, ironically, that Marx and Engels had regarded
as having the most potential for socialist revolution on account of its
unmatched industrialisation and burgeoning proletariat. Here, where the
influence of Marxist internationalism was felt less strongly than on the
continent, patriotic and national sentiment was a significant presence in
the discourse of left-wing political opinion of all shades, from Labour MPs
to communist revolutionaries.[1] This sentiment took a variety of forms. At
a general level it showed itself in the constitutional conservatism of the
Labour party, which was committed to socialist progress through the agency
of parliament, eschewing both revolutionary agitation and doctrinaire repub-
licanism.[2] More particularly, it was evident in proposals for the establishment
of a citizen army and the maintenance of a strong navy in the face of the
German threat, both of which were strongly favoured by Hyndman's SDF.[3]
In addition, much left-wing social reformism was animated by what might
be termed 'welfare patriotism' – a love of country that found expression in
the promotion of legislation to improve the lot of ordinary Englishmen and
women. It was in this spirit that Ben Tillett appealed to his audience in a
speech at Bridgwater in November 1913:

---

[1] Ward, *Red flag*.
[2] M. Pugh, 'The rise of Labour and the political culture of Conservatism, 1890–1945',
History lxxxvii (2002), 523–6.
[3] H. M. Hyndman, *Further reminiscences*, London 1912, 393–402; H. Quelch, *Social-
democracy and the armed nation*, London 1900.

If they valued their race and nation ... then surely, when they realised there were two million mothers in the slums of this country living under conditions of disease and starvation, their souls would revolt against the degraded condition dehumanising the most beautiful of God's creation – (applause). Capitalists said they would take their capital away from the country, but he would point out that money did not make a nation great.[4]

Tillett's was the type of patriotism described by Durkheim as 'directed towards the interior affairs of the society and not its exterior expansion ... societies can have their pride, not in being the greatest or the wealthiest, but in being the most just, the best organized and in possessing the best moral constitution'.[5] It was not, of course, a patriotism confined to Labour and socialist opinion, being shared by many Liberal social reformers too.[6] But it did have a special appeal for those on the left, who (following a line of socialist thought running back to Robert Owen) held an environmentalist view of human nature: improve the material conditions of life in England, and the character of the English people will improve as a consequence. As this chapter will show, land reform was an integral part of a wider project of welfare patriotism, one directed at the strengthening of the nation through the improvement of the condition of the people. It was informed by appreciation of the material hardship suffered by the working class; but was also inspired by patriotic visions of the English past, which presented a picture of national life standing in sharp contrast to contemporary reality.

Socialism and the English national past

Labour and socialist ideology is customarily regarded as directed at effecting dramatic change, breaking from old ways and moving forward into socialist modernity. Yet, while this was certainly true in the late nineteenth- and early twentieth-century English context, readings of history nevertheless loomed large in left-wing discourse. For some socialists this was partly due to the influence of a Marx-inspired dialectical view of history as driven by changes in the means of production – changes that would ultimately bring about the demise of capitalism. Hyndman, to take one example, saw history as valuable insofar as it provided a centuries-spanning narrative of class conflict in England, which could be correlated with the more general narrative supplied by Marx and Engels to form a basis for practical action – a means by which

4   *TE*, 4 Nov. 1913, 7.
5   A. Giddens (ed.), *Durkheim on Politics and the state*, Cambridge 1986, 204.
6   M. Hampton, 'The press, patriotism, and public discussion: C. P. Scott, the *Manchester Guardian* and the Boer War, 1899–1902', *HJ* xliv (2001), esp. p. 191; Readman, 'Patriotism and the general election of 1900', 48–51.

Englishmen could realise their true situation, so facilitating the inevitable revolution from below.[7]

Mapped onto the sphere of land politics, this perspective implied opposition to policies deemed contrary to the unfolding dialectic of history; of these policies, the legislative promotion of peasant proprietors stood out as most disagreeable of all. Hence, despite all their admiration for aspects of fifteenth-century life, Hyndman and Morris condemned the widespread desire 'to return to the old forms of industrial production' as hopelessly 'reactionary' and in any case doomed to fail: 'we cannot, if we would, so put the hands upon the dial of human development'.[8] This argument was especially prominent in socialist discourse in the mid-1880s, in the context of the 'three acres and a cow' agitation promoted by Chamberlain and Collings. At this time the SDF was assiduous in condemning the 'shallow empirics' and 'silly proposals' of the Birmingham radicals as futile efforts to counteract the operation of ineluctable economic laws.[9] (As will be recalled, many Conservatives were saying much the same thing – although they of course did not see economic progress as the engine of revolution.) In a July 1885 article on 'The peasant proprietary fraud', the working-class SDF activist Harry Quelch presented those like Collings who hankered after the sturdy yeomanry of yore as simply trying to defeat calls for land nationalisation by creating 'a class of so-called small proprietors which will act as a rampart for landlordism against the forces of the advancing revolution'.[10]

Quelch's reading of Collings's motives was a perceptive one, and underlined the left's objection to small ownership as politically reactionary: for socialists, economic individualism and political conservatism were inextricably linked, the one being an inevitable product of the other. This objection grew stronger over time, as Tories came to share the view that a large class of peasant proprietors – small capitalists, in effect – would help to protect the entire capitalist system from revolutionary attack. With the passage of the 1892 Smallholdings Act, Quelch was convinced that the Unionists now realised that 'the peasant proprietary class form the greatest and most powerful bulwark of landlordism'.[11] It was an argument that was maintained in socialist discourse until 1914, being taken up by the ILP and the Fabian Society, with the latter's 1905 policy programme on *The revival of agriculture* describing peasant proprietors as 'stubbornly and timorously conservative'.[12] And despite the absence of a land nationalisation pledge in the Edwardian

---

[7] H. M. Hyndman, *The historical basis of socialism in England*, London 1883, esp. pp. 434ff.

[8] H. M. Hyndman and W. Morris, *A summary of the principles of socialism*, London 1884, 61.

[9] *Justice*, 29 Mar. 1884, 5; 14 Feb. 1885, 1.

[10] *Justice* 18 July 1885, 2.

[11] *Justice*, 6 Jan. 1894, 4.

[12] Fabian Society, *The revival of agriculture*, London 1905, 14.

Labour party's official programme, its leadership's hostility to small occupying ownership was abundantly clear. Speaking in the Commons debate on Collings's 1907 Purchase of Land Bill, Ramsay MacDonald declared that

> If the Bill proposed merely to re-establish peasant proprietors and yeoman farmers under the same economic conditions as they occupied before they were destroyed, his Party would oppose it. Any such proposal would be flying in the face of nature. The peasant proprietor and the yeoman farmer of the old conditions could not possibly fight against the great economic forces inimical to them which now existed.[13]

Yet despite all this antipathy to the peasant proprietor as an outdated, politically conservative relic of a defunct economic system, patriotic evocations of a bygone 'Merrie England' were widespread in left-wing discourse. These fused with the millenarian pastoralism evident in pictorial representations of May Day, most famously those of Walter Crane, which were an important element of socialist iconography from the mid-1890s on and regularly appeared in publications like the ILP's *Labour Leader* and the SDF's *Justice*.[14] (Indeed, for a time, the masthead of the latter was decorated with archaic rural motifs.)

As leader of the Independent Labour Party (ILP) and the first Labour MP, Keir Hardie once declared 'every departure of whatever kind from the pastoral simplicity which characterised the even tones of the lives of the men of old' to be 'a burden and a curse', and in 1895 prophesised that after socialism had been achieved in England 'the youngsters will dance around the May-pole, whilst our young people will dance Sir Roger de Coverly and the many round dances sacred to the memory of the village green'.[15] This sort of temporally non-specific allusion to a lost rural communitarianism, the spirit of which could be revived through socialism, owed much to the influence of Blatchford's *Merrie England*. Written in homely, accessible prose by the editor of the *Clarion*, a popular socialist newspaper, this book reached an enormous number of readers.[16] Its message was that England had taken a wrong turn in its history, towards oppressive industrialism and the vulgar commercialism of the 'Manchester School', and away from a life lived in more harmonious relation to nature.[17] Influential as it was, however, Blatchford's book did not provide much in the way of historical detail: though it

---

[13] *Hansard*, 4th ser., 1909, clxx. 824–5.
[14] E.g., *LaL*, 5 May 1894, 5; *Justice*, 2 May 1903, 5.
[15] Cited in Ward, *Red flag*, 23, and Howkins, *Poor labouring men*, 107.
[16] First published in instalments in the *Clarion* in 1892–3, a cheap 1*d.* edition sold over 700,000 copies in the last few months of 1894 and a subsequent 3*d.* version achieved sales of almost 1,000,000: R. Blatchford, *Merrie England*, London 1976, publisher's foreword at p. v.
[17] Blatchford, *Merrie England*, 4–11.

was clear that 'Merrie England' was a memory of the past as well as a hope for the future, the precise provenance of this memory was never spelled out.

Other socialists, however, engaged with history with more specificity, pointing to the late Middle Ages, and the fifteenth century in particular, as the time when ordinary English people enjoyed a 'Golden Age' of freedom and prosperity. Here, the writings of Morris were undoubtedly significant, especially *A dream of John Ball* (1886–7) and *News from Nowhere* (1891). As these works demonstrated, Morris's Utopian vision of a post-industrial, ruralised, communist England was inspired by aspects of the medieval past, not least the craft gilds, which he saw as prototypically socialist organisations.[18] But while heavily tinged with Golden Age medievalism, Morris's vision lacked a coherent historical focus: he did not extol the virtues of a single point in time above all others (notwithstanding its fourteenth- and fifteenth-century resonances, *News from Nowhere* featured a revival of the Anglo-Saxon moot, as well as futuristic innovations like self-propelled 'force-barges' on the Thames).[19] This being the case, it was arguably Hyndman who bore most responsibility among socialists for the idea that 'Merrie England' was a description particularly appropriate to late medieval national life. In Hyndman's narrative, which he set out in his books *England for all* (1881) and *The historical basis of socialism in England* (1883), the peasant risings of Wat Tyler and others had brought about the end of serfdom, inaugurating a time of 'rough plenty' and 'perfect freedom' for the common man; an England 'merrie ... for Englishmen as a whole, not merely for the landlords and capitalists at the top'.[20] As Hyndman emphasised, one of the crucial factors behind the maintenance of this felicitous state of affairs was the land system, which afforded a self-sufficient livelihood to a race of masterless men. Free access to the soil, as conferred by the benevolent pre-Reformation Church and the existence of common rights, fostered prosperity, happiness and all the best elements – self-reliance, independence, vigorousness – of the English national character.[21]

In the hands of socialists, recourse to the past also helped to make the case that socialist ideology was not an alien, un-English ideology, as many of its critics alleged, but had roots stretching down deep into the history of the nation. For Hyndman, the record of popular resistance to oppression dating back to the fourteenth century peasants' revolt provided evidence that socialism was indigenous to England, and not incompatible with patriotic feeling. Notoriously, Hyndman neglected to acknowledge his debt to Marx in *England for all*, an omission that might well have been due to a

---

[18] W. Morris, '*A dream of John Ball*'; '*The pilgrims of hope*'; '*News from Nowhere*', ed. A. L. Morton, London 1977.

[19] Ibid.

[20] Hyndman, *Historical basis*, 1–4, and *England for all* (London 1881), Brighton 1973, 7–10.

[21] Idem, *Historical basis*, 22.

desire to present socialism in as English as possible a light. In a revealingly defensive passage early in his next book, he pointed out that

> It is well to show that the idea of socialism is no foreign importation into England. Tyler, Cade, Ball, Kett, More, Bellers, Spence, Owen read to me like sound English names: not a foreigner in the whole batch. They all held opinions which our capitalist-landlord House of Commons would denounce as direct plagiarisms from 'continental revolutionists'. We islanders have been revolutionists however, and will be again, ignorant as our capitalists are of the history of the people.[22]

Like Hyndman, Morris was also convinced that the beginnings of modern socialist thought could be located deep in English history; and he gave substance to this conviction in *A dream of John Ball* by putting revolutionary sentiments in the mouths of the peasant rebels.[23] Other socialists followed suit, among them the propagandists of the SDF/SDP. One 1909 pamphlet even produced an extract from a speech made by Ball, which it implied was a faithful record of words he addressed to the men of Kent all those centuries ago: 'Good people! Things will never be well in England so long as they be villeins and gentlemen! ... They have leisure and fine houses; we have pain and labour, and the wind and rain in the fields. And yet it is of us and our toil that these men hold their estates.' The lesson here was that Ball's words, though 500 years old, 'may yet be addressed ... by the democracy ... to the landed and capitalist class in England now'.[24] More prosaically, there was also the idea that the conditions of life in the medieval Golden Age amounted to a sort of primitive collectivism, from which England subsequently drew back but which still had value as inspiration for future progress – not least because it underlined the native quality of socialism. Writing in the *Labour Leader* in 1908, the prominent ILP leader (and hero-worshipper of Morris) J. Bruce Glasier claimed that while there was oppression in the medieval period, this was 'external' in character; it did not penetrate down into the quotidian texture of life, as did its modern-day capitalist equivalent, which alienated men from their labour and demoralised the national spirit:

> It is not the oppression from without, but the oppression from within that destroys the soul of men and nations. And here we arrive at the kernel of the matter. *The secret of the freedom and of the genius and art of olden times, which monarch, noble, or priest could not destroy, is found in the* Socialism *which prevailed in the towns and the villages, and in the guild fraternities.*[25]

Thus, Glasier concluded, the memory of this golden age imparted a lesson for the future: 'Not only ... was "Merry England" once a reality, but its reality

---

22 Ibid. 4.
23 Morris, *A dream of John Ball*.
24 A. W. Humphrey, *Land and the people's property*, London [1909], 6.
25 J. B. Glasier, 'Was there once a Merry England?', *LaL*, 21 Aug. 1908, 1.

... is full of promise and instruction to us concerning the merrier England that is to be'.

The vision of a pastoral 'Merrie England' of the past functioned as inspiration for future progress and evidence of the Englishness of English socialism. But if socialism was not foreign to English history, and if its first stirrings had been felt in centuries long gone, what accounted for the lack of progress leftwards in more recent times? Expressed in general terms, the socialist answer to this question was that the development of capitalism had brought the 'golden age' to an end, so setting in train the progressive immiseration of the working class. Described in greater detail, however, such an answer assigned a particularly important part to the advance of (capitalist) landlordism. Here there were affinities with Liberal-radical narratives of dispossession: a sturdy race of country-dwellers was transformed into a debased slum-dwelling proletariat through the extinction of popular rights in the soil. But while Liberals pointed to the eighteenth- and early nineteenth-century enclosure movement or (less frequently) the Norman Conquest as marking the crucial *caesura*, socialists were more inclined to point to events in the Tudor past.[26] Once again, Hyndman provided the most complete account. In his interpretation the fall of the barons after the Wars of the Roses threw many of those who lived on their estates into lives of pauperism and vagrancy, a situation that was later exacerbated by the sixteenth-century enclosure of land for sheep farming. Caused by rising demand for wool, this shift from tillage to pasturage swelled the ranks of the landless, as not only was sheep farming far less labour intensive than arable, but many small farmers also lost their common rights in the process. On top of this, Henry VIII's dissolution of the monasteries took land that had been used for the whole community's benefit and placed it in the hands of noblemen; an act which was, according to Hyndman, 'the greatest injury inflicted on the poor which our history records'.[27] In this analysis, the loss of popular rights in the land was key: it robbed Englishmen of their freedom and independence, forcing them and their descendants from self-sufficient production into wage-slavery. The result was the transformation of the nation's identity. As Hyndman and Morris explained,

Under the rule of the Tudors England changed from a country where in the main the mass of the people lived on their own land, were happy, contented, well-fed, and well-clothed, producing and working up enough food and raw material for their own use, and thinking little of exchange, into a country where people were gradually being driven off the soil, their ancient rights destroyed, their means of production and land taken by others and exchange for profit was becoming the rule of the time; a property-less folk compelled

---

[26] On socialists' relative lack of interest in the 'Norman yoke' see Ward, *Red flag*, 24–5.

[27] Hyndman, *England for all*, 12–16 at p. 15; Hyndman and Morris, *Summary*, 19–22.

187

to work for the farmer's profit, or forced to compete against one another in the cities for wages to keep body and soul together, replaced to a large extent the sturdy yeomen, craftsmen, and labourers of old days. Pauperism became an integral portion of the English social system, and the lot of the many one never-ending servitude under the guise of freedom.[28]

In this interpretation, later injustices – such as the enclosures of the eighteenth and nineteenth centuries – further extended the damage done; but the critical moment in the history of popular dispossession had come centuries earlier. Appreciation of the dispossession and the transformation it wrought fed into a patriotic project of restitution and national renewal through land reform. This project was not merely the preoccupation of socialist intellectuals and ideologues, but also formed an important element of the politics of many mainstream Labour party politicians.

National dispossession and the language of left-wing land politics

For socialists, history supplied a sad story of national dispossession, a chronicle of how the masses of the people were deprived of the stake in the soil that was their birthright. In this way the past could be used to explain the present, and in particular the modern-day Englishman's exclusion from the land of his native country, which was presented as penetrating many aspects of his daily life. It was not just that men were prevented from getting hold of land to cultivate free from the shackles of capitalist domination; the whole countryside was closed to the people of England: parks were reserved for the private enjoyment of the rich, footpaths were stopped, village greens were stolen, fishing and the gathering of flowers or berries was prohibited, and so on. This explains why many socialists were strong supporters of the landscape preservation movement, which they regarded as a struggle for the assertion of communal rights in the land, against the claims of private property.[29] Publications like *Justice* paid a good deal of attention to commons and footpaths, and socialist organisations orchestrated a number of protests against landlordly high-handedness in access disputes.[30]

Shutting footpaths and denying access to open spaces provided evidence of the pervasive iniquity of the land system, illustrating how it had a negative effect on the day-to-day existence of ordinary people. Many Liberals thought similarly, of course, but socialists drew the moral that it was not just 'landlordism' that was the problem, but the institution of private prop-

---

[28] Hyndman and Morris, *Summary*, 55.
[29] See, for example, H. S. Salt, *On Cambrian and Cumbrian hills*, London 1908, ch. vii.
[30] One prominent example was the controversy over a road leading to the summit of Winter Hill, near Bolton: *Justice*, 12 Sept. 1896, 5; 17 Sept. 1896, 8; P. Salveson, *Will yo' come o' Sunday mornin'? The 1896 battle for Winter Hill*, Bolton 1996.

erty in land. This fed into calls for land nationalisation, or reforms tending towards this end, which were often presented in the form of a demand that Britain (or England) should 'belong to the British'. In *Britain for the British*, his 1902 follow-up to *Merrie England*, Blatchford gave powerful expression to this demand.[31] But it also occupied a significant place in the idiom of platform rhetoric. As independent Labour candidate for Colne Valley at the by-election of 1907, Victor Grayson chose to begin his official address with Karl Marx's words, 'Workers of the World, unite! You have a world to win, and only your chains to lose.' But such strident internationalism was offset by patriotic feeling when it came to the question of the land, with Grayson declaring

> it to be a gross injustice that nearly the whole of the land of Great Britain should be in the hands of an insignificant number of people, whose huge rent-rolls enable them to live luxuriously on the labour of landless men and women. The land of a country should belong to the people of that country.[32]

Such rhetoric was not always backed up with reference to history: Labour politicians were quite capable of arguing, on *a priori* grounds, that the system of landownership was a fit object of patriotic condemnation – natural rights, legal precepts or simple welfare patriotism could all be invoked. In H. Brockhouse's 1909 ILP pamphlet, *The curse of the country*, it was argued that historical injustices, while relevant, were not essential to the case for land nationalisation; the damage landlordism inflicted on the community was sufficient grounds for its abolition.[33] But, more often than not, the past was called upon to give substance to claims that landlordism was based on robbery, and that land nationalisation – or at least radical reform – was necessary to restore the nation's stake in the soil. Such an approach bore a strong resemblance to that of the Edwardian Liberal party, and indeed leftist discourse used some of the same historical sources as that of the Liberals (Hasbach and the Hammonds featured prominently).[34] But not all leftist discourse drew on the past to the same extent. In general, there seems to have been a positive correlation between support for land nationalisation and reference to the sad tale of national dispossession. The SDF was a case in point. Having always backed land nationalisation as a just policy of 'restitution',[35] the party's propaganda on the land question at the 1906 election drew heavily on history. In Northampton, where two candidates stood, much was made of the idea that 'the people' had been 'robbed of their heritage by Whig and Tory land-sharks', with voters being urged to cast their ballots

---

31 R. Blatchford, *Britain for the British*, London 1902, 52–4.
32 *Election addresses*, reel 8: by-election addresses (1905–10).
33 H. Brockhouse, *The curse of the country*, London 1909, 2–3.
34 C. V. J. Griffiths, 'Labour and the countryside: rural strands in the British Labour movement, 1900–1939', unpubl. DPhil. diss. Oxford 1996, 32–42.
35 Hyndman and Morris, *Summary*, 60.

'for the purpose of becoming owners again of the property which was stolen from their forefathers'.[36]

It was a similar story with the ILP, which had also supported land nationalisation from the beginning. The party's original policy manifesto declared support for nationalisation on the grounds that 'we desire to restore to the whole people the common heritage that kings have stolen and bestowed on their favourite lackeys and harlots, from whom our great landlords are descended'.[37] This theme persisted in ILP discourse until 1914. In his *Socialism, the dukes and the land* [1909], the prominent ILP propagandist William Anderson deployed history to support the claim that as private property in land was essentially theft (much of it having been stolen through the agency of aristocratic parliaments), its forcible restoration to the people was entirely justified.[38] To provide evidence in support of his party's radical position, Anderson delved into the family histories of prominent noblemen who were especially vocal in their opposition to land taxes and valuation, arguing that much of their estates had been bestowed upon their ancestors after the dissolution of the monasteries, or during the enclosure movement – often as a reward for sycophancy towards the crown; and such ill-gotten gains had been the cause of national hardship over centuries.[39]

The long memory of the left in this regard was also evident in the electioneering appeal of ILP candidates. It was especially prominent on those relatively rare occasions when the party contested an agricultural constituency. In Gloucestershire, where Labour secured a tenuous foothold before 1914, Charles Fox pushed the narrative of national dispossession to the fore. Chairman of the Gloucester ILP, Fox stood as candidate for Tewkesbury in January 1910, mounting a campaign that combined good socialist hostility to small ownership, Blatchford-like patriotic sloganeering and keen appreciation of the historical injustice visited on the nation by landlordism:

THREE-FOURTHS OF GREAT BRITAIN ARE OWNED BY ELEVEN THOUSAND MEN. OVER FORTY MILLIONS OF OUR PEOPLE HAVE NO INHERITANCE in what is fondly called 'Our native land so dear'. Merely increasing the number of landowners, as in Ireland, will not solve the difficulty; but the gradual transfer of all land and minerals to the ownership and control of the whole people. **BRITAIN MUST BELONG TO THE BRITISH**, and not to a small fraction of them.

Whatever use the landlords may have been in the past, when they held the soil in exchange for the duty of defending the country, we cannot any more afford the luxury of a class who neither use their estates well themselves, nor allow the workers access to the land.

[36] *The Northampton Pioneer*, special election edition 1906, 1.
[37] *LaL*, 17 Oct. 1891, 8.
[38] W. C. Anderson, *Socialism, the dukes and the land*, London [1909], 12.
[39] Ibid. 11–12.

The laws have hitherto been made by the wealthy and powerful in the interests of property and privilege. The common land that once covered a third of England has been stolen by Act of Parliament, and the burden of armaments thrown upon the backs of the whole people. With landlordism entrenched in the Upper House it is folly to fill up the People's Chamber with landlords and capitalists. **STRENGTHEN THE LABOUR PARTY AND NATIONALISE THE LAND.**[40]

However, the propaganda of ILP men fighting hopeless contests in the shires was one thing; that of mainstream Labour politicians elsewhere in the country was quite another. Following the line taken by the party leadership, which steered clear of unambiguous endorsement of land nationalisation as policy, most candidates and MPs did not employ language like that of Fox. Yet allusion to the history of dispossession and calls for the repatriation of stolen land did crop up from time to time, especially in the language of the Labour movement in provincial towns with large rural hinterlands. At the Taunton by-election of February 1909, the Labour candidate Frank Smith used the memory of dispossession as a rhetorical device to rebut Conservative accusations of socialist expropriation. In one barnstorming speech he attacked his Tory opponent, William Peel, whose 'party had stuck on the hoardings bills about Socialism being spoliation and robbery'. But such accusations were absurd, Smith claimed, as spoliation and robbery

> had been the history of this country – (applause). If they asked him (Mr Smith) for an example he pointed them to the land of this country (applause). Was the land of the nation the property of a few titled men who because they had been in the place of the power for the making of the laws had secured its possession – (No) ... If they voted for Mr Peel would he enable them to recover their lost heritage? – (No.)[41]

Here, such rousing populism was not linked to any very detailed explication of land policy, but things could be different elsewhere. One such example is provided by Norwich, where George Roberts was the leading figure in the city's Labour movement and MP between 1906 and 1923. Though a mainstream (indeed progressively rightwards-leaning) figure, Roberts – a member of the ILP until 1914 – was a keen supporter of radical land reform in the direction of nationalisation, and acted as chairman of the Labour Land Enquiry in 1912–14. In his campaign at the 1904 by-election he argued that 'the land should revert to the people to whom it belonged', drawing on the past crimes of landlordism to make his case.[42] 'From the 16th century right down to modern times', he told the meeting announcing his candidature, 'the work of expropriating the people from the land had been carried on

40 *Election addresses*, reel 5 (Jan. 1910).
41 *TE*, 23 Feb. 1909, 2.
42 *EDP*, 12 Jan. 1904, 8.

... The landlords had passed hundreds of enclosure Acts to legalise their thefts.' It followed that restitution through reform was required and the best way of achieving this was to return representatives of the working class to the Commons; in this way the narrative of national dispossession could be linked to the Labour party's central claim that workingmen required representation in parliament. Roberts repeated this argument at later elections, even going so far as to supplement his allusions to past 'robbery' on the part of landlords with legal learning: in one speech he quoted extensively from Coke, Pollock and Blackstone to make the point that English law had never recognised the existence of absolute property in land.[43]

For all their recourse to the past, Labour and socialist supporters of land reform – like their Liberal counterparts – did not seek a return to pre-industrial conditions of life. Left-wing opinion was after all unanimous in rejecting the yeoman proprietor as representing an outdated and regrettably individualistic form of economic organisation, the revival of which would have a counterproductive and reactionary effect. Even among the most enthusiastic champions of 'Merrie England' medievalism, the past did not provide a blueprint for future progress. To be sure, it had many lessons to teach, including the idea that socialism was historically 'English'; and at a more general level it gave an account of the advance of capitalist oppression – a story in which the extinction of the people's stake in their native soil played a key part. As a Marxist who believed in the inevitable onward march of history driven by economic forces, Hyndman did not hanker for a return to the conditions of the fifteenth century; but these conditions did throw into sharp relief the alienation of life in modern England, where workers toiled as dependent appendages of mechanised capitalism. For Hyndman and other Marxist socialists, history was a means by which the proletariat could be apprised of its true position, of the genealogy of its degradation, and from such self-knowledge would spring national renewal through revolution.

Morris, another revolutionary socialist with his eye on the past, took a similar view. Although Morris drew heavily on history in his writings, he never believed that a return to bygone ways of life was possible or desirable. For all its historical resonance, News from Nowhere represented a vision of a future England, in which certain centuries-old values, practices and organisations were preserved or revived (handicraft, for example) in combination with aspects of industrial modernity.[44] This is evident from Morris's treatment of machinery. Like Edward Carpenter and other ethical socialists, Morris was not hostile to machines in themselves; his objection was to their use in the context of a capitalist system where they caused the

---

[43] Ibid. 5 Jan. 1906, 6.
[44] The oft-made claim that News from Nowhere is a purely medieval Utopia is absurd, as the Church and feudalism, the two key elements of medieval society, are absent: A. D. Culler, The Victorian mirror of history, New Haven 1985, 239.

degradation and alienation of their operatives.[45] 'We should', he felt, 'be the masters of our machines and not their slaves, as we are now. It is not this or that tangible steel or brass machine which we want to get rid of, but the great intangible machine of commercial tyranny.'[46] It followed that modern machinery was entirely acceptable outside the context of industrial capitalism: in the socialist Utopia of *Nowhere*, machines run by a new source of power (perhaps electricity) are used in large-scale enterprises like mills, and also in the homes of the Utopians, where they are employed for tedious and unpleasant tasks. In this way labour would be saved to the extent that the working day would be reduced to four hours, so setting free the creative energies of the people.[47]

Morris's attitude to machinery was consonant with that of left-wing opinion generally. For all his hostility to contemporary industrial capitalism, Blatchford was a keen advocate of scientific methods and innovation; he did not propose any reversion to a pre-modern economy. In *Merrie England*, the development of 'water power and electricity' was presented as a means of combating 'the smoke nuisance' of English cities while at the same time furthering economic progress.[48] Similarly, left-wing politicians held out much hope for technological advances, providing they were directed towards the good of the nation rather than the selfish interests of exploitative entrepreneurs. With regard to the land question, some, like the SDF, proposed to impose a collectivised industrialism on the countryside by introducing large-scale municipal (or state) farms, it being argued that this would promote social justice while maximising productivity through mechanisation and other benefits of economies of scale. Most did not go as far as this, however. Drawing on the burgeoning technical literature on the subject, Labour (including the ILP) argued that modern science and technology could be applied with good effect to small-scale cultivation: chemical fertilisers, electrical power, mechanisation and so on could all be used by smallholders, especially in the context of co-operative methods of organisation (which provided the benefits of scale economies without necessitating large farms).[49] Here, continental intensive farming practices were especially influential, with the Labour Party's Land Enquiry Report drawing heavily on the example of Denmark, a country to which the Enquiry Committee travelled to collect evidential support for its proposals.[50]

As suggested by its Land Enquiry Report, Labour's vision was of a peopled countryside overspread by communities of smallholders, holding their farms

---

45 R. Watkinson, 'The obstinate refusers: work in *News from Nowhere*', in S. Coleman and P. O'Sullivan (eds), *William Morris and* News from Nowhere, Bideford 1990, 96–9.
46 P. Thompson, *The work of William Morris*, London 1967, 250.
47 Morris, *News from Nowhere*.
48 Blatchford, *Merrie England*, 18, 21–2.
49 Brockhouse, *Curse of the country*, 1.
50 Labour party, *Labour party and the agricultural problem*.

on secure tenancy from the state or local authority, and cultivating the soil using up-to-date agricultural methods, assisted by co-operation (which itself would restore community spirit to the villages). This formed part of a wider decentralised vision for the nation – a vision which did not reflect rejection of the 'urban' or the 'industrial' in favour of the 'rural', but a desire to combine the best elements of town and country life. It was a vision that had strong affinities with that of Morris, whose News from Nowhere gave expression to these desiderata, describing a land where the city was free of congested slums, being 'invaded' by the countryside in the form of woods, gardens and other open spaces; and where, conversely, 'the town invaded the country' by infusing it with intellectual vigour, creative dynamism and technological progress.[51] This was also a vision that had strong affinities with that of the emerging Garden City movement, with which many on the political left were associated. Primarily conceived as a means of ameliorating urban overcrowding and rural depopulation, the pre-1914 Garden City plan involved low-density urban settlement, green spaces and the like, but also the widespread development of allotments and smallholdings in the city's hinterland.[52]

But while socialists believed that the Garden City movement would do some good, land reform in conjunction with other legislation (like railway nationalisation) was their preferred means of giving substance to such visionary ideas. By granting public authorities sweeping powers of compulsory purchase, urban overcrowding could be relieved, unemployment reduced and the English people set free to live productive lives spread out more widely over the land of their native country. This was the perspective of the Fabians, whose technocratic proclivities and faith in the transformative power of the central state did not prevent them arguing for a revival of agriculture and rural life oriented around a decentralised Garden City-type model. While emphatic that it would be 'futile' to attempt to halt the industrialising tendencies of the day, Fabians were convinced that agriculture should not be allowed to collapse and looked to socialist reform to rectify the balance between town and country. In 1905 the report of the Fabian Agricultural Committee argued that there was no binary opposition between land reform and urban renewal, claiming that the revival of agriculture through socialist legislation would also benefit towns, stimulating the decentralisation of population and industry:

> With the revival of agriculture would come also the revival of the small towns which at present decay with the decay of rural industry. In this way ... the towns would be 'spread over the country' and a stimulus given to the decen-

---

[51] K. Kumar, 'A pilgrimage of hope: William Morris's journey to Utopia', Utopian Studies v (1994), 101–2.
[52] E. Howard, Garden cities of to-morrow, London 1902, esp. pp. 2–5, 22; T. Adams, Garden city and agriculture, London 1905.

tralisation of manufacture. Round the suburbs would run a ring of farms, and within their precincts many of the workers on the nearer large holdings might reside. The outer village-clusters would be closely connected with them by motor services and light railways. In all these ways the best elements of town and country life would be interfused. The rural districts would be more closely settled, and while the general health of the nation would be improved, dullness and apathy would be eliminated from country life.[53]

This vision of a merging of the 'best elements of town and country life' was reiterated in a further Fabian land report of 1913.[54] It also featured in the language of Labour party politicians, who were still more committed to a decentralised resettlement of the nation – what MacDonald called 'a scheme of repatriation' to be achieved through local authority-supplied farm colonies, smallholdings, housing reform and the like.[55] In his 'Towards socialism' series of articles for the *Labour Leader*, published in 1908, J. Bruce Glasier declared that

> The restoration of the land to the people and the people to the land will not destroy, but recreate and greatly sweeten and ennoble the towns. They will no longer be the enemies of the villages and the fields, but will become friends with them, co-operating and benefiting mutually by each other's help. The towns will re-energise the country, and the country will refresh and nourish the towns. The towns will spread themselves out into the gardens and fields, and the fields and gardens will stretch pleasantly into the towns. That is the law of adjustment which Socialism will fulfil.[56]

In the eyes of Labour land reformers, what was required was not a reversion to pre-modern pastoralism or any repudiation of the city and industrial modernity, but a restoration of national socio-economic balance.[57] Under the influence of untrammelled capitalism and landlordism, cities had become grossly overcrowded while rural areas languished in bucolic backwardness, their populations ebbing away to urban slums and far-flung colonies. The solution was not tinkering reform within the parameters of the *status quo*, or idealistic plans for state farms, but rather far-reaching but practicable measures to facilitate the redistribution of England's population.

---

[53] *Revival of agriculture*, 22.
[54] H. D. Harben, *The rural problem*, London 1913, 5–6.
[55] *Leicester Daily Post*, 18 May 1905, 5; Tichelar, 'Socialists, Labour and the land', 133.
[56] *LaL*, 14 Aug. 1908, 1.
[57] On this idea see also F. Trentmann, 'Wealth versus welfare: the British Left between free trade and national political economy before the First World War', *HR* lxx (1997), 82.

Welfare patriotism and national renewal

Animated by a desire to see Englishmen and women re-people the land in new decentralised communities that combined the best elements of urban and rural life, the land reform project of the left was a project of national renewal, and one that also drew strength from sentiments of welfare patriotism. Labour and socialist politicians regarded the injustices inflicted on the people over centuries by the advance of capitalism as having had negative effects on the health and well-being of the nation that true patriots ought to abhor. As Ramsay MacDonald explained in a speech during the Taunton by-election of 1909,

> [R]ural England had been depopulated by reason of landlord rapacity – because the great landlords in the past saw that sheep paid better than peasants. The great landowners had shut the people out of the land; they had stolen the commons, and now they were even stealing the highways by means of the use of motor cars. (Laughter & applause.) No wonder the people were poor, and that physical deterioration had sapped the strength of the nation. The other side claimed to be the patriotic party, but their patriotism consisted in making everything tend to their own profit. He said by all means be patriotic and worship their country, but had they ever known a patriotic people cribbed, cabined, and confined in factories? He held that the Labour party was the patriotic party, because they stood for the emancipation and liberty of the workers.[58]

In the language of the left, such welfare patriotism was often contrasted with the hollow, jingoistic patriotism of their opponents. During his election campaign at Norwich in 1906, George Roberts linked his opposition to the recently-concluded Boer War with his support for land reform, making the point that it was wrong to invade other countries and take their land while England's own natural resources lay underdeveloped, to the detriment of the nation's health and character. 'The Labour party', he told an audience at the city's Agricultural Hall,

> maintained that whilst England ... had gone scouring about the globe in search of fresh markets we had failed to properly develop the consuming power of our own people, to properly cultivate our own land, and to utilise our own resources. True patriotism lay in using to the fullest advantage the land and resources of our own country before we sought to acquire territory in other parts of the globe. (Loud applause).[59]

In a sense, this sort of rhetoric echoed the 'home colonisation' cry of contemporary Liberals. But it also reflected a tendency within the Labour party towards autarkic economic nationalism – a rejection of trade and commerce

---

58 *TE*, 23 Feb. 1909, 3.
59 *EDP*, 10 Jan. 1906, 6.

for home production that had much in common with some agrarian Tories. And for Roberts, whose thought certainly did tend in this latter direction, the problem was that while Britain and British trade was expanding overseas, land and labour languished in idleness at home.

Following the good socialist axiom that labour added to land was the source of all wealth, other party members took up similar views, focusing particular attention on the unemployed, who searched in vain for work while land was left underused by building speculators and landlords. The solution seemed clear: bring unemployed labour and unemployed soil together. Various schemes were proposed to achieve this, with the creation of so-called 'land colonies' proving especially popular. Indeed, Keir Hardie used his maiden speech in the Commons to call for government encouragement of 'home colonies' to combat the unemployment problem, and went on to make similar suggestions throughout his career.[60] Labour proposals for unemployment bills in years following typically included provisions for the establishment of farm colonies.[61] The party leadership's views reflected considerable support for the idea among Labour grassroots opinion in the 1890s and 1900s (in Bradford, to take one example).[62] Aside from land colonies, land reform more generally was advocated as a remedy for unemployment, particularly in ILP circles.[63] Public ownership of land for smallholdings, as well as outright nationalisation, was presented as a way of curtailing the monopolistic practices that denied men access to land – and hence work. Speaking in the debate on the King's Speech in February 1909, Will Crooks made an impassioned call for state action to make more land available for the unemployed:

> We have wealth, and there is land enough to maintain every man, woman and child in the country ... We say to the Tariff Reformers: Have you ever thought of turning your attention to the land? 'We really love the workman' – apart from what you 'do' him for. Do you really love him? Do you really care for an Imperial race? Turn your attention to the land! Remember that you import in foodstuffs £4 per head of the population. What work we could find for our people if we were not looking about for excuses for not finding work![64]

Crooks's reference to 'an Imperial race' here touches on an aspect of Labour's reformism – in land policy and in other areas – which historians have been

---

[60] I. Mclean, *Keir Hardie*, London 1975, 46; *Hansard*, 4th ser., 1904, cxxx. 457–8.
[61] For example, the 1909 draft Unemployment Bill. See Labour party, *Report of the ninth annual conference of the Labour Party*, London 1909, appendix 1, 'special conference on unemployment, 27 Jan. 1909'.
[62] K. Laybourn, '"The defence of the bottom dog": the Independent Labour Party in local politics', in D. G. Wright and J. A. Jowitt (eds), *Victorian Bradford*, Bradford 1982, 230–3.
[63] See, for example, T. Mann, *The programme of the I.L.P. and the unemployed*, London 1895.
[64] *Hansard*, 5th ser., 1909, i. 154.

reluctant to discuss. For some on the left, concern about the health and character of the English 'race' was an integral part of their welfare patriotism. In the context of debates about the land question, this took the form of fears that the capitalist economic system was promoting physical and moral degeneration, with the monopoly of real property being accorded a key role in this process. For those of this cast of mind, current arrangements had racially negative effects in both town and country. In urban areas they fostered unsanitary overcrowding and high levels of competition for jobs, which had a depressive effect on wages and by extension on health, while in rural areas they promoted depopulation, with fit men and women leaving the land for English slums or overseas colonies. Given their environmentalist view of human nature – the view that (as Blatchford put it) 'man is a creature of circumstances'[65] – a number of socialist politicians were inclined to regard such conditions as fraught with national danger; for what sort of creature would the future Englishman be if corrective action were not taken?

The SDF, in particular, had few doubts as to the answer to this question: if the people were not soon restored to their heritage in the soil through land nationalisation 'the standard of the English race' would 'become a negligible quantity'.[66] This was the verdict of the Northampton SDF in 1906; as its newspaper lamented,

> [t]he people have been effectively divorced from the soil which their fathers and forefathers tilled and made fertile, and the ever-growing and spreading towns and cities have become congested with the struggling crowds of dispossessed ones, forced by economic circumstance to exchange the free, open, health-giving life of the country for the foetical, unhealthy, body-dwarfing and soul-destroying life of the towns.[67]

Such views were not unrepresentative; indeed they reflected those of the SDF leadership. Since his Tory Democrat days Hyndman had been concerned about racial degeneration. If his memoirs are to be believed, in 1881 he even called on the aged Disraeli (whose literary work, especially *Sybil*, he admired), treating the old statesmen to a fireside harangue about the socialist crusade that he was in the process of launching. 'Well, we cannot go on as we are without national decay and eventual collapse', Hyndman asseverated, before continuing,

> Our people are being crushed into the cities, where they lose their bodily and mental vigour, or the more capable of them emigrate straight from the country to the colonies, and leave only the weaklings to perpetuate the race at home. The process of deterioration is going on steadily. There are fewer

---

[65] Blatchford, *Merrie England*, 51–2. Blatchford himself was in no doubt that the conditions of the poor were causing race deterioration: *Britain for the British*, 19.
[66] *Northampton Pioneer*, Mar. 1906, 4.
[67] Ibid.

agriculturalists every year, and the recruiting ground for healthy inhabitants of the cities is thus being reduced every year. All can see that the physique of the population is falling off. And at the very same time we are grasping more territory than before.[68]

If it seems unlikely that this is an accurate verbatim record of what Hyndman actually said on this occasion, it is undeniable that these words reflected long-held views. His *Historical basis of socialism* contained much discussion of the degenerative effects of industrial capitalism and landlordism on the ordinary people of England – and therefore on 'the real strength and well-being of the nation'.[69] Such concerns were repeated still more trenchantly in his later writings.[70]

In common with their Liberal and Tory counterparts, socialist support for land reform as a means of bolstering the fibre of the English race can be placed in the context of the 'national efficiency' movement, which developed considerable momentum in the aftermath of the Boer War. The poor physical fitness of many would-be recruits made an impact on socialist as well as Liberal and Conservative opinion. In 1903 *Justice* ran a series of articles urging the need to get 'back to the land' for the sake of racial health.[71] The picture they painted was little short of apocalyptic: capitalism might have brought 'commercial prosperity', but it had also caused a situation in which the nation had to confront 'an empire rotting at its heart; a decadent and dying race; a people torn from the land, forced into the overcrowded slums of our great cities to provide food for profit for the master class, and perishing of anaemia, adulterated food and foul air'.[72] And while not all socialists used such colourful language, the perspective offered by *Justice's* articles occupied a significant place in socialist discourse. Closely connected to the national efficiency movement, Fabianism provides a particularly important case in point. Tellingly, while the Fabians' rural reports of 1905 and 1913 claimed that smallholdings were now more profitable than large farms, it was made explicit that economic considerations did not provide the reason for reform. Instead, legislation for the provision of smallholdings, cottages and a minimum agricultural wage was justified on the grounds of national need, as a way of halting rural depopulation and by so doing improving character and health.[73] The Labour party leadership also expressed such views from time to time. In his *Socialism and society* of 1905, Ramsay MacDonald complained that capitalists and landlords were indifferent to 'the deterioration of the physique of the people', as this had no immediate impact on profits. 'Indeed', he went on, 'profits and rents can really be made out of the very condi-

68 H. M. Hyndman, *The record of an adventurous life*, London 1911, 243.
69 Idem, *Historical basis*, 158–9. See also pp. 311–25.
70 See, for example, idem, *Record*, 296–303.
71 *Justice*, 24 Jan. 1903, 1; 9 May 1903, 1; 12 Dec. 1903, 4.
72 *Justice*, 11 July 1903, 1.
73 Harben, *Rural problem*, 52–6; Fabian Society, *Revival of agriculture*, 5.

tions which hasten this deterioration'; but if cramming people into slums benefited landlords' rent-rolls, such capitalistic practice ran counter to the national welfare and this justified state intervention.[74]

As was the case in Hyndman's writings and *Justice*'s 'Back to the land' articles of 1903, the left's patriotic concern for the welfare of the race was often accompanied by assertions that England was dangerously dependent on foreign sources of food. Blatchford argued strenuously that Britain's exposure to 'the risk of almost certain starvation during a European war' justified the dismantling of the land system. This system, he claimed, prevented national self-sufficiency in food because of its capitalistic focus on profit (not least rent) ahead of production.[75] Addressing his fictional interlocutor Mr Smith (a 'hard-headed workman, fond of facts') in *Merrie England*, Blatchford spelled out the perversion of patriotism perpetrated by supporters of the *status quo*:

> Tory orators and Jingo poets are fond of shouting of the glories of the Empire and the safety of our possessions; and reams of paper have been covered with patriotic songs about our 'silver streak' and our 'tight little island'. But don't you see Mr. Smith, that if we lose our power to feed ourselves *we destroy the advantages of our insular position*? Don't you see that if we destroy our agriculture we destroy our independence at a blow, and become a defenceless nation?[76]

As we have seen, Liberals and (especially) Conservatives harboured anxieties similar to Blatchford's. But in the language of the left, such concerns chimed with a socialist emphasis on production rather than trade and finance – and in particular with the ideological conviction that land was the ultimate source of all wealth. This conviction fed assertions that the neglect of the land under capitalism, which laid waste the countryside and crowded the people into towns, cut at the taproot of national existence. The ILP was especially fond of making such claims, which were presented as arguments against private property and in favour of land nationalisation. Declaring the private property-based land system to be 'rotten', Charles Fox told readers of the *Labour Leader* in 1913 that

> [t]o everyone his own immediate industry and conditions seem all important, but in reality the industry of agriculture and the conditions under which it is carried on are vital to the whole population of the country. It is a bald statement of fact that no nation can exist for long without a sound rural basis.[77]

With their emphasis on the need for self-sufficiency in food, such arguments were strongly suggestive of autarkic economic nationalism, and despite Labour's declared support for Free Trade after 1903 there was a definite

---

[74] J. Ramsay MacDonald, *Socialism and society*, 2nd edn, London 1895, 144–5.
[75] Blatchford, *Britain for the British*, 98–9, 116–17; *Merrie England*, 11–13.
[76] Idem, *Merrie England*, 14.
[77] *LaL*, 10 Oct. 1913, 558.

tendency in this direction within socialist thought, as Frank Trentmann has shown.[78] It is certainly true that anti-commercialist sentiment suffused left-wing debate and from this it was a fairly short step to the type of position represented by Collings and some radical Unionists, with their rejection of liberal market internationalism in favour of the maximisation of domestic production protected by tariff walls. Blatchford regarded the rivalry between different countries on the world stage as really a struggle for the supply of food, and was hot in his condemnation of 'Manchester School' advocates of Free Trade who had sacrificed agriculture – and thereby national safety – on the altar of 'cheapness' and capitalistic money-getting.[79] *Clarion* propaganda echoed this line, arguing that 'the idea of turning everything into money' had been 'carried too far' and the course of true patriotism was to turn away from commercialism, trade and the profit impulse, and towards domestic production – the production of food in particular.[80] In this interpretation, England's economic system had spawned a host of inter-related national evils: 'Manchester School' capitalism at home prompted lust for new markets and empire overseas, the corollary to which was the underdevelopment of home resources and dependency on food imports; this in turn threatened racial deterioration and starvation in time of war, which promoted militarism and imperialism in an attempt to shore up the nation's increasingly precarious position. For the sake of commerce and empire, *Clarion* pamphleteers thundered, '[w]e have given up the land which should give us bread', and in this way the free trading 'Imperialism of the Stock Exchange' was imperilling 'our very existence as a nation'.[81]

An important element of the solution socialists of this bent proposed to remedy England's existential crisis was to turn inwards, away from the 'evil policy of self-aggrandisement' towards a 'policy of self-conquest' through land reform.[82] The rhetoric used here had some kinship with that employed by Edwardian Liberal exponents of 'home colonisation', but the crucial difference in perspective was socialist antipathy to commercial capitalism and even – in some cases – to Free Trade itself. This, then, was a version of Little Englander welfare patriotism that positioned itself in opposition to liberal market economics, which it presented as the handmaiden of imperial expansion and national malaise at home. Thus it followed that it was 'blasphemy from the point of view of patriotism' for 'Rule Britannia politicians' to clamour for the opening of foreign markets, while at the same time millions of their fellow-countrymen were languishing in degradation and want at home: '[I]t is to the opening up and development of our *home market*

---

[78] Trentmann, 'Wealth versus welfare'.
[79] Blatchford, *Merrie England*, esp. pp. 6–11, 40–3, and *Britain for the British*, 97ff.
[80] W. Sowerby, *The agricultural deadlock*, London 1896.
[81] A. M. Thompson, *Towards conscription*, London 1898; W. Jameson, *The coming fight with famine*, London 1896.
[82] Jameson, *Coming fight*.

right here in our own country, amongst our own people, that we must turn, and turn quickly, if we are to avert that national shipwreck that seems to threaten.'[83] And as labour applied to the soil was held to be the source of all real wealth, one especially effective way of doing this, it was argued, was to re-people the countryside and replace the capitalist system with co-operative communities of smallholdings (or, in the case of the SDF, municipal farms).

It might be objected that the ideological position just outlined was confined to the extremes of Labour discourse. But while the SDF was undeniably fairly marginal by the 1900s, the same cannot be said of Blatchford or his influential *Clarion* movement, whose newspaper outsold all others on the left until 1914.[84] Neither can it be said of the ILP, a number of whose members held leadership positions within the Labour party in the 1900s. Many of these individuals combined advocacy of land reform (including nationalisation) with an anti-commercial, autarkic economic stance and attitudes to Free Trade that ranged from equivocal to openly critical. In 1903 Philip Snowden expressed the view that

> [t]he idea of the Manchester School that we should devote ourselves to building up a foreign trade, that England should be the workshop of the world, was a mistake. The tendency all over the world is for manufactures to settle down where the raw material is grown. Each country must devote itself to developing its natural resources. This is the new policy that we must adopt.[85]

It followed from this that land, as the primary natural resource, merited the attention of socialist legislation. For Snowden this meant land nationalisation, which he described as the 'only possibility of national salvation' as it would make 'our nation a self-sustaining nation'.[86] 1903, however, was the year of Labour's electoral pact with the Liberals and also that in which Chamberlain launched his Tariff Reform crusade. Yet, while there is little doubt that these developments caused Labour to draw back from outright advocacy of economic autarky bolstered by radical land reform, attitudes to Free Trade remained equivocal, despite the party's official opposition to protection.

Snowden's own position here is worthy of further comment. At the 1904 party conference he moved a resolution condemning Chamberlainite Tariff Reform while simultaneously declaring that although 'Free Trade is ... beneficial to industry ... under Free Trade, as under Protection, the position of

---

83 L. Hall, *Land, labour & liberty*, London 1899, 10–11.
84 The *Clarion's* circulation reached 60,000: J. Rose, *The intellectual life of the British working classes*, New Haven 2001, 48.
85 This is cited in Trentmann, 'Wealth versus welfare', 78.
86 Ibid.

the working classes remains deplorable'. In his speech supporting this resolution, which was passed, Snowden insisted that neither Free Trade nor Tariffs would enable workers to earn a decent living; what they needed were collectivist reforms, including land reform. 'They would notice that the resolution stood by Free Trade', Snowden told the conference. But, he went on,

> It did that because they knew that Free Trade was the best fiscal policy for a commercial country. They knew, however, that all was not well with the industrial and social conditions of the people, but to exchange Free Trade for Protection would aggravate every social evil and inequality. The strength of Mr. Chamberlain's position lay in his insistence on the existence of a large amount of poverty in the country, and that they were falling away from that first commercial position that they had occupied for so long. It was not sufficient, therefore, that they should oppose Mr. Chamberlain in the same way as orthodox Free Traders, by a mere negative opposition or by rhetorical platitudes about the glorious destinies and traditions of the Free Trade era.[87]

Unlike many of their Liberal counterparts, Labour politicians did not regard Free Trade as the foundation of social progress. After all, few on the left were comfortable with the idea that liberal market economics was of much real benefit to the working class, though they might have some temporary value as a stopgap, a least worst option as it were, in the specific context of 1900s commercialism. As Ramsay MacDonald explained in 1905, the fiscal campaign of the Unionists and the mismanagement of Conservative governments since 1895 might 'have raised into a temporarily renewed value the classical economic doctrines of Liberalism'. However, he continued, 'these doctrines, whilst making excellent fortified camps for defensive purposes, are of no use to an army on the march. Free Trade solves no social problems'.[88]

Examination of the left's approach to the land question reveals some similarities with that of the Liberals. Indeed, some historians have suggested that, in policy terms, there was little difference between the position of the Labour and Liberal parties in the 1900s. As Michael Tichelar and Ian Packer have emphasised, Labour's own Land Enquiry of 1912–14 followed much the same lines as Lloyd George's: both advocated a minimum agricultural wage, more smallholdings and improved housing provision for labourers.[89] This can be interpreted as evidence of the strength of traditions of popular Liberalism within the Labour movement, so providing support for the 'currents of radicalism' thesis, which argues for continuity between nine-

[87] *Labour party foundation conference and annual reports, 1900–1905*, ed. H. Pelling, London 1967, 166–7.

[88] MacDonald, *Socialism and society*, 152.

[89] Tichelar, 'Socialists, Labour and the land'; Packer, *Lloyd George, Liberalism and the land*, 162–77.

teenth-century radicalism and twentieth-century Labourism.[90] For scholars who take such a view, Labour's response to the Land Campaign was essentially a radical Liberal rather than a distinctively socialist response; and it has been suggested that this hampered the party's electoral appeal before 1914. In his study of Leicester politics, Bill Lancaster has highlighted the popularity of land reform among members of the town's ILP, and noted the prominence of land reform in MacDonald's election campaigns of 1900 and 1906, claiming that these were indications of policy failure. Hampered by internal divisions and the conservatism of many Leicester workingmen, the Labour programme consisted of 'welfare palliatives' and 'the old shibboleth of land reform', rather than a coherent socialist appeal.[91]

There is much to be said for this line of interpretation. Labour land policy was close to that of the Liberals and, as Packer shows, Liberal initiatives like the Land Campaign did play a part in the electoral containment of the left before 1914.[92] However, the emphasis on commonality of approach threatens to obscure the very real differences that did exist. For a start, even if the leadership ruled it out as practical policy in the short term, Labour – unlike the Liberals – was committed to land nationalisation as an ultimate goal, as was indicated in the party's Land Enquiry Report.[93] But more significantly, there were important ideological differences, which the existing scholarship with its emphasis on high politics and parliamentary goings-on has tended to neglect. Labour land policy – though outwardly similar to that of the Liberals – was underpinned by a rather different economic vision for the nation, one that was ambivalent about Free Trade, hostile to the values of the 'Manchester School' and leaned towards autarkic nationalism. Liberal Land Campaigners wanted to stimulate the capitalist market economy through reform to put land on 'a business footing'; needless to say, this was not a view with which many Labour politicians had much sympathy. Also, while both the Liberals and the left looked back into national history to provide inspiration for their patriotic schemes of land reform, their visions of the past, and the lessons they drew from it, contrasted quite considerably. For a start, Liberals tended to extol the virtues of Anglo-Saxon or pre-enclosure (but post-Reformation) England, while the socialist 'Golden Age' was predominantly a late medieval one. Furthermore, for Liberals (and some radical Unionists), the smallholder of pre-enclosure times provided an example of the ideal type of Liberal 'free-born Englishman' – thrifty, upright, politically independent but not apt to revolutionary agitation. The emphasis here was on individual rights and

---

[90] E. F. Biagini and A. J. Reid (eds), *Currents of radicalism: popular radicalism, organised labour, and party politics in Britain, 1850–1914*, Cambridge 1991.
[91] B. Lancaster, *Radicalism, cooperation and socialism: Leicester working-class politics, 1880–1906*, Leicester 1987, 158, 166–8, 179.
[92] Packer, *Lloyd George, Liberalism and the land*.
[93] Labour party, *Labour party and the agricultural problem*, 3.

liberties. For those on the left, however, the emphasis was more on community and collective organisation. The Golden Age and the peasant revolts that brought it about were presented as prototypically socialist, harbingers of a yet more Golden Age to come – one to be achieved through the defeat of capitalism by Labour, a triumph in which the restoration of the land to the nation would play a crucial part.

Conclusion

Political discourse on the English land question was deeply coloured by patriotic rhetoric and ideas. Overlooked by historians, this fact is of considerable significance. Indeed, the demonstrable contemporary importance of debates on land politics is in large part attributable to the prominence, in these debates, of language that was informed by patriotic sentiment and addressed issues of patriotic resonance. This does much to explain why Free Trade in Land, land tenure reform, allotments and smallholdings legislation, the Liberal Land Campaign and the like excited interest, even passion, among people at the time. These issues were dealt with in part I of this book. Many of them related to fears about national decline. Liberals and (especially) Unionists were concerned for the constitutional stability of the nation at a time of democratisation and growing support for social radicalism, and proposed legislation to widen the basis of property ownership as part of the solution. Similarly, fears for the degradation of the nation's health and character (which many radicals attributed to landlordism) provided a further patriotic stimulus to land reform. Liberals, and those Unionists who harboured such anxieties, proposed measures to stem the flow of rural depopulation, give the countryman an independent (and hence character-forming) life on the land, and prevent the speculative holding of vacant land in urban areas, which only served to exacerbate slum overcrowding and by extension the process of racial deterioration. A further set of national issues related to the state of English agriculture, about which there existed a great deal of contemporary concern. For some politicians, Conservatives in particular, such concern assumed existential proportions; that is to say, they worried that the decline of the agricultural industry, if allowed to continue, would spell doom for England as a great nation. In their interpretation, Britain had become over-reliant on the 'urban' pursuits of commerce and trade at the expense of food production, an imbalance that not only threatened the character and physique of the race, but also raised the possibility of being starved into submission in the event of war. National decline of a rather different sort occupied the minds of those land reformers who sought a reconstruction of the system of landownership. For these supporters of land tenure reform and Free Trade in Land, as well as the far more radical land nationalisers and land taxers, monopolistic landlords were parasites who sapped the energies of the nation by denying Englishmen their rightful stake in the soil. This was presented as an unjust and unpatriotic alienation of birthright, destructive of character and citizenship. It followed from this that were remedial action not taken on behalf of the democracy, England risked national eclipse in the manner of ancient Rome, whose collapse was caused by a system of *latifundia* that had denied the people free access to land.

Taken together, then, responses to the issues thrown up by the land question were actuated by patriotic concern. To put it more precisely, they were, in their different ways, directed towards national renewal. In the context of anxieties thrown up by rural depopulation, agricultural depression, urban overcrowding and unemployment, the rise of socialism, military setbacks in South Africa, international competition and so on, land reform offered a means of revitalising the nation while simultaneously forging new and effective appeals to a mass electorate. Even mainstream Conservative opinion came to take this perspective, for circumstances were no longer conducive to complacent acceptance of the *status quo*. And as shown by the progressively popular bent of Conservative agrarian policy, land reform proposals were framed by a conception of the political nation as democratic in character. The Third Reform Act not only brought an increase in direct pressure on political parties through the enfranchisement of agricultural labourers, many of whom supported radical schemes of land reform, it also changed contemporary definitions of the 'national'. The nation and what it connoted were henceforth typically conceived in democratic terms. This meant that it was increasingly difficult – and electorally unwise – to defend the existing land system, which by the 1900s was widely regarded as a 'feudal' anachronism, even among mainstream Conservative opinion. In denying ordinary Englishmen access to the soil of their own country it seemed out of kilter with constitutional arrangements, which through the widened franchise allowed ordinary Englishmen access to the political nation.

The advent of a democratic conception of nationhood also coloured the national visions that informed the politics of land, which were the focus of part II of this book. Like the national issues of part I, these visions of Englishness took various forms. But one common denominator was their reliance on ideas of the rural past – ideas of the past, moreover, that in most cases put the ordinary Englishman centre stage. Liberals and radicals, from moderate advocates of Free Trade in Land to supporters of land nationalisation, mythologised a pre-enclosure past, where cottagers and small farmers, secure in their rights of commons, lived independent and morally virtuous lives. As for their opponents, it is true that a myth-history of a socially stable 'Merrie England' was a significant component of Unionist agrarianism, especially in the early part of the period. But from the 1890s on, a more popular vision of a *quondam* 'yeoman past' began to take hold on Conservatives as well as Liberal Unionists. This vision inspired Unionist reform proposals like the 1892 Smallholdings Act, as well as the more wide-ranging policies advocated in the 1900s, all of which aimed to encourage social stability through the diffusion of property ownership. Unsurprisingly, popular conceptions of the national past also inspired socialist and Labour politicians. The late nineteenth- and early twentieth-century left upheld a myth of a late medieval 'Golden Age' before the advent of modern capitalism – a time animated by a spirit of collectivism and community solidarity. For its exponents, this vision of a lost proto-socialist nation demonstrated the English roots of English socialism, and served as inspiration for land nationalisation and other reforms to restore the people's inheritance in the soil. As shown in chapter 8, the ideological content of Labour and socialist discourse on the land question had affinities with that of the Liberals, which also drew on a felicitous image of the rural past, a subsequent narrative of dispossession and the need for national restitution. But notwithstanding socialist emphasis on collective organisation, as opposed to Liberal stress on individual freedoms, the historical vision of the left was bound up with a production-orientated condemnation of 'Manchester School' commercialism that tended towards autarkic economic nationalism. In this respect many socialists were closer to radical Unionists like Collings than they were to the Liberal party.

Three broader conclusions suggest themselves. The first has implications for the methodology of political history. Increasingly, though to varying degrees, historians of modern British politics are directing their attention to the study of language and rhetoric, or 'discourse'. As a consequence, there is a growing recognition that, crucially, the politics of the past were about public debate and that the ideological content of politicians' appeals there merits more attention than it has hitherto been given. This implies a focus on published as opposed to unpublished primary sources. Philip Williamson's biography of Stanley Baldwin, which is based on its subject's public utterances, provides an excellent example of this trend as it is affecting the study of 'high' politics.[1] Other work, such as Jon Lawrence's in the field of electoral history, has drawn attention to the importance of the ideological content of what politicians said on the stump. As the work of Lawrence illustrates, deterministic interpretations of voting behaviour based on class have been supplanted by those which stress the role played by language in securing popular support, both at local and national level.[2]

This book has sought to support these trends in the historiography. As a study of political discourse, it recognises that archival records are of only limited use for the study of ideology.[3] In politicians' papers, tactical considerations often loom very large, and so accounts that are heavily reliant on private correspondence can give the impression that such considerations were the dominating motive force behind political action. Yet, in fact, late nineteenth- and early twentieth-century politics were largely about political speech. In the context of the democratisation of the political nation,

---

[1] P. Williamson, *Stanley Baldwin*, Cambridge 1999. See also Bentley, *Lord Salisbury's world*.
[2] J. Lawrence, *Speaking for the people: party, language and popular politics in England, 1867–1914*, Cambridge 1998.
[3] On this see M. Bentley, 'Ideology, doctrine and thought', in M. Bentley and J. Stevenson (eds), *High and low politics in modern Britain*, Oxford 1983, 141.

oratorical ability was seen as the key index of political authority, with no amount of administrative competence being able to make up for lacklustre speechifying.[4] This reflected a more widespread belief that public debate and rhetoric was central to the day-to-day business of politics. Praising a speech by Lloyd George in October 1908, the *Daily News* declared that

> It is a superficial view of politics which regards it merely as the business of inventing legislation and guiding the machinery of administration ... Politics ... are also the art of persuasion, and no leader can be great, whatever be his constructive power as a legislator or his organizing talent as an administrator, who fails in the task of inspiring the democracy in whose name he acts. Politics are collective thinking, and the Government which neglects to think aloud will fail in its work, and deserve to fail.[5]

To a large extent, then, politics before the Great War were about what politicians said. The truth of this is illustrated by political debate on the land question, which derived much of its contemporary significance not from the fact that it was connected with important pieces of legislation that radically altered the shape of society, but because it addressed wider issues of patriotic and 'national' concern, such as the character of the 'freeborn Englishman', the health of the 'race', the issue of food supply in time of war and so on.

Examination of the ideological content of the language of land politics reveals much about late nineteenth- and early twentieth-century political discourse more generally. The advance of democracy in both country and town prompted political responses from both main parties, and land policy played an important part here. For the Liberals, land reform was a key element in a democratic and patriotic onslaught on rural Conservatism. With its emphasis on popular rights and the nation's welfare it formed part of a wider critique of Tory sectionalism. Defending the national interest against the selfish claims of landlords, clergymen, brewers and industrialists, this stance was in line with Liberal traditions of patriotism. And while its impact was delayed by preoccupation with home rule, internal party problems and Boer War jingoism (which swept the Unionists to victory in 1900), the 1906 general election saw it burst to the forefront of the political scene. The Conservative's response to this challenge was to popularise their political appeal, with their party reconceptualising itself as the party of property in general, not just that of the elites.[6] Land policy was crucial to this refashioning. In the two or three decades after 1880 the Conservative line on the land question moved from traditionalist defence of the *status quo* to patriotic advocacy of radical reform premised on the notion that yeoman or peasant proprietorship was a vital national good. Tentative initiatives such as the 1892 Smallholdings Act were followed by more sweeping proposals, culmi-

---

[4] G. H. L. Le May, *The Victorian constitution*, London 1979, 154.
[5] *DN*, 2 Oct. 1908, 6.
[6] Cf. Green, *Crisis*.

nating in those put forward – to good electoral effect – in the aftermath of devastating defeat in English county constituencies in 1906.

This clash of competing patriotic discourses sheds particular light on contemporary Liberalism, and herein lies the second major conclusion of this book. Historians have made much of the idea that in the 1890s and 1900s Liberal thought and policy was transformed by the ideology of 'The New Liberalism'.[7] According to their interpretation, the increasingly dominant radical section of the party fell under the influence of thinkers like J. A. Hobson and L. T. Hobhouse, and abandoned *laissez-faire* principles for social democratic collectivism. As Stefan Collini has written, 'The term "radical" itself came to denote … support for a policy of social reform which was to a greater or lesser extent Collectivist. "Reform" came increasingly to mean "social reform".'[8] The agrarian policies and measures promoted by Liberals have been seen as part of this shift to the left. For Matthew Fforde, 'the collectivist spirit was ever present' in resolutions, especially those concerning land reform, at NLF conferences from the time of the Newcastle Programme onwards.[9]

It is certainly true that legislation such as the 1907 Smallholdings Act or the measures proposed by Lloyd George's Land Campaign were incompatible with *laissez-faire* principles, but these principles were never as important to Liberal government or doctrine as is sometimes made out.[10] As Jonathan Parry has shown, nineteenth-century Liberalism was founded on an agenda that aimed at class reconciliation.[11] The Irish and Scottish land legislation passed by Liberal governments in the 1870s and 1880s, which ran counter to *laissez-faire*, were informed by this agenda. So too were late Victorian and Edwardian proposals for the reform of the English land system. Presented as a project of national integration, Liberal policy on the English land question was a patriotic endeavour consonant with the time-honoured aims of Liberalism. Even in the 1900s it was relatively little influenced by the 'new Liberal' collectivism identified as so important by historians.[12]

The third conclusion is more tentative, and bears on historical understanding of national identities in Britain at this time. Political discourse on the English land question was freighted with various patriotic issues. For Liberal, Conservative and Labour politicians, the land question was a vehicle for debate about the physique and national character of the people, the 'Englishman's' liberties and freedoms, the nature of the national past,

[7]   See, for example, Clarke, *Lancashire*, and *Liberals*; Emy, *Liberals, radicals and social politics*; Harris, *Unemployment*; and Collini, *Liberalism and sociology*.
[8]   Collini, *Liberalism and sociology*, 42.
[9]   Fforde, *Conservatism*, 49.
[10] Biagini, *Citizenship and community*.
[11] This is a theme pursued in Parry, *Rise and fall*.
[12] Also consonant with the long continuities of Liberal political argument, the language employed in the presentation of education policy and the defence of Free Trade casts similar doubt on the purchase of 'new Liberal' ideas: Readman, 'Liberal party'.

the idea of agriculture as the quintessential 'national industry', among other things. Furthermore, politicians' responses to the land question were underpinned by ruralised visions of the national past. At a basic level this lends support to the claim that rural life and the countryside were closely associated with contemporary conceptions of Englishness, as is borne out by the simple fact that political debates on the land question were conducted using patriotic language. It seems likely that these debates would not have involved this sort of language were it the case that English identity had little to do with land or the rural. However, this observation will only get us so far. After all, it is of course the case that nationalistic language was employed in other circumstances; it can scarcely be said that it was only to be found in the field of land politics. Indeed, in recent years, scholars have located English and British identity in a bewildering variety of political and cultural contexts: in religion, in gender and race relations, in encounters with the 'Other', in imperialist discourse, in the politics of the constitution and elsewhere. So, while the evidence presented here does lend credence to the view that agrarian discourse was an important vehicle for conceptions of English national identity in the late Victorian and Edwardian periods, the question as to the precise extent of its importance must remain open. Whether or not it will ever be answered satisfactorily is a moot point, and depends on further research on the significance of other elements of national identity (the constitution, for instance).[13] That said, however, some preliminary observations can usefully be offered.

First of all, there is the question of Britishness, which Linda Colley's seminal work has established as a key category of historical analysis. One of Colley's arguments was that from the early nineteenth century onwards, Britishness increasingly came to be defined in terms of empire, as global *imperium* brought Britain into identity-shaping contact with alien others.[14] This argument, which of course owes much to the writing of Edward Said, has been extended and amplified by other scholars: claims that the experience of imperialism played a key role in the formation of British identities are now commonplace in the historical literature.[15] It is perhaps the case, however, that these claims have been taken too far. Bernard Porter has recently called into doubt the extent of the empire's impact on British social and cultural life; and while Porter's conclusions seem overdrawn, his work is suggestive none the less.[16] Whatever the strength of the relationship

---

[13] J. P. Parry has suggested that a 'constitutional conception of Englishness' was central to national identity in the mid-Victorian period: 'Impact of Napoleon'.

[14] L. Colley, *Britons*, New Haven 1992, and 'Britishness and otherness: an argument', *JBS* xxxi (1992), 309–29.

[15] For a recent example see A. Burton (ed.), *After the imperial turn*, Durham, NC 2003; cf. E. W. Said, *Orientalism*, London 1978.

[16] B. Porter, 'Empire and British national identity, 1815–1914', in H. Brocklehurst and R. Phillips (eds), *History, nationhood and the question of Britain*, Basingstoke 2004, 259–73, and *The absent-minded imperialists: empire, society and culture in Britain*, Oxford 2004.

between empire and Britishness, it would certainly appear that connections between empire and Englishness were far weaker (few contemporaries spoke of an 'English empire'). If Britishness looked outward to empire, Englishness looked inward, focusing on insular patriotic concerns and conceptions of national belonging. The present study supports this perspective. Political debate on the land issue postulated introspective and rural ideas of English identity and patriotism that did not draw upon imperial conceptions of nationhood. Indeed, as shown in chapter 7, even agrarian Conservatives seemed to prefer countrified visions of national identity to imperial alternatives.

The insular Englishness present in political discourse reflected contemporary cultural preoccupations that were similarly inward-looking. Cultural concern with land, landscape and the rural was based on the maintenance of a sense of continuity with an imagined English past. This was a past of self-sufficient yeomen, freedom-giving commons and 'Merrie England' folk culture. It was of a piece with a more general concern with England's island history current at the turn of the twentieth century. Elements of this concern included the continued popular interest in Anglo-Saxon England, the beginnings of mass heritage tourism and the fashion for historical pageantry, which developed into something of a craze before the First World War.[17] Although much remains to be written on this subject, it seems clear that popular interest in English heritage involved patriotic celebration of the national past with the empire largely left out: most historical pageants, for example, made little if any reference to overseas territories coloured pink on the map.[18] This is not to say that the domestic impact of empire was insignificant. Imperial issues could certainly excite popular passions, for instance during the Boer War of 1899–1902. And, as the example of the 'Khaki' election of 1900 shows, they could at times also provide a focus for the politics of patriotism.[19] But the empire was not an integrated element of English national identity – or at least, not as significant an element as has often been claimed. Periodically, it might have provided opportunities for patriotic flag-waving, but it did not feature prominently in the quotidian fabric of national belonging. Discourses of land and nation, on the other hand, played a more important role in this regard – as shown by the patriotic resonance of the political debates surveyed in this book.

Was this the case throughout the rest of the United Kingdom? In Scotland, it is arguable that the empire was more closely connected to national

See also Parry, 'Impact of Napoleon'; Rose, *Intellectual life*, ch. x; and P. Harling, 'The centrality of locality: the local state, local democracy, and local consciousness in late-Victorian and Edwardian Britain', *Journal of Victorian Culture* ix (2004), 216–35.

17 Readman, 'landscape preservation', and 'Place of the past'.
18 Idem, 'Place of the past', 185–7.
19 Idem, 'Conservative party'.

identities than it was in England,[20] while links between land and nation were less strong. Although ethnic nationalism was mobilised behind the cause of the crofters, whose folk-memory of the clearances could be integrated into Celticist narratives of dispossession, Ewen Cameron's work has demonstrated that the Scottish land question was more a 'parochial' than a national one. Very largely confined to the Highlands, it did not prove a powerful driver of Scottish national sentiment and was in any case essentially solved by the passage of the 1886 Crofters' Act. This measure, which established a system of 'dual ownership' on the Irish model, was generally accepted as satisfactory by Highland people, as shown by the petering out of popular agitation for more radical reform in the mid-1890s.[21]

Connections between land and nation were stronger in Wales, where nationalists drew on the myth of the *gwerin* – a nonconformist, classless and largely rural Welsh democracy united in opposition to Anglican landlords and their 'alien' Church. Some campaigners for Welsh land reform undoubtedly conceptualised their proposals as patriotic: freeing the people from the territorial control of the landed aristocracy could be presented as conducing to national liberation. Yet, on the whole, the Welsh land reform project as championed by Liberals was not so heavily charged with patriotic ideas as were other issues of concern to nationalists. As Kenneth Morgan commented some time ago, 'the land question was only an intermittent theme of national protest in Wales' (significantly, it hardly featured in the 1906 election), with even the 'crusade for higher education' playing a much more important role in the nationalist movement.[22] Morgan's point is well taken. Parliamentary debates on Welsh land reform were often carried out with little reference to Welsh national claims.[23] And while landlords were a focus of nationalist complaint, this was informed more by their connection with the Anglican Church than their status as agents of territorial despotism.[24]

Ireland, of course, presents a different picture. Here, the connections between the land and the national questions were undeniably strong. As Philip Bull and others have demonstrated, between the 1860s and the 1880s land became associated with a distinctive idea of Irish identity, one predicated on the united opposition of all sections of Irish rural society – farmers, shopkeepers, Catholic clergy – to the Protestant landed ascendancy.[25] It was

---

[20] J. M. Mackenzie, 'Empire and national identities: the case of Scotland', *TRHS* 6th ser. vii (1998), 215–31.

[21] Cameron, *Land for the people?*

[22] K. O. Morgan, 'Welsh nationalism: the historical background', *Journal of Contemporary History* vi (1971), 161.

[23] See, for example, *Hansard*, 4th ser., 1897, xlvi. 1014–44.

[24] Indeed, as David Howell and Matthew Cragoe have shown, when it came to agrarian matters, landlord-tenant relations were typically good: Howell, *Land and people*; M. Cragoe, *An Anglican aristocracy: the moral economy of the landed estate in Carmarthenshire, 1832–1895*, Oxford 1996.

[25] Bull, *Land, politics and nationalism.*

this that the Land League mobilised in its mass agitation of 1879–82, so drawing land and nationalism closer together, and this association remained important throughout the period leading up to 1914. That said, however, the extent of its importance can be exaggerated, particularly after 1882 and Charles Stewart Parnell's shrewd transformation of the Land League into the home rule-focused Irish National League. George Wyndham's Land Act of 1903 effectively solved the Irish land question, by providing a mechanism through which the territorial control of the landlords could be (and was) put to an end. Yet it is surely significant that this measure had little effect on the nationalist movement. In Ireland the national movement was linked to land politics, but in the final analysis was not dependent upon it for sustenance.

Viewed in the wider British context, the patriotic content of the English land question appears of considerable historical significance. Indeed, it could be argued that the languages of land and nation examined in this book formed part of a wider discourse of English nationalism. This was not a nationalism that sought any alteration of the relationship between nation and state, as in the case of its Irish equivalent, for example, but was rather directed at preserving the historical character of English national identity amid the transformations of modernity. Preoccupation with idealised visions of the rural past – that of the sturdy yeoman of pre-enclosure times, for example – formed an important part of this nationalist project, manifesting itself in a range of cultural developments (such as landscape preservationism), as I have argued elsewhere.[26] But it also manifested itself in the politics of land, with Liberal, Conservative and socialist policy all being informed by conceptualisations of visions of an older, rural, England.

That this was the case does not lend support to the argument that a sort of anti-modern Little Englandism animated late Victorian and Edwardian discourses of Englishness. Indifference or hostility to empire and veneration of the rural did not imply reactionary nostalgia and abhorrence of change. Nor did it imply any simplistic privileging of 'country' over 'town'. True, the countryside might have been more important in constructions of English national identity, but this does not mean that contemporaries regarded urban modernity as necessarily degrading or somehow anti-national. In political as well as cultural history, scholars need to adopt a more sophisticated approach to interpreting the relationship between 'rural' and 'urban' language and preoccupations. This relationship, bound up with the wider relationship between 'the past' and 'the present', cannot be characterised as one of binary opposition.[27] In land politics they were inseparable – not least because many land reform proposals dealt with the modern-day problems of town as well as country life (the issue of slum overcrowding is a case in point). Indeed, it might be said that debates on the land question derived a good part of their

---

[26] Readman, 'Place of the past', and 'Landscape preservation'.
[27] See D. Matless, *Landscape and Englishness*, London 1998, for a sensitive treatment of this point with regard to interwar British culture.

'national' resonance from the fact that they addressed issues of concern to urban as well as rural dwellers. And while it is true that the conceptions of national identity present in political discourse on land and landscape drew upon familiar ideas about the rural past, they did so partly out of necessity: much of the English past was inescapably rural in character. It may be, in fact, that a sense of historical continuity was the essential repository of English ideas of nationhood in the late nineteenth and early twentieth centuries; at a time of great change Englishmen and women regarded the preservation of links to the past as a means of maintaining a coherent sense of national belonging.[28] The agenda of land reform was in accordance with this perspective. Reviving the spirit of 'Merrie England', or Anglo-Saxon rural self-government, or the 'sturdy yeoman' in forms adapted for modern conditions were seen as means by which the *telos* of Englishness could be preserved on into the future. But this did not denote any widespread renunciation of 'town' in favour of 'country'. For Liberal, Conservative and socialist politicians land reform was an integrative patriotic project, one which sought to fuse the best aspects of an imagined rural life of the past with those of the increasingly urbanised present.

[28] Readman, 'Place of the past'.

Bibliography

Unpublished primary sources

Birmingham University Library
Austen Chamberlain papers
Joseph Chamberlain papers

Cambridge University Library
British political party general election addresses, Brighton 1984–5 (microfilm)
National Liberal Federation, *Annual reports and council proceedings, 1877–1936*, Hassocks 1975 (microfiche)

Kendal, Cumbria Record Office
WDX/422 Papers and cuttings relating to preservationist activity in the Lake District

London, British Library
Central Land and Housing Council leaflets
Land Union leaflets
Rural Labourers' League, selection of leaflets

London, House of Lords Record Office
Political papers of Herbert, 1st Viscount Samuel

Oxford, Bodleian Library
Archives of the British Conservative party
Pamphlets and leaflets

John Johnson collection of printed ephemera
'Allotments and small holdings' (boxes 1, 2)
'Creeds, parties, policies' (boxes 6, 7, 18, 19)
'Elections' (box 6)
'Housing and town planning' (boxes 1–12)
'Land and the people' (boxes 1–11)
'Land tax and valuation booklets' (box 1)

Reading, Centre for Rural History, University of Reading
Commons and Footpaths Preservation Society, *Reviews of* [G. J. Shaw Lefevre], *Commons, forests and footpaths*

Woking, Surrey History Centre
Onslow papers
Robert Hunter papers

Published primary sources

Reference works
Craig, F. W. S., *British parliamentary election results, 1885–1918*, Dartmouth 1989
Labour party foundation conference and annual reports, 1900–1905, ed. H. Pelling, London 1967
Law reports (1892)

Official documents and publications
Hansard, 3rd, 4th, 5th series
Report of the Select Committee on Small Holdings, PP 1888–90
Report of the inter-departmental committee on physical deterioration, 1904 (Cd. 2175)
Report of the Royal Commission on Supply of Food and Raw Material in Time of War, PP 1905 (Cd. 2643–5)
Report of the departmental committee appointed by the Board of Agriculture on small holdings in Great Britain, 1906 (Cd 3277)

Newspapers and periodicals
Albany Review
Birmingham Daily Post
Blackwood's Magazine
Cable
Cambridge Chronicle
Cambridge Independent Press
Chambers's Journal of Popular Literature, Science, and Art
Clarion
Commonwealth
Contemporary Review
Daily Express
Daily News
Edinburgh Review
Empire Review
English Labourers' Chronicle
Fortnightly Review
Henley and South Oxfordshire Standard
The Homeland
Independent Review
Labour Leader
Land and Labour
Land and People
Land Values
Law Quarterly Review
Leicester Daily Post
Liberal Magazine
Liberal Monthly
Lincoln Gazette

Lincolnshire Chronicle
Manchester Guardian
Monthly Review
The Nation
National Liberal Club Political Economy Circle Transactions
National Review
National Union Gleanings
Nature Notes
New Liberal Review
New Review
Nineteenth Century
North American Review
Northampton Pioneer
Oxford Times
Peterborough Advertiser
Primrose League Gazette
Punch
Quarterly Review
Rural World
Speaker
Spectator
The Times
Village Search-Light
Westminster Gazette
Westminster Review
Yorkshire Post

Collected papers, speeches etc.

The crisis of British Unionism: Lord Selborne's domestic political papers, 1885–1922, ed. G. Boyce, London 1987

Mr Chamberlain's speeches, ed. C. W. Boyd, London 1914

The red earl: the papers of the fifth earl Spencer, 1835–1910, ed. P. Gordon, Northampton 1981–6

Spencer, H., Collected writings, III: Social statics (1851), London 1996

Winston S. Churchill: his complete speeches, 1897–1963, ed. R. R. James, New York 1974

Contemporary books, articles and pamphlets

A Unionist agricultural policy, London 1913

Acland, A. H. D., 'What can be done for our country villages', New Review iv (1891), 320–31

Adams, T., Garden city and agriculture, London 1905

Agricultural Organisation Society, Second annual report of the Agricultural Organisation Society, Leicester 1902

Allotments and Small Holdings Association, Public meeting at Bridgwater, London 1890

Anderson, W. C., Socialism, the dukes and the land, London [1909]

Anon, 'Lord Tollemache's cottage farms', *Chambers's Journal* 5th ser. ii (1885), 769–72

—— 'The one black mark and the one stain upon the glorious reign of the queen', n.p. 1897

—— 'Our food supply in time of war', *Blackwood's Magazine* clxxiii (1903), 275–85

Arnold, A., *Free land*, London 1880

—— 'Free land and peasant proprietorship', *NC* vii (1880), 297–317

—— *The land and the people*, Manchester 1887

Aronson, H., *Our village homes*, London 1913

Austin, A., 'Why I am a Conservative', *NR* vi (1885), 564–5

Barker, J. E., 'The land, the landlords and the people', *NC* lxvi (1909), 549–67

—— 'The land, the people and the general election', *NC* lxvi (1909), 389–406

—— 'Every man his own landlord', *FR* lxxxvii (1910), 123–39

Bateman, J., *The great landowners of Great Britain and Ireland* (1883), Leicester 1971

Bathurst, C., *To avoid national starvation*, London 1912

Bear, W. E., 'The true principle of tenant-right', *CR* xli (1892), 645–55

—— *An agricultural Rip Van Winkle*, London 1893

Blatchford, R., *Merrie England* (London 1893), London 1976

—— *Real socialism*, London 1898

—— *Britain for the British*, London 1902

Borring, F. M. de, 'The peasant proprietor of the south', *NR* vii (1885), 345–57

Brockhouse, H., *The curse of the country*, London 1909

Brodrick, G. C., 'The law and custom of primogeniture', in J. W. Probyn (ed.), *Systems of land tenure in various countries*, new edn, London 1881, 93–168

—— 'Local government in England', in J. W. Probyn (ed.), *Local government and taxation in the United Kingdom*, 2nd edn, London 1882, 5–87

—— *The reform of the English land system*, London 1883

Buxton, C. R., 'Small holdings', *Commonwealth* x (1905), 141–5

—— Small holdings: the English bill', *Albany Review* i (1907), 368–73

Campbell, G. D., 8th duke of Argyll, 'Agricultural depression, II', *CR* xli (1882), 381–403

A carrier's boy [E. Hamshire], *The source of England's greatness and the source of England's poverty*, 4th edn, Ewhurst 1892, in D. Stemp (ed.), *Three acres and a cow: the life and works of Eli Hamshire*, Cheam 1995, 85–182

Chalmers, M. D., *Local government*, London 1883

Chamberlain, A., *Politics from inside*, London 1936

Chamberlain, J. and others, *The radical programme* (1885), ed. D. A. Hamer, Brighton 1971

Channing, F. A., 'Latest lights on small holdings', *Monthly Review* xxvii (1907), 26–35

Churchill, W., *The people's rights* (1909), London 1970

Cobden Unwin, Mrs [J.], *The land hunger*, London 1913

Collings, J., *Land reform* (1906), new edn, London 1908

—— '"An island fortress"', *NR* lvi (1910), 48–58

—— *The colonization of rural Britain*, London 1914

Commons Preservation Society, *Reports of proceedings*, London 1868–

Constable, H., *Some hints for political leaflets addressed to the agricultural labourer*, London 1894

Creighton, M., *Historical lectures and addresses*, London 1903

Dicey, A. V., 'The paradox of the land law', *Law Quarterly Review* xxi (1905), 221–32

Dicey, E., 'The Conservatism of to-day', *QR* clxxx (1895), 549–76

Ditchfield, P. H., 'Parish councils', *NR* xviii (1891), 252–8

—— *English villages*, London 1901

—— *The old English country squire*, London 1912

Eighty Club, *Social problems*, London 1891

English Land Restoration League, *Special report, 1891*, London 1891

—— *Among the agricultural labourers with the red vans*, London 1895

Fabian Society, *The revival of agriculture*, London 1905

Finch-Hatton, M. E. G., 12th earl of Winchilsea, 'Agricultural union', *NR* xx (1893), 587–93

Fisher, H., *The English land question*, London 1883

Froude, J. A., 'Uses of a landed gentry', in his *Short studies on great subjects* (1867–83), ed. D. Ogg, London 1963, 255–77

Gearey, C., *Rural life*, London 1899

George, H., *Progress and poverty* (1880), New York 1987

Gomme, G. L., *Primitive folk-moots*, London 1880

—— *The village community*, London 1890

Goschen, G. J., *Political speeches*, Edinburgh 1886

Graham, P. A., *The rural exodus*, London 1892

Grant, C., *The small holdings and allotments handbook*, Bristol 1908

Green, F. E., *The awakening of England*, London 1912

—— *A history of the English agricultural labourer, 1870–1920*, London 1920

Green, J. L., *English country cottages*, London 1899

Greenwood, H., *Our land laws as they are*, 2nd edn, London [1891]

Greg, P., 'The new radicals', *NR* v (1885), 158–72

Haggard, H. Rider, *A farmer's year*, London 1899

—— *Rural England*, 2nd edn, London 1906

—— *Rural Denmark and its lessons*, London 1911

Hall, L., *Land, labour & liberty*, London 1899

Hammond, J. L. and B. Hammond, *The village labourer*, London 1911

Harben, H. D., *The rural problem*, London 1913

Hardie, J. Keir, 'The Independent Labour party', in Reid, *New party*, 375–86

Hasbach, W., *A history of the English agricultural labourer* (1894), London 1908

—— 'The new death duties in England', *North American Review* clx (1895), 95–108

Heath, R., 'The rural revolution', *CR* lxvii (1895), 182–200

Herbert, A., 'Three planks of progress', in Masterman and others, *To colonise England*, 130–4

[Hobhouse, C. E.], 'The problems of land and labour', *MG*, 9 Oct. 1913, 8.

Hobson, J. A., *Imperialism* (1902), 3rd edn, London 1988

Hodgson, W. B., 'The disease', in Masterman and others, *To colonise England*, 2–55

Howard, E., *Garden cities of to-morrow*, London 1902

Humphrey, A. W., *Land and the people's property*, London [1909]

Hunter, R., *Footpaths and commons and parish and district councils*, London 1895
—— 'Places of interest and things of beauty', *NC* xliii (1898), 570–89
—— 'Communal occupation and enjoyment of the land', *NC* lxii (1907), 494–508
—— *The preservation of places of interest or beauty*, Manchester 1907
Hyndman, H. M., *England for all* (1881), Brighton 1973
—— *The historical basis of socialism in England*, London 1883
—— *The record of an adventurous life*, London 1911
—— *Further reminiscences*, London 1912
—— and W. Morris, *A summary of the principles of socialism*, London 1884
Impey, F., *Three acres and a cow*, new edn, London 1887
—— 'Lord Tollemache', *New Review* ix (1893), 299–313
—— *Small holdings in England*, London 1909
Jameson, W., 'Land monopoly', in Reid, *New party*, 145–75
—— *The coming fight with famine*, London 1896
Kay, J., *Free trade in land*, 2nd edn, London 1879
Labour party, *Report of the ninth annual conference of the Labour Party*, London 1909
—— *The Labour party and the agricultural problem*, London 1914
The land: the report of the Land Enquiry Committee, 3rd edn, London 1913
Land Law Reform Association, *Sixteenth annual meeting*, London 1903
—— *Seventeenth annual meeting*, London 1904
—— *Eighteenth annual meeting*, London 1905
Land Nationalisation Society, *Opinions of leading thinkers*, London 1890
—— *Programme*, London 1890
—— *Eleventh annual meeting*, London 1892
—— *A parliamentary candidate's catechism*, London 1892
—— *Property and the land question*, London 1892
—— *Thirteenth annual meeting*, London 1894
—— *To landless Britons*, London 1895
Leach, A. F., *The English land question*, London 1883
Leadam, I. S., *Agriculture and the land laws*, I: *Ownership*, London 1881
Levy, H., *Large and small holdings* (1904), Cambridge 1911
Lewes, C. L., 'How to secure breathing spaces', *NC* xxi (1887), 677–82
Liberal Publication Department, *The condition of the rural population*, London 1891
—— *The case for dissolution: a speech delivered by the Right Hon. Sir H. Campbell-Bannerman*, London 1905
Lilly, W. S., ' "Collapse of England" ', *FR* lxxi (1902), 771–84
Lindsay, H. S. L., *Lord Wantage*, London 1907
Lloyd George, D., *Better times*, London 1910
Macaulay, T. B., *The history of England from the accession of James the Second*, London 1858
MacDonald, J. Ramsay, *Socialism and society*, 2nd edn, London 1895
Maine, H., *Village communities in the east and west*, London 1871
—— *Popular government*, 2nd edn, London 1886
Mallock, W. H., *Property and progress*, London 1884
—— *The old order changes*, London 1886

Mann, H. H., 'Life in an agricultural village in England', *Sociological Papers* i (1904), 163–93

Mann, T., *The programme of the I.L.P. and the unemployed*, London 1895

Mansfield, H. R., 'The rural exodus', in Masterman and others, *To colonise England*, 186–93

Masterman, C. F. G., 'Towards a civilisation', *IR* ii (1904), 497–517

—— *The condition of England*, London 1909

—— and others, *To colonise England*, London 1907

Maude, F. N., 'The internal organisation of the nation in time of war', *CR* lxxxi (1902), 36–45

Mill, J. S., *Principles of political economy*, London 1848

—— *Principles of political economy*, 7th edn, London 1877

Miller, H. E., *The Small Holdings Act, 1892*, London 1892

Millin, G. F., *Life in our villages*, 3rd edn, London 1891

Molteno, P. M., *A plea for small holdings*, London 1907

Mond, A., 'The increment tax', *NC* lxvi (1909), 377–88

Morley, J., *The life of Richard Cobden*, London 1881

Morrell, P., 'The administration of the Small Holdings Act', *Nation* iv (28 Nov. 1908), 338–9

Morris, W., *A dream of John Ball; The pilgrims of hope; News from Nowhere*, ed. A. L. Morton, London 1977

Moss, S., *The English land laws*, London 1886

National Liberal Club, *Address on land-tenure reform by James Rowlands, MP*, London 1906

National Union of Conservative and Constitutional Associations, *Specimen leaflets issued by the Rural Labourers' League*, London n.d.

Newman, F. W., *The land as national property*, London 1892

Ogilvie, W., *Birthright in land* (1782), London 1891

Ogilvy, A. J., *Land nationalisation*, London 1890

Onslow, W. H., 4th earl of Onslow, *Landlords and allotments*, London 1886

Parker, G., *The land for the people*, London 1909

—— 'Small ownership, land banks, and co-operation', *FR* lxxxvi (1909), 1079–91

—— 'Small ownership: new light on old difficulties', *NC* lxx (1911), 573–87

—— 'British land and British emigration', *NC* lxxii (1912), 964–76

—— 'A word for small ownership in reply to Lord Lincolnshire', *NC* lxxii (1912), 421–31

—— 'Land reform and the chancellor', *NC* lxxiv (1913), 273–82

Peart-Robinson, W., *Burning questions*, London 1895

Pedder, D. C., *Where men decay*, London 1908

[Petty-Fitzmaurice, H. C. K. and H. H. Smith], 'Land incomes and landed estates', *QR* clxvi (1888), 210–39

Pratt, E. A., *Agricultural organisation*, London 1912

Pretyman, E. G., 'The land question: a reply to Mr. Lloyd George', *Empire Review* xxvii (1914), 1–14

Price-Heywood, W. P., *The land monopoly*, London 1906

Prothero, R. E., *The pioneers and progress of British farming*, London 1888

Quelch, H., *Social-democracy and the armed nation*, London 1900

Rees, J. A., *Our aims and objects* (1903), 12th edn, London 1912

Reeve, H., 'Plain truths and popular fallacies', ER clxii (1885), 558–90

Reid, A. (ed.), *The new party*, London 1894

Richards, R. C., 'Some economic and commercial aspects of the land question', *National Liberal Club Political Economy Circle Transactions* ii (1894), 160–1.

Riddell, Lord, *More pages from my diary, 1908–1914*, London 1934

Roe, G. M., 'Great Torrington Commons', *Report and Transactions of the Devonshire Association for the Advancement of Science, Literature, and Art* xxxi (1899), 156–69

Rogers, J. E. Thorold, *The economic interpretation of history*, London 1888

Roundell, C. S., *Parish councils*, London [1894]

Rowntree, B. S., 'Rural land reform', CR civ (1913), 609–23

—— and M. Kendall, *How the labourer lives*, London 1913

Rural Labourers' League, *Fourth annual report*, London 1893

Russell, R., *First conditions of human prosperity*, London 1904

Salt, H. S., *On Cambrian and Cumbrian hills*, London 1908

Samuel, H., *Liberalism*, London 1902

—— 'The village of the future', *IR* iii (1904), 391–404

Scrutton, T. E., *Land in fetters*, Cambridge 1886

—— *Commons and common fields*, Cambridge 1887

Shaw Lefevre, G. J., Lord Eversley, 'The question of the land', NC xviii (1885), 513–31

—— *Agrarian tenures*, London 1893

—— *English commons and forests*, London 1894

—— *Commons, forests and footpaths*, 2nd edn, London 1910

Sidgwick, H., *The elements of politics*, 2nd edn, London 1897

Slater, G., *The English peasantry and the enclosure of common fields*, London 1907

Sowerby, W., *The agricultural deadlock*, London 1896

Spurr, H. A., 'The cockneyisation of England', *New Liberal Review* v (1903), 273–83

Thomas, E. and H. L. Richardson, *The heart of England*, London 1906

Thompson, A. M., *Towards conscription*, London 1898

Thornton, W. T., *A plea for peasant proprietors*, London 1848

Trevelyan, C., 'Land taxation and the use of land', in W. T. Stead (ed.), *Coming men on coming questions*, London 1905, 358–72

Tuckwell, W., *Reminiscences of a radical parson*, London 1905

Turnor, C., 'A constructive agricultural policy', NR liv (1909), 590–600

—— *Land problems and national welfare*, London 1911

Verinder, F., *The land question*, Manchester 1901

Verney, F. P., 'Peasant properties in France', NR x (1887), 549–64

Vinogradoff, P., *Villainage in England* (1892), Oxford 1968

Wallace, A. R., *Land nationalisation* (1882), London 1892

—— *My life*, new edn, London 1908

—— 'Economic and social justice', in A. Reid (ed.), *Vox clamantium*, London 1894, 166–97

Watson, R. S., *The reform of the land laws*, London 1905

Wheelwright, J., *Landlordism*, London 1896

White, E., *Land reform and emigration*, London 1884

Wicksteed, C., *Village politics and cottage farms*, London n.d.

Wilkinson, S., 'Does war mean starvation?', *NR* xi (1902), 472–9

Secondary sources

Addison, P., *Churchill on the home front, 1900–1955*, London 1992

Adonis, A., 'Aristocracy, agriculture and Liberalism: the politics, finances and estates of the third Lord Carrington', *HJ* xxxi (1985), 871–97

Anderson, B., *Imagined communities*, rev. edn, London 1991

Ashby, M. K., *Joseph Ashby of Tysoe, 1859–1919*, Cambridge 1961

Baldwin, S., *On England*, London 1926

Bentley, M., 'Ideology, doctrine and thought', in Bentley and Stevenson, *High and low politics*, 123–53

—— *Lord Salisbury's world: Conservative environments in late-Victorian Britain*, Cambridge 2001

—— and J. Stevenson (eds), *High and low politics in modern Britain*, Oxford 1983

Bew, P., *Land and the national question in Ireland, 1858–82*, Dublin 1978

Biagini, E. F., *Liberty, retrenchment and reform: popular Liberalism in the age of Gladstone, 1860–1880*, Cambridge 1992

—— and A. J. Reid (eds), *Currents of radicalism: popular radicalism, organised labour, and party politics in Britain, 1850–1914*, Cambridge 1991

Blewett, N., *The peers, the parties and the people: the general elections of 1910*, London 1972

Brudenell-Bruce, C. S. C. [7th marquess of Ailesbury], *The wardens of Savernake Forest*, London 1949

Bull, P., *Land, politics and nationalism*, Dublin 1996

Burchardt, J., *The allotment movement in England, 1793–1873*, Woodbridge 2002

Burrow, J. W., '"The village community" and the uses of history in late nineteenth-century England', in N. McKendrick (ed.), *Historical perspectives*, London 1974, 255–84

—— *A Liberal descent: Victorian historians and the English past*, Cambridge 1981

Burton, A. (ed.), *After the imperial turn*, Durham, NC 2003

Cameron, E. A., *Land for the people? The British government and the Scottish Highlands, c. 1880–1925*, East Linton 1996

Cannadine, D., *The decline and fall of the British aristocracy*, New Haven 1990

Clark, A., 'Gender, class, and the nation: franchise reform in England, 1832–1928', in J. Vernon (ed.), *Re-reading the constitution*, Cambridge 1996, 230–53

Clarke, P. F., *Lancashire and the new Liberalism*, Cambridge 1971

—— *Liberals and social democrats*, Cambridge 1979

—— and K. Langford, 'Hodge's politics: the agricultural labourer and the Third Reform Act in Suffolk', in Harte and Quinault, *Land and society*, 119–36

Coats, A. W., 'The historist reaction in English political economy, 1870–90', *Economica* xxi (1954), 143–53

Coetzee, F., *For party or country: nationalism and the dilemmas of popular Conservatism in Edwardian England*, Oxford 1990

Colley, L., 'Britishness and otherness: an argument', *JBS* xxxi (1992), 309–29

—— *Britons*, New Haven 1992

Collini, S., *Liberalism and sociology: L. T. Hobhouse and political argument in England, 1880–1914*, Cambridge 1979

Cornford, J. P., 'The parliamentary foundations of the Hotel Cecil', in R. Robson (ed.), *Ideas and institutions of Victorian Britain*, London 1967, 268–311

Cragoe, M., *An Anglican aristocracy: the moral economy of the landed estate in Carmarthenshire, 1832–1895*, Oxford 1996

—— *Culture, politics and national identity in Wales, 1832–1886*, Oxford 2004

Culler, A. D., *The Victorian mirror of history*, New Haven 1985

Cunningham, H., 'The language of patriotism, 1750–1914', *History Workshop Journal* xii (1981), 8–33

—— 'The Conservative party and patriotism', in R. Colls and P. Dodd (eds), *Englishness*, London 1986, 283–307

Davis, R. W., *Political change and continuity, 1760–1885: a Buckinghamshire study*, London 1972

—— 'The mid-nineteenth-century electoral structure', *Albion* viii (1976), 142–53

Dewey, C., 'Images of the village community: a study in Anglo-Indian ideology', *Modern Asian Studies* vi (1972), 291–328

—— 'Celtic agrarian legislation and the celtic revival: historicist implications of Gladstone's Irish and Scottish land acts, 1870–1886', *P&P* (1974), 30–70

Douglas, R., *Land, people and politics: a history of the land question in the United Kingdom, 1878–1952*, London 1976

Dunbabin, J. P. D., 'The politics of the establishment of county councils', *HJ* vi (1963), 226–52

—— *Rural discontent in nineteenth-century Britain*, London 1974

Dutton, D., *'His Majesty's loyal opposition': the Unionist party in opposition, 1905–1915*, Liverpool 1992

Eastwood, D., 'Contesting the politics of deference: the rural electorate, 1820–60', in Lawrence and Taylor, *Party, state and society*, 27–49

Emy, H. V., 'The Land Campaign: Lloyd George as a social reformer', in A. J. P. Taylor (ed.), *Lloyd George*, London 1971, 35–68

—— *Liberals, radicals and social politics, 1892–1914*, Cambridge 1973

Fforde, M., *Conservatism and collectivism, 1886–1914*, Edinburgh 1990

Finn, M., *After Chartism: class and nation in English radical politics, 1848–1874*, Cambridge 1993

Fisher, J. R., 'The Farmers' Alliance: an agricultural protest movement of the 1880s', *AgHR* xxvi (1978), 15–25

—— 'The limits of deference: agricultural communities in a mid-nineteenth century electoral campaign', *JBS* xxi (1981), 90–105

—— 'Agrarian politics', in E. J. T. Collins (ed.), *The agrarian history of England and Wales*, VII: *1850–1914*, Cambridge 2000, i. 321–57

Ford, D. J., 'W. H. Mallock and socialism in England, 1880–1918', in K. D. Brown (ed.), *Essays in anti-labour history*, London 1974, 317–42

Freeden, M., *The new Liberalism*, Oxford 1978

Gardiner, A. G., *The life of Sir William Harcourt*, London 1923

Gerard, J., 'Lady bountiful: women of the landed classes and rural philanthropy', *Victorian Studies* xxx (1987), 183–209

Giddens, A. (ed.), *Durkheim on Politics and the state*, Cambridge 1986

Gilbert, B. B., 'David Lloyd George: the land, the Budget, and social reform', *American Historical Review* lccci (1976), 1058–62

Gould, P. C., *Early green politics: back to nature, back to the land, and socialism in Britain, 1880–1914*, Brighton 1988

Gourvish, T. R. and A. O'Day (eds), *Later Victorian Britain, 1867–1900*, Basingstoke 1988

Grainger, J. H., *Patriotisms*, London 1986

Green, E. H. H., *The crisis of Conservatism: the politics, economics and ideology of the British Conservative party, 1880–1914*, London 1995

Grigg, J., *Lloyd George: the people's champion, 1902–1911* (1978), London 2002

Hall, C., *White, male and middle-class: explorations in feminism and history*, Oxford 1992

—— and others, *Defining the Victorian nation: class, race, gender and the British Reform Act of 1867*, Cambridge 2000

Hampton, M., 'The press, patriotism, and public discussion: C. P. Scott, the *Manchester Guardian*, and the Boer War, 1899–1902', *HJ* xliv (2001), 177–97

Hanham, H. J., *Elections and party management: politics in the time of Disraeli and Gladstone*, London 1959

Harling, P., 'The centrality of locality: the local state, local democracy, and local consciousness in late-Victorian and Edwardian Britain', *Journal of Victorian Culture* ix (2004), 216–35

Harris, J., *Unemployment and politics*, Oxford 1972

Harte, N. and R. Quinault (eds), *Land and society in Britain, 1700–1914*, Manchester 1996

Hastings, A., *The construction of nationhood*, Cambridge 1997

Havinden, M. A., *Estate villages*, London 1966

Higgins, D. M., '"Mutton dressed as lamb?" The misrepresentation of Australian and New Zealand meat in the British market, c. 1890–1914', *Australian Economic History Review* xliv (2004), 161–84

Hill, C., *Puritanism and revolution*, London 1958

Hirst, F. W., *Alexander Gordon Cummins Harvey: a memoir*, London 1926

—— *Gladstone as financier and economist*, London 1931

Horn, P., *Labouring life in the Victorian countryside*, Dublin 1976

Howard, C. H. D., 'Joseph Chamberlain and the "unauthorised programme"', *EHR* lxv (1950), 477–91

Howell, D., *Land and people in nineteenth-century Wales*, London 1978

Howkins, A., *Poor labouring men: rural radicalism in Norfolk, 1872–1923*, London 1985

Hutchinson, J., *The dynamics of cultural nationalism*, London 1987

Jaggard, E., *Cornwall politics in the age of reform, 1790–1885*, Woodbridge 1999

Jenkins, T. A., 'Hartington, Chamberlain and the Unionist alliance, 1886–1895', *Parliamentary History* xi (1992), 108–38

Jones, A., 'Word and deed: why a *post*-poststructuralist history is needed, and how it might look', *HJ* xliii (2000), 517–41

Joyce, P., 'History and post-modernism I', *P&P* cxxxiii (1991), 204–9

—— *Democratic subjects*, Cambridge 1994

Keynes, S., 'The cult of King Alfred the Great', *Anglo-Saxon England* xxviii (1999), 225–356

Kumar, K., 'A pilgrimage of hope: William Morris's journey to Utopia', *Utopian Studies* v (1994), 89–197

—— *The making of English national identity*, Cambridge 2003

Lancaster, B., *Radicalism, cooperation and socialism: Leicester working-class politics, 1880–1906*, Leicester 1987

Lawrence, J., *Speaking for the people: party, language and popular politics in England, 1867–1914*, Cambridge 1998

—— and M. Taylor (eds), *Party, state and society: electoral behaviour in Britain since 1820*, Aldershot 1997

Laybourn, K., '"The defence of the bottom dog": the Independent Labour Party in local politics', in D. G. Wright and J. A. Jowitt (eds), *Victorian Bradford*, Bradford 1982, 223–44

Le May, G. H. L., *The Victorian constitution*, London 1979

Lloyd, T., 'Uncontested seats in British general elections, 1852–1910', *HJ* viii (1965), 260–5

Lucas, J., 'Conservatism and revolution in the 1880s', in J. Lucas (ed.), *Literature and politics in the nineteenth century*, London 1971, 173–219

Lynch, P., *The Liberal party in rural England, 1885–1900*, Oxford 2003

Mackenzie, J. M., 'Empire and national identities: the case of Scotland', *TRHS* 6th ser. viii (1998), 215–31

McLean, I., *Keir Hardie*, London 1975

Malchow, H. LeR., *Agitators and promoters in the age of Gladstone and Disraeli*, New York 1983

Mandler, P., 'Against "Englishness": English culture and the limits to rural nostalgia', *TRHS* 6th ser. vii (1997), 155–75

—— 'The consciousness of modernity? Liberalism and the English "national character", 1870–1914', in M. Daunton and B. Rieger (eds), *Meanings of modernity: Britain from the late-Victorian era to World War II*, Oxford 2001, 119–44

—— 'The problem with cultural history', *Cultural and Social History* i (2004), 94–117

Marsh, P. T., *Joseph Chamberlain*, New Haven 1994

Martin, D., 'Land reform', in P. Hollis (ed.), *Pressure from without in early Victorian England*, London 1973, 131–58

Matless, D., *Landscape and Englishness*, London 1998

Miller, D., *On nationality*, Oxford 1995

Moore, D. C., *The politics of deference: a study of the mid-nineteenth century political system*, Hassocks 1976

Morgan, K. O., 'Welsh nationalism: the historical background', *Journal of Contemporary History* vi (1971), 153–72

Morris, A. J. A., *C. P. Trevelyan, 1870–1958*, London 1977

Newby, H., *The deferential worker: a study of farm workers in East Anglia*, London 1977

—— *Country life: a social history of rural England*, London 1987

Offer, A., *Property and politics, 1870–1914*, Cambridge 1981

Orwin, C. S. and W. F. Darke, *Back to the land*, London 1935

Oxford dictionary of national biography

Packer, I., 'The Conservatives and the ideology of landownership, 1910–1914', in M. Francis and I. Zweiniger-Bargielowska (eds), *The Conservatives and British society, 1880–1990*, Cardiff 1996, 39–57

—— *Lloyd George, Liberalism and the land: the land issue and party politics in England, 1906–1914*, Woodbridge 2001

Parry, J., *The rise and fall of Liberal government in Victorian Britain*, New Haven 1993

—— 'The impact of Napoleon III on British politics, 1851–1880', *TRHS* 6th ser. xi (2001), 147–75

—— *The politics of patriotism: English Liberalism, national identity and Europe, 1830–1886*, Cambridge 2006

Pelling, H., *Social geography of British elections, 1885–1910*, London 1967

Phillips, G. D., *The diehards: aristocratic society and politics in Edwardian England*, Cambridge, MA 1979

Porter, B., *The absent-minded imperialists: empire, society and culture in Britain*, Oxford 2004

—— 'Empire and British national identity, 1815–1914', in H. Brocklehurst and R. Phillips (eds), *History, nationhood and the question of Britain*, Basingstoke 2004, 259–73

Pugh, M., 'The rise of Labour and the political culture of Conservatism, 1890–1945', *History* lxxxvii (2002), 514–37

Quinault, R., 'Joseph Chamberlain: a reassessment', in Gourvish and O'Day, *Later Victorian Britain*, 69–92

Readman, P., 'The 1895 general election and political change in late Victorian Britain', *HJ* xlii (1999), 467–93

—— 'The Conservative party, patriotism, and British politics: the case of the general election of 1900', *JBS* xl (2001), 107–45

—— 'Landscape preservation, "advertising disfigurement", and English national identity, c. 1890–1914', *Rural History* xii (2001), 61–83

—— 'The Liberal party and patriotism in early twentieth century Britain', *TCBH* xii (2001), 269–302

—— 'The place of the past in English culture, c. 1890–1914', *P&P* clxxxvi (2005), 147–99

—— 'Conservatives and the politics of land: Lord Winchilsea's National Agricultural Union, 1893–1901', *EHR* cxxi (2006), 25–69

—— 'Jesse Collings and land reform, 1886–1914', *HR* lxxxi (2008), 292–314

Reed, M., 'Nineteenth-century rural England: a case for "peasant studies"', *Journal of Peasant Studies* xiv (1986), 78–99

Rose, J., *The intellectual life of the British working classes*, New Haven 2001

Russell, A. K., *Liberal landslide: the general election of 1906*, Newton Abbot 1973

Said, E. W., *Orientalism*, London 1978

Salveson, P., *Will yo' come o' Sunday mornin'? The 1896 battle for Winter Hill*, Bolton 1996

Samuel, R. (ed.), *Patriotism*, London 1989

Scotland, N., *Agricultural trade unionism in Gloucestershire, 1872–1950*, Cheltenham 1991

—— 'The National Agricultural Labourers' Union and the demand for a stake in the soil, 1872–1896', in E. F. Biagini (ed.), *Citizenship and community: Liberals, radicals and collective identities in the British Isles, 1865–1931*, Cambridge 1996, 151–67

Searle, G. R., *The quest for national efficiency*, Berkeley 1971

Shannon, R., *The age of Salisbury, 1881–1902*, London 1996

Short, B., *Land and society in Edwardian Britain*, Cambridge 1997

Shpayer-Makov, H., 'The appeal of country workers: the case of the Metropolitan Police', *HR* lxiv (1991), 186–203

Skelley, A. R., *The recruitment and terms of conditions of the British regular, 1859–1899*, London 1977

Smith, A. D., *Nationalism and modernism*, London 1998

—— 'National identity and myths of ethnic descent', in J. Hutchinson and A. D. Smith (eds), *Nationalism*, London 2000, iv. 1394–429

Smith, N. R., *Land for the small man: English and Welsh experience with publicly-supplied small holdings, 1860–1937*, New York 1946

Snell, K. D. M., *Annals of the labouring poor: social change and agrarian England, 1660–1900*, Cambridge 1985

Stearn, R. T., 'Lindsay, Robert James Loyd-, Baron Wantage (1832–1901)', *ODNB*

Sykes, A., *Tariff reform in British politics, 1903–1913*, Oxford 1979

Taplin, K., *The English path*, Ipswich 1979

Taylor, M., 'Imperium et libertas? Rethinking the radical critique of imperialism during the nineteenth century', *JICH* xix (1991), 1–23

—— *The decline of British radicalism, 1847–1860*, Oxford 1995

Thirsk, J., *Alternative agriculture*, Oxford 1997

Thompson, F., *Lark Rise to Candleford* (1945), London 1973

Thompson, F. M. L., 'Land and politics in the nineteenth century', *TRHS* 5th ser. xv (1965), 23–44

—— 'Landowners and the rural community', in G. E. Mingay (ed.), *The Victorian countryside*, London 1981, ii. 457–74

Thompson, P., *The work of William Morris*, London 1967

Tichelar, M., 'Socialists, Labour and the land: the response of the Labour party to the Land Campaign of Lloyd George before the First World War', *TCBH* viii (1997), 127–44

Trentmann, F., 'Wealth versus welfare: the British left between free trade and national political economy before the First World War', *HR* lxx (1997), 70–98

Van Zanden, J. L., 'The first green revolution: the growth of production and productivity in European agriculture, 1870–1914', *EcHR* xliv (1991), 215–39

Viroli, M., *For love of country: an essay on patriotism and nationalism*, Oxford 1995

Ward, P., *Red flag and Union Jack: Englishness, patriotism and the British left, 1881–1924*, London 1998

—— *Britishness since 1870*, London 2004

Watkinson, R., 'The obstinate refusers: work in *News from Nowhere*', in S. Coleman and P. O'Sullivan (eds), *William Morris and News from Nowhere*, Bideford 1990, 91–106

Wiener, M. J., *English culture and the decline of the industrial spirit, 1850–1980*, Cambridge 1991

Williamson, P., *Stanley Baldwin*, Cambridge 1999

Winfrey, R., *Great men and others I have met*, Kettering 1943

Unpublished theses

Brown, J., 'Ideas concerning social policy and their influence on legislation in Britain, 1902–11', PhD diss. London 1964

Ellins, R. E., 'Aspects of the new Liberalism, 1895–1914', PhD diss. Sheffield 1980

Fforde, M., 'The Conservative party and real property in England, 1900–1914', DPhil. diss. Oxford 1985

Fisher, J. R., 'Public opinion and agriculture, 1875–1900', PhD diss. Hull 1972

Griffiths, C. V. J., 'Labour and the countryside: rural strands in the British Labour movement, 1900–1939', DPhil. diss. Oxford 1996

Hogg, S., 'Landed society and the Conservative party in the late nineteenth and early twentieth centuries', DPhil. diss. Oxford 1972

Quinault, R., 'Warwickshire landowners and parliamentary politics c. 1841–1923, DPhil. diss. Oxford 1975

Readman, P. A., 'Patriotism and the general election of 1900 in Britain', MPhil. diss., Cambridge 1998

Savage, D. C., 'The general election of 1886 in Great Britain and Ireland', PhD diss. London 1958

Simon, A., 'Joseph Chamberlain and the unauthorized programme', DPhil. diss. Oxford 1970

Ward, S. B., 'Land reform in England, 1880–1914', PhD diss. Reading 1976

Wilks, W. I., 'Jesse Collings and the "back to the land" movement', MA diss. Birmingham 1964.

Index